The Vaněk Plays
Four Authors, One Character

The Vaněk Plays

FOUR AUTHORS, ONE CHARACTER

Edited by
Marketa Goetz-Stankiewicz

UNIVERSITY OF BRITISH COLUMBIA PRESS
VANCOUVER 1987

THE VANĚK PLAYS
© The University of British Columbia Press 1987

This book has been published with the help of a Canada Council grant.

The author wishes to thank the Social Sciences and Humanities Research
Council of Canada for the generous support provided to this volume,
which was administered through the University of British Columbia's
Research Office.

Canadian Cataloguing in Publication Data

Main entry under title:
The Vaněk plays

   ISBN 0-7748-0280-4 (bound). — ISBN 0-7748-0267-7 (pbk.)
   1. Czech drama - 20th century - Translations into English. 2. English
drama - Translations from Czech. I. Goetz-Stankiewicz, Marketa, 1927—
PG5145.E5V35 1987   891.8'625'08   C87-091187-2

International Standard Book Number 0-7748-0267-7 (PBK)
                              0-7748-0280-4 (Bound)
Printed in Canada

Contents

Illustrations

For Jiřina Šiklová

*"Call me what instrument you will,
though you can fret me,
you cannot play upon me."*

Hamlet, III.ii

Introduction

"A tragedy that repeats itself is a farce. . . . Thank God biology can't repeat itself."

(JOSEF ŠKVORECKÝ)

"Big nations consider themselves the masters of history and thus cannot but take history, and themselves, seriously. A small nation does not see history as its property and has the right not to take it seriously."

(MILAN KUNDERA)

"Since we pay a rather harsher price [than people in the West] for our interest in the destiny of the world, we may also have a stronger need to make light of ourselves, to desecrate the altar, as Bakhtin so superbly describes it."

(VÁCLAV HAVEL)

THE PLAYWRIGHTS

When the main character of Kafka's novel *America* was asked by a woman employee of the Hotel Occidental where he came from and when he answered "from Prague," she called out with delight: "Oh, then we are country-men . . . . I'm from Vienna!" This was—in fictional as well as historical time—about 1912. Today, an immigrant from Vienna would react very differently in the same situation. The two imperial cities, Vienna and Prague, related for hundreds of years by their political fate as well as cultural development, are now separated by a border which is not merely the border between two countries (like, say, that between France and Germany or Canada and the United States) but between two vastly different political systems which divide Europe into an Eastern and a Western half. Though a short distance apart, the two cities belong to two dramatically distinct societies—the open society of the democratic West and the coercive society of the totalitarian East. Of the four playwrights whose works comprise this volume, two live in Prague (Havel and Dienstbier) and two, since 1978, in Vienna (Kohout and Landovský). In other words, two are still "at home," surrounded by their own language and culture (though that culture is being put to a hard test of survival); the other two have had to make the adjustment to another language and a culture which, though growing from related roots, has undergone the same changes that all the consumer societies of Western Europe have undergone since the Second World War.

The life stories of all four writers—future biographers are likely to fill many pages with aspects of these true-to-life accounts—have the compo-nents of political thrillers. There are prisons and enforced labour, house-searches, constant watches, exile, ruthless acts of censorship, ostracism, harassment, confiscation of valuable manuscripts, and even a poisoned dachshund. However, these life stories also contain (and perhaps in this sense, too, they strangely resemble the generally optimistic tenor of popular thrillers) brotherly sacrifice, noble deeds of friendship, patterns of deep loyalties, and unshakable ethics which transcend not only the authors' above-mentioned difficulties in living but also—on a less tangible level—the tightly closed political border.

Václav Havel (born 1936), the recipient of several literary prizes, including, in 1986, the prestigious Erasmus Prize awarded by the Netherlands, is a well-known international writer whose plays are staged in the many lan-guages in London and New York, Stockholm and Paris, Tel Aviv and Vienna, Zurich and, surprisingly, Warsaw. In addition to more than a dozen plays, of which *The Memorandum* (1966) is perhaps the best known and of which the most recent, *Temptation* (1985), is possibly the most profound and challenging—

intellectually, philosophically, and dramatically—Havel has been writing a steadily increasing number of essays on topics of urgent concern to our modern world, from peace to power, from ecology to the nature of faith. The best known of these essays is "The Power of the Powerless"(1978), in which Havel eloquently analyses the pressures exerted on an individual in a totalitarian society.

In his plays, Havel demonstrates over and over again how a phrase or a slogan can be employed—consciously as well as unconsciously, strategically, as well as carelessly—to destroy a reasoning process, to obfuscate reality. In his essays written with circumspect, thoughtful clarity, Havel has provided the contemporary international politico-cultural scene with aphoristic formulations which have already spawned commentaries by others. Apart from the above-mentioned "the power of the powerless," the reader may take note of his musings on modern man's need for "a renewed rootedness in the universe;" ponder the implications of "totalitarianism entering every vein and artery of the social organism;" or the "rut of seriousness" eroding causes, no matter how just. The reader may also consider the tragedy of a society, albeit well fed and adequately clothed, which is "living in a lie;" as well as Havel's own attempt—shared by his character Vaněk, around whom this volume is moulded—at "living in truth" (a title given to a selection of twenty essays, six by Havel himself, the others by friends and colleagues, which appeared in 1987).

Havel's *Letters to Olga*, written to his wife during his four-and-a-half-years' prison sentence between 1979 and 1983, are eloquent documents of a thinking man's attempt to formulate and to try to answer—under very difficult physical and spiritual circumstances—some of the most private but also the most general questions of human life, from the salutary results of tea-drinking to the nature of human identity; from the quality of a man's moods to the essence of truth. His autobiographical *Dálkové rozhovory* of 1986 (to appear in Paul Wilson's translation as "At a Distance") is another artistic document, rousing for its intellect, moving for its unassuming honesty.

Pavel Kohout (born 1928) is a writer of many talents. Less philosophical and searching than his colleague Havel, he has written an extraordinary number of lively dramatic texts and prose works, many of which have been translated into other languages and performed from Germany to Greece and the United States, from Finland to Japan and Canada. In the late 1970's, after having spent a year in Vienna, where he had been invited to act as consultant and director at the venerable Wiener Burgtheater, he was forcibly prevented from re-entering Czechoslovakia and was thus compelled to start life "in exile." With unfading energy and resourcefulness Kohout has managed to continue writing, even while surrounded by a new language. His dramatic adaptations still catch the imagination of countless audiences. Just as his dramatization of Jules Verne's *Around the World in Eighty Days* delighted Prague audiences in 1962, so his version of Rostand's *Cyrano de Bergerac* delights audiences in Brussels today.

Of his original plays, *August August, August* (its English language première took place in Minneapolis, in May 1986) is the most popular (to date it has had over 2,400 performances in several languages); though his *Poor Murderer*, an adaptation of a short story by Andrejev, had a successful run on Broadway in the 1976-77 season. A Czech literary critic once wrote that "Kohout was given to the Czech theatre, so that there would not be any peace and quiet." There is truth in this ironic adage: Kohout does keep things on the move. He is every inch a man of the theatre, happy to direct his own plays as well as those of others because his whole work (including his prose writings, of which several have been published in English translation) is permeated by the intense awareness that the actual text is only one part of the whole structure of the play, that the word is only one of the many means to reach an audience. This is where Kohout, despite his exile from his native environment, has a professional advantage over his colleagues in Prague, one that is as obvious as it is absurd: he is able to see his plays performed on stage. Pavel Kohout is also the only playwright represented here who has begun to write in another language: *Safari* is the first play he has actually composed in German. Kohout's work glows in many colours, some of them loud, even gaudy. Yet one thing is certain: with an uncanny sense for topicality, he uses every aspect of the stage with unfailing histrionic intuition.

For Pavel Landovský (born 1936), who also now lives in Vienna without the possibility of returning to Prague, exile presents a particular problem: he is an actor turned playwright. In Prague, Landovský was an eminent member of the theatre Činoherní Klub, starred in several films, and immortalized the image of several dramatic characters. His unforgettable features were well-known to Prague theatre audiences from the late 1950's to the late 1970's. Since language is the most important professional tool for an actor, Landovský's talents have obviously been severely curbed. However, with half a dozen exhilarating comedies to his credit, Landovský's claim as a playwright is substantiated. His spirited farce *Detour,* which appeared in English translation in *Dramacontemporary: Czechoslovakia* (New York, 1985), is as lively a proof of this as is *Arrest* in this volume. As Landovský writes in his note on the Vaněk plays, he was actually the first to "borrow" the dramatic figure of the shy and polite forbidden writer Vaněk from his friend and colleague Havel, and introduce it in 1976 into his biting comedy *Sanitární noc* (which I have translated elsewhere as *Closed for Disinfection* and which is not included in this volume only because it is not a one-act play).

There circulates a story which, if it is not true, ought to be because it vividly illustrates the nature of Landovský's ebullient talents and character. When he complained to Pavel Kohout in Vienna that he was never considered for more prominent parts at the Burgtheater because of his deficiency in German, Kohout, with typical resourcefulness, suggested that Landovský write a dramatic text with a mute character in it and thus create a role for himself. Landovský did just that, and we now have *Arrest* with its wordless but magnificently theatrical character of the gypsy Matte.

Jiří Dienstbier's (born 1937) writing career has many aspects to it. After working as editor with the Czechoslovak broadcasting network, he became its Far Eastern correspondent in the 1960's and subsequently correspondent in the United States. Apart from the many essays and commentaries he wrote in his capacity as correspondent and observer in many countries, he contributed to a number of journals of opinion and literary publications, and wrote a book on events in Indonesia. Forbidden to publish since 1969 and fired from broadcasting, he became spokesman for Charter 77[1] in 1979. Three of his plays, a number of essays, and a collection of international political essays circulate in Czechoslovakia in *samizdat*[2] editions. As he notes in his comment on the Vaněk figure, he was imprisoned together with Havel and spent the years from 1979 to 1982 in prison. His play *Reception* is inspired by this experience.

THE PLAYS

In his essay written for this anthology, Václav Havel tells us that *Audience* and *Unveiling*, the two plays in which the character Vaněk first appeared, were originally written to entertain a few friends. It did not then occur to the author that these private playful musings would conquer the international theatre scene. Their unexpected success taught Havel, as he writes in the "Afterword" to the Czech edition of his plays (published by Sixty-Eight Publishers in Toronto in 1977), that it was essential for him to write with a concrete audience in mind, rather than envisaging a faceless international reader; that he must "lean on what I know, on my own concrete living background, and that only by means of this authenticity I could—perhaps— provide a more general comment as witness of a certain period." And so, drawing on his personal experience, he wrote the three one-act plays that have come to be produced more often and in more countries than any other of his plays. They are also the works which inspired Havel's three colleagues to "borrow" his central character and write their own plays around him— truly an uncommon, if not a unique, occurrence in modern theatre.

The eight plays, written in an unplanned, indeed an impulsive way in the course of a decade, surprisingly fall into what seems a logical pattern of development as if they were part of a preconceived scheme. In Havel's *Audience,* Vaněk is working in a brewery, still living at home, though already regarded and watched as a subversive person, harmful to the state and noxious to its community of citizens (as a result, his boss, the Brewmaster, is faced with an unusual professional problem: he is expected to inform the authorities about the "subversive" activities of the suspect employee—a difficult task indeed, if it is to be performed regularly).

In *Unveiling,* Vaněk is visiting successful and "normalized" friends, who distinguish themselves from him by being able to travel abroad to the West, by serving international exotic food, and by being generally well adapted and definitely "with it," politically and in every other way. In *Protest,* the playwright meets a "colleague"—a writer who is successful in the society that has ostracized Vaněk. Their hour-long discussion—containing Staněk's masterly display of "dialectically argued objectivity"—is resolved by a change in the momentary but by no means in the basic situation. In Havel's three plays Vaněk deals with private individuals. However, their weaknesses, strategies, and blunders—which become blatantly obvious during the action—are soon revealed as the meek echoes of the workings of a vast hierarchy of powers, the upper echelons of which remain unfathomable and hence, like the power-structure referred to by Kafka's gatekeeper, unchallenged and unassailable. Kohout's Vaněk (*Permit* and *Morass*) no longer copes with private individuals; he is obliged to tackle the authorities, a dog-licence office, on the one hand, and a bureau for drivers licences *cum* police station, on the other. In these plays, the power structure becomes more concrete and with it the employees' need to conform dutifully.

In Landovský's *Arrest* and Dienstbier's *Reception,* Vaněk has ended up where his steadfastness has inevitably led him—in prison. Again, it is the other prisoners who catch and hold our attention. Not only are they interesting characters in themselves, but they also provide a fascinating picture of the Czech variety of a police-state prison. As we laugh our way through the rambunctious comedies, the dark shadows of more serious, indeed tragic, issues retreat into the background, only to emerge more insistently when we become aware that the hilarious goings-on on stage are a comic reflection of the vast political and social issues which hover over our divided world.

In *Safari,* Pavel Kohout's play written especially for this anthology, Vaněk is for the first time exposed to the "liberal" society of a Western democracy. Having been spirited to Vienna, Vaněk now faces a panel of artists and intellectuals who have been invited by the media to take part in a televised talk-show and interview with the famous "dissident" writer from the neighbouring

"Eastern bloc" country. Again, the playwright is more interested in revealing Vaněk's surroundings than in the amiable "anti-hero" himself. In a rollicking hour of acerbic fun, Kohout explores standard types of mass-media minds: their relativistic values, their confused notions of freedom, their clichéd ideas of what a "forbidden" writer is all about, and their adamant refusal to learn anything that would rock their respective ideological boats.

And so we realize that, despite their unplanned nature, the Vaněk plays have come full circle and thus reflect the shape of some of the plays themselves (say, *Audience, Unveiling, Morass*), which are structured in such a way that at the end they could begin again, thus forming a circular link in an endless chain reminiscent of Beckett's *Waiting for Godot.* At the end of *Safari,* the hapless writer Vaněk goes back to his home country where—the thought is inevitable—he will again embark on a cycle of similar experiences. In fact, he might, if permitted by the authorities, again begin working as a labourer, say, in a brewery . . . .

FERDINAND VANĚK AND THE OTHERS

Vaněk is a shy, unpretentious man whose intelligence never really shows, although it is often referred to by the other characters. After all, most of them know—for better or for worse—that although he has been ostracized by the régime, he is a formidable writer. However, although Vaněk knows how to put words on paper, he cannot handle them in conversation. It is the others who talk and tell him what they want, know, hope, and fear. Sometimes they even tell him what he himself is all about, and he never manages to counter their arguments. None of the four authors gives Vaněk the chance to show verbally what he is supposed to stand for. His spoken part inevitably consists of unfinished sentences, fragmentary apologies, murmured remarks, repetitions. The venerable Viennese actor Joachim Bissmeier (who acted the enormously difficult part of Vaněk in all three Havel plays as well as in Kohout's *Permit* with the subtle understanding and meticulous control it requires) said in an interview that "the rules of the part are established very precisely"; Vaněk is "the catalyst, it is the others who bring the problems."

In a way Vaněk practices what George Steiner called the "retreat from the word." Vaněk's experience has taught him that he can no longer be committed to the resources of language as a dependable instrument with which to convey reality. When he tries to use language with precision and circumspect caution, in order not to formulate anything that might not correspond to the truth, he is met by torrents of language, obfuscating and void-filling, or strategic and calculated to produce a certain effect. Language as the instrument that can bring the mind into contact with reality—as classic and medieval philosophy have taught us—is no longer valid. Silence becomes the chief defence against the falseness of language. The silence that Vaněk practices becomes a more eloquent tool of communication than the thousands of words used by the others.

It is this largely silent man who gradually reveals himself as controlling the situation on a deeper level, though, on the surface, he seems to be manipulated by it. While the other characters psychologically—and therefore also linguistically—twist and turn, Vaněk remains himself and emerges from each play unchanged in his basic attitudes. Soon it dawns on the audience that this awkward, fumbling man could not be moved by ten horses, nor by a powerful political hierarchy, to do something he considers wrong. This strength in weakness, this "power of the powerless" (in the words of Havel's famous essay), becomes the intellectual focus as well as the moving spirit of the plays.

There is another interesting thing that happens in the receptive process. As we watch (or read) the plays, we are bound to realize that we steadily give more attention to the characters who surround Vaněk rather than to him. He somehow takes on the quality of the quiet eye of a hurricane where things remain the way they were and where there is shelter from the roaring and shifting turmoil all around. And yet we must be cautious about the implications of this image. A hurricane wreaks destruction; there is no doubt about it. But the people who surround Vaněk are not really evil. They are merely all too human in their pathetic weakness, their petty greeds, their creeping fears, their anxious hearts trained on the passing chances to grasp a shred of an advantage for themselves. There are, let it be quite clear, no "villains" in the Vaněk plays. And it is in part this very fact that makes the plays such good and challenging pieces of theatre. To be sure, it would be less disturbing to watch a clear display of evil as the counterpart of the gentle, movingly awkward, and obviously sorely wronged writer Vaněk, who is bound to draw sympathy, even affection, from readers or audience. However, this is not what we get. None of the four writers provides the comforting service of pitching poor nice Vaněk against brutal representatives of political power. If that were the case, we would be free to lodge our righteous resentment fairly and squarely on the representatives of the "other" side—the persecutors, oppressors, exploiters. We would place ourselves just as fairly and squarely in Vaněk's camp, certain of what is good and bad, our ethical judgments supported by an uncluttered, streamlined view of good against evil. But such a reassuring, cowboy-movie pattern does not emerge from the intensely searching literature of Central Europe.

In this way, as if despite himself, Havel has created a new hero for Czech literature, an antipode to Hašek's Good Soldier Švejk, who is silent where Švejk talks, whose stories, unlike Švejk's are never told, whose unsung life, unlike Švejk's colourful adventures, remains concealed in the background. In recent years Švejk has been variously compared and contrasted with Kafka's characters, and it has been said, by the eminent Czech philosopher Karel Kosík, that one posits the positive and the other the negative scale of human values. Vaněk also posits a scale of human values by not subscribing to the false values of those who surround him. It is the others who spout "values": a good life, a safe income, a need to make do with the powers that be (after all, a wise old proverb teaches us that one ought to make the best of any situation), plus a dash of cynicism about the messiness of human affairs. What's wrong with these values? Ferdinand Vaněk does not voice criticism of them, but he makes it perfectly clear that he will not live by them. Thus, without expounding "right" values but by constantly, yet modestly, even unconsciously, displaying the absence of "wrong" values, Vaněk posits his own scale of values, which can best be defined by what it is *not*: it is not materialistic, not opportunistic; it is not intolerant and not arrogant; it is the very opposite of facile conformism and strategic reasoning.

THE "DISSIDENT"

The word "dissident" is used frequently and largely unthinkingly by the Western press and media. What exactly is meant by it? If we try to suggest an image behind the modish word, we might envisage, say, a frowning young man with a placard, pacing up and down in front of a government building; or perhaps a fiery-eyed young woman in a humid cellar, late at night, editing human-rights activist pamphlets; or else a venerable grey-haired citizen, standing upright at court, defying a bribed judge's verdict; or else . . . ? Perhaps the only fair thing is to allow every reader to choose the image that fits the word "dissident" in his or her own mind. Of course, the cases of famous "dissidents"—no matter under which régime—contribute to moulding the popular image. We might think of the renowned physicist Andrei Sakharov's "internal exile" in the Soviet union imposed in 1980; of Polish labour leader Lech Wałęsa addressing a crowd of workers in the shipyards of Gdansk during the strike of 1980; of the Czech student Jan Palach setting himself on fire to protest the invasion of his country by Soviet troups in 1968. Yet these examples, vivid as they are, do not really define the concept of "dissident" either. They refer to drastically different situations, and their common denominator is too abstract to yield a useful definition.

There is another problem which clouds the issue. If a "dissident" happens to be a writer—as is often the case—there exist many designations for what he produces. We find references to "parallel," "underground," "uncensored," "illegal," "independent" or "*samizdat*" literature. Each of these designations leads to problems in connotation and inevitably creates confusion. For example, "unofficial" literature means something different in each age and political situation; "underground" literature gives the impression that it is non-literary (we may think of pamphlets); "illegal" literature is confusing in the sense that, for example, the works of some Czech writers (though very few) have appeared both in *samizdat* typescripts and in works issued by state-sponsored publishing houses.[3]

If such uncertainty reigns with regard to what to call their writings, what are we to call the authors themselves? Does the word "dissident" not add to the confusion rather than lessen it? Besides, neither the forbidden writers of Central-Eastern Europe nor those who have emigrated and now write in the West feel comfortable with the term "dissident," although they are surely aware of the fact that this label has been given with the best intentions to point out their difficult and courageous attitude and behaviour.

I will mention three examples of writers' attempts to illuminate the misleading nature of the word "dissident." Milan Kundera, who left Czechoslovakia in 1975 and now lives and writes in Paris, said in an interview (*Index on Censorship* 6:6, 1977): "I must confess I don't like the word 'dissident,' particularly when applied to art. It is part and parcel of that same politicising, ideological distortion which cripples a work of art . . . . The importance of this art (the art that comes from Prague or Budapest) does not lie in the fact that it accuses this or that political régime, but in the fact that on the strength of social and human experience . . . it offers new testimony about human conditions."

Secondly, there is Josef Škvorecký, now living and writing in Toronto, Canada, who in his note on the "Writer/Dissident" (in *Na brigádě*, 1979) argues with typical wry irony that the true "dissident" writer should actually be called a "socialist writer" in Marxist terminology: he acts according to the dictates of the freedom of will which, as Hegel taught the Marxists, is the understanding of necessity. The "dissident," after all, does just that—he understands this necessity and behaves according to it—namely, he says and writes what he perceives to be the truth.

The third voice in this context comes from Czechoslovakia, from one of the writers represented in this volume who himself is being constantly referred to as a "dissident" writer. Václav Havel, less ironic than Škvorecký, less aphoristic than Kundera, and guided by his usual circumspect rationality as well as first-hand experience of the circumstances, tries in "The Power of the Powerless" (1978) to define the main qualities of people who are called "dissidents" by the Western mass media. Havel's main points are the following: Firstly, such persons make their critical opinions known publicly, albeit within the severely limited possibilities at their disposal. Secondly, they have reached a stage in which they are taken more or less seriously by their government, and even their persecution causes certain complications for this government. Thirdly, their critical engagement extends beyond a narrow circle and has therefore taken on a political character. Fourthly, these people are for the most part intellectuals (Havel calls them "men of the pen") whose only political means is their writing; the attempts of others, namely, non-writers, to "live in truth" rarely penetrate beyond their country's borders and are by and large unknown in the West. Fifthly, Westerners refer more frequently to the political engagement of these people than to their activity as writers. Havel himself knows from personal experience that at some point—and he did not realize exactly when this came about—people in the West began to regard him less as a writer than as a "dissident" who in his spare time also wrote some plays. "Dissidentism," Havel writes, "somehow creates the impression that it is a kind of profession rather than a state of mind that makes a person reason and act in a certain way." In fact, it usually happens that it is only after a person has consistently behaved in a certain way, and has done so from an inner urge and conviction, that he suddenly realizes that this will probably earn him the label of "dissident." People with first-hand experience of Central Eastern Europe are aware of this. In his essay "Does Central Europe Exist?" (*New York Review of Books,* 9 October 1986) Timothy Garton Ash calls Havel "a playwright catapulted by circumstances and the dictates of conscience into the role of dissident but not at all by temperament a political activist." To be a dissident, we conclude, therefore, is an existential attitude arising from certain ethical convictions or, as Havel puts it, from the conscious decision "to live in truth."

EIGHT PLAYS: A CONSTELLATION

It is important to realize that these eight plays are related to each other not merely by the figure of Vaněk but by the whole surrounding social context. The audience (or reader) is constantly made to feel that there are real lives being lived, say, on the street running past the apartment where Vaněk visits his well-adjusted friends; beyond the office where he tries to obtain breeding papers for his dog; in the village near the brewery where he rolls beer barrels; outside the prison where he serves a sentence for "subversive activities." Throughout the text, moreover, there are references to other Czech writers (forbidden as well as "official" ones); popular singers (those banned from their profession as well as those successfully pursuing it); we are made aware of a world that contains political dissidents like Sakharov, literary figures of the past like Ibsen and of the present like Samuel Beckett. Moreover, there are references to the authors who wrote the very plays we are watching or reading and to events from their real lives which become part of the plays. We are, for example, amused by references to Pavel Landovský's not-too-restrained drinking habits (*Audience*); we are made to wonder about Pavel Kohout's youthful flirtation (or more?) with Communism (*Morass*); we learn about the official offer made to Václav Havel by the Czech authorities to leave the country (taking along his possessions) and about his decision to refuse to do so and to go to prison instead if his friends were not released as well (*Reception*); and we hear about Kohout's poisoned dachshund (*Permit*) and Vaněk's (or Havel's?) never "giving a damn about what the others did" (*Arrest*). Real figures and true occurrences thus merge with the events on the stage in what seems a singular blend of fact and fiction, of the world as a stage and the stage as a world reflecting in its concentrating mirror images the complex, personal, political, and ethical issues of the contemporary world. Yet, it must be stressed again, the plays bear their burden of ideas exceedingly lightly. Never weighed down by the serious issues they raise, they vibrate with the histrionic and intellectual exuberance of the playwrights' comic genius.

The fictional figures, too, provide a connecting line by re-emerging in the play of a different author or flashing across its background. For example, Staněk, the well-adjusted playwright who manages to provide the most convincing arguments for not signing the dissident letter in Havel's *Protest,* is referred to in Kohout's *Permit* as having attended a formal occasion in the Czech National Theatre; the gypsy Sherkezy, who rolls barrels in *Audience* and tends to arrive at work tipsy (though we never actually see him on stage), has ended up in prison in *Reception,* where he tattoos the prisoners with imaginative variations of the Hradčany Castle; in fact, we have the pleasure of seeing his artwork on the Brewmaster's hairy chest. In *Audience,* Vaněk is warned not to associate with Kohout, in *Protest* and *Morass,* he is told not to go drinking with Landovský, whom Michael, the impeccable host of *Unveiling,* calls "a failure." The Brewmaster, who in *Audience* repeatedly asks Vaněk to bring the actress Bohdalová for a visit to the brewery, complains in *Reception* when he meets Vaněk in prison that the latter had not kept his promise, had not brought the actress, and he, poor Brewmaster, had never had the pleasure of seeing her in person. An early Stalinist poem written by Kohout as a young man is quoted by an apparatchik twenty-five years later as the very work that influenced him to embark on a marriage that had turned out less than ideal (*Morass*). The Brewmaster, who in *Audience* tried (unsuccessfully) to make Vaněk help him to compose reports on his, Vaněk's, subversive activities, has become more efficient in *Reception*; he suggests that Vaněk write an "ideologically clean" skit for the prison May celebrations, to be submitted to the authorities under the Brewmaster's name and subsequently performed by the prisoners in one of their classroom hours. A film about the liberation by the Soviets in 1945—which is being shot in the next prison compound and causes havoc during the final stages of *Arrest*—is likely to be the kind of film that was shown to the leftist poet in *Safari* on one of his red carpet visits to Prague.

THE TRANSLATIONS

Much could be said about the craft of translation (or is it an art?—scholars have not been able to make up their minds on this question for centuries), but this is not the place. So let me only say this: it is much more difficult to translate well than is commonly realized. A translation can make or break a text. And, it is even more difficult to translate for the stage. The spoken word wields extraordinary power, and where a reader's eye might leniently pass by an awkward turn of phrase or stiffly unreal dialogue, the highly tuned collective ear of a theatre audience will quickly pick up a false tone, an alien phrase in the mouth of a character, or a laboured reference to something that obviously belongs to a different context. Moreover, an actor having to work with a translated text will be acutely aware of every false note which would throw off his characterization.

Only two of the translations in this volume have been on stage; Václav Havel's *Protest,* among other performances, was staged at the Public Theater on Broadway in the fall of 1983; Pavel Kohout's *Permit* was "workshopped" (as theatre people like to put it) by the Kitsilano Theatre Company of Vancouver, Canada. Havel's *Audience* and *Unveiling* (under the title of *Private View*) were performed in New York together with *Protest* in Vera Blackwell's translation. In this volume, however, the plays appear in a translation by Jan Novak, a writer in his own right. All eight plays, it must be stressed, were translated with a performance and an audience in mind. For, if I may give voice to a conviction which seems to contradict the whole sense of this volume, a play belongs on a stage rather than between the covers of a book.

Considering their intention to create living, speakable language, the translators were faced with a formidable task: prisoners' tough talk, bureaucratic jargon of all shades and colours, political innuendo, cultural and literary references, plays on words, and linguistic jokes are just a few of the problems they encountered. They, therefore, had not merely to translate but rather to transform the text and recreate it in a new context, trying to make up for the loss of some meanings by moulding new ones in tune with our own social and cultural context. At the same time, they strove to preserve as much as possible of the original flavour, the unique brand of Czech humour, the particular chiaroscuro-effect of mingled comic and tragic elements which makes up the stuff of life for the inhabitants of that small country at the very centre of Europe. By and large they strove to strike a balance between loyalty to the author and responsibility toward the new readers—or the new audiences—who have to be guided into the dramatic situation and acquainted with the particular idiom of the plays' characters with a light and yet decisive touch.

THE AUTHORS ON THE VANĚK PLAYS

The comments by the four authors speak for themselves. They certainly reveal the different artistic temperaments and intellects of the playwrights, but they also express varying perceptions of the Vaněk figure. Václav Havel, who was the first to conceive Vaněk, emphasizes that, though he has some of the author's personal traits and represents some of his experiences, Vaněk is not a self-portrait. Rather he is a dramatic principle which causes his environment to react and reveal itself. However, the other three writers, all aware that they have put the stamp of their own artistic personalities on their Vaněk figures, are obviously not able to remove their conception of the character from their experience of Václav Havel himself. Kohout, calling Vaněk Havel's "fictional twin brother," stresses the character's childlike soul and "chastity" (Kohout insisted on using this word, perhaps in order to express the timeless and rarefied nature of this quality). Landovský sees Vaněk as a "symbol" of Havel: instead of delving into past layers of the language, he expands Vaněk's quality by abstracting it. Dienstbier, who is possibly less intense in his thoughts about Havel (perhaps because he not only currently shares his fate as "dissident" but also has personal contact with him that is denied to the writers who live abroad) tells us that he has taken up two of Havel's dramatic figures (he also revived the Brewmaster from *Audience*) because he wanted to make a point about true ethical commitment having to be practical rather than remaining suspended in abstract theory.

What all this boils down to is that the figure of Ferdinand Vaněk—actually a dramatic paradox because he does not wield the word, a dubious hero because he hardly acts, a suspect model because he knows better what *not* to do than what to do—provokes by merely existing and proving to a corrupt world that a "good" existence is still possible. It is the way to show this possibility of "goodness" which the other three writers absorbed into their work. Karl Kraus once wrote that one must "dig up words by their roots" in order not to be drawn into the murky pool of cliché. In that sense, the word "goodness" is to be taken here. By resisting the use of the language gone dead under the weight of facile, unexamined usage, Vaněk proves the falseness (the "deadness" to truth) of the language by which most of the other characters in the plays live. This is what the three writers who borrowed the figure of Vaněk inherited from Havel. This is why in their comments they try, by different means, to stress the general aspect of the figure. That Vaněk captured their attention because he not only came from the pen of their colleague and friend but also resembled him in a basic way, is a lucky incident both for Czech literature and for contemporary literature and theatre as such. Without this incident we would not have this remarkable string of plays. It also shows that in a time when every writer strives for individualism, there exists—no matter how fragile—a common idea of human value. That this idea reaches beyond the stringent calls for human rights whirling agonizingly around our globe is clear. That it comes from a country situated precariously at the very borderline of a vast division is a fact that deserves more thought.

NOTES TO THE INTRODUCTION

1. Charter 77, a human rights document issued in Czechoslovakia in January 1977 which was designated in its Declaration as a movement for "a free, informal, open community of people of different convictions, different faiths and different professions, united by the will to strive, individually and jointly, for the respect of civil and human rights in our country and in the world." This declaration, signed by 240 writers, artists, and intellectuals resulted in immediate and long-range repressive measures by the Czechoslovak government against its supporters and signatories. For an eloquent and fully documented account of this, see H. Gordon Skilling, *Charter 77 and Human Rights in Czechoslovakia* (London: Allen & Unwin, 1981).

2. The works of so-called "dissident" writers, as well as any writings considered "subversive" by state censorship are, of course, barred from publication in Czechoslovak state-run publishing houses. Such writings circulate "underground" in typescript. Several series of these "unpublishable" works now exist, *Edice petlice* (Padlock Edition) being the most widely known. The designation *samizdat* (meaning "self-made" in Russian) literature has become most widely used for this kind of writing. For the problem of finding an appropriate name, see the above section on the "Dissident."

3. I am indebted for this thought to Dr. Vilém Prečan, Executive Director of the Documentation Centre for the Promotion of Independent Czechoslovak Literature in Schwarzenberg, Federal Republic of Germany.

VÁCLAV HAVEL

Audience

Translated by Jan Novak

CHARACTERS

Brewmaster
Ferdinand Vaněk

PLACE

A Brewery Office

(Brewmaster's office. Stage right, there is a door. Above it hangs some sort of a framed certificate. A wardrobe and a filing cabinet, on top of which there is a collection of beer bottles, stand stage left. Upstage, on the back wall, a large crude painting portrays the good soldier Švejk and the inn-keeper Palivec. A decorative sign under it proclaims: LIVING IS EASY WHERE BREWERS KEEP BUSY. An office desk and three chairs take up the centre of the stage. The desk is littered with stacks of various forms, several empty beer bottles, and beer glasses. A case of beer lies on the floor beside the desk. An undefined mass of junk is piled up along the walls and in the corners—broken valves, an old radio, a broken-down coat rack, stacks of yellow newspapers, galoshes, and so on. As the curtain rises, the Brewmaster is sitting by the desk in a work smock, supporting his head in his hands, and snoring loudly. Moments later, someone knocks on the door. The Brewmaster wakes up immediately.)

BREWMASTER	Come in—
	(Vaněk enters, wearing a heavy workcoat and boots.)
VANĚK	How are you—
BREWMASTER	Oh, Mr. Vaněk! Come on in! Have a seat—
	(Vaněk sits down timidly.) How about a beer?
VANĚK	No, thank you—
BREWMASTER	Oh, come on! Why not? Go ahead and have one—
	(Brewmaster pulls a bottle out of the case, opens it, pours beer into two glasses, pushes one in front of Vaněk while downing the other one quickly.)
VANĚK	Thank you—
	(Brewmaster pours himself another glass. Pause.)
BREWMASTER	Well? So how is it goin'?
VANĚK	Fine, thank you—
BREWMASTER	Like there was any choice, right?
VANĚK	Right.
	(Pause.)
BREWMASTER	So what are you up to today? Rollin' the full barrels?
VANĚK	No, the empties actually—
BREWMASTER	A little better than them full suckers, ain't it?
VANĚK	Yes, it is—
	(Pause.)
BREWMASTER	So who's pushin' the ballbusters today?
VANĚK	Sherkezy[1]—
BREWMASTER	He made it in this morning?
VANĚK	Yes, he just came in—

BREWMASTER	Plastered as usual?
VANĚK	Somewhat maybe—
	(Pause.)
BREWMASTER	Drink up! Why ain't you drinkin'?
VANĚK	Thank you, but I'm not used to drinking beer—
BREWMASTER	You bein' serious?! Well, don't worry, we gonna break you in over here. Oh yeah, you gonna get used to drinking beer, no problem. We all drink it here, everybody—it's kind of like a tradition or something we got in this brewery—
VANĚK	I know—
	(Pause.)
BREWMASTER	And don't you let it get you down—
VANĚK	I am not down—
	(Pause.)
BREWMASTER	So how's everything else?
VANĚK	Such as what?
BREWMASTER	Like everything in general—
VANĚK	Oh, not too bad, thank you—
	(Pause.)
BREWMASTER	So you like it here?
VANĚK	I do—
BREWMASTER	Things could always be worse, right?
VANĚK	I guess—
	(Brewmaster opens another bottle and pours himself beer.)
BREWMASTER	A guy'll get used to just about anything, right?
VANĚK	Yes—
	(Pause.)
BREWMASTER	So kill that, will ya!
	(Vaněk empties his glass; Brewmaster refills it.)
VANĚK	Oh no, not any more, please—
BREWMASTER	What are you talkin' about? You ain't even started tastin' it yet! *(Pause.)* So what about the people here? You gettin' along with everybody?
VANĚK	Fine, thank you—
BREWMASTER	If you don't mind me givin' you a little tip, I wouldn't wanna get too close to any of these people here—Me, I don't trust anybody! People are real assholes! Real assholes! You'd better believe it. So you just do your job—don't get into no deep discussions—that really ain't worth it— especially in your case—
VANĚK	I understand—
	(Pause.)
BREWMASTER	In point of fact, what the hell was this stuff you been writin'—if you don't mind me askin'?
VANĚK	Theatre plays—

BREWMASTER	Theatre plays, huh? So they played 'em in some theatre somewhere, or what?
VANĚK	Yes—
BREWMASTER	Oh, yeah, yeah—So theatre plays, huh? Listen, that bein' the case, you oughta write somethin' about our brewery here. Somethin' like about somebody like Bureš—D'you know Bureš?
VANĚK	Yes—
BREWMASTER	Hell of a character, ain't he?
VANĚK	Yes—
	(Pause.)
BREWMASTER	But anyway, I betcha this never even crossed your mind, right?
VANĚK	What do you mean?
BREWMASTER	Well, that you gonna end up rollin' em in a brewery one day—
VANĚK	Well— *(noncommittal.)*
BREWMASTER	Them is the paradoxes of life, right?
VANĚK	Well—
BREWMASTER	Boy, I'll tell you!
	(Pause.)
BREWMASTER	You said you're rollin' the empties today?
VANĚK	Yes—
BREWMASTER	But yesterday it was them full suckers—I saw you myself—
VANĚK	Sherkezy was off yesterday—
BREWMASTER	Oh yeah, right—
	(Pause.)
	Well, we ain't never had a writer in here yet—And we've had 'em all, I tell ya! Like take Bureš! D'you know what he used to be? A gravedigger! That's where he learned to tip 'em and that's why he came to us here—That guy's full of stories, I tell ya!
VANĚK	I know—
BREWMASTER	So what the hell were them plays about?
VANĚK	Mostly about office people—
BREWMASTER	Oh, office people, huh? For real? Well—
	(Pause.)
	D'you take your break yet?
VANĚK	Not yet—
BREWMASTER	Well, you can take it later. Just tell the guard at the gate that you been in my office—
VANĚK	Thank you—
BREWMASTER	And quit thanking me all the time, will ya?
	(Pause.)
	Anyway, I do respect you—

VANĚK	Respect me? Why?
BREWMASTER	It's gotta be a bitch—After you been sitting at home all your life—where it's nice and warm—sleeping as long as you wanted to every morning—and now outta the blue this—Seriously now, that I gotta lotta respect for— *(Pause.)* Excuse me— *(Brewmaster gets up and leaves. Vaněk quickly pours his beer into the Brewmaster's glass. A few moments later, the Brewmaster returns, zipping up his fly. He sits back down.)* So you like used to actually know all kinds of actresses when you used to write for them theatres?
VANĚK	Of course—
BREWMASTER	So d'you know Bohdalová,[2] too?
VANĚK	Yes—
BREWMASTER	I mean you personally?
VANĚK	Yes—
BREWMASTER	So maybe you could invite her over one of these days for a few beers—We'd get Bureš in on it, too—Could be hell of a good time, what do you think?
VANĚK	Well— *(Pause.)*
BREWMASTER	Don't you let it get you down!
VANĚK	I'm not down— *(Brewmaster gets up, opens another bottle, and pours himself beer. Pause.)*
BREWMASTER	You know that young guy from upstairs? You know who I'm talkin' about?
VANĚK	Mlynarik?
BREWMASTER	Watch your step around that guy— *(Pause.)* And Karel Gott,[3] d'you know him, too?
VANĚK	Yes, I do. *(Pause.)*
BREWMASTER	It's too bad you wasn't here some five years ago! You would've seen a hell of a gang here! Today, it ain't nothin' like it no more. Yeah, we used to have a good time around here. A bunch of us used to get together at the maltroom—myself, this guy Kaja Maranek, he's gone, Honza Peterka, the girls from the bottling plant—we even been known to party all night long—and we still got everything done, too! Just go and ask Honza Peterka, see what he says—
VANĚK	He's already told me about it— *(Pause.)*
BREWMASTER	Is there a lotta dough in them plays?

VANĚK	It varied a lot—
BREWMASTER	Well, you gotta clear at least five thousand, right?
VANĚK	It all depends on how many theatres produce it—Sometimes you make quite a bit of money—At other times, you don't make any at all—
BREWMASTER	Like for a whole month even?
VANĚK	Even several months—
BREWMASTER	So it's got its drawbacks, too, don't it? Just like everything else, right?
VANĚK	Yes—
BREWMASTER	But anyway, them's the paradoxes, right?
VANĚK	Uh, huh—
BREWMASTER	Boy, I tell you—
	(Pause.)
	You're not drinkin' a goddam thing!
VANĚK	But I am drinking.
	(Brewmaster opens another bottle and pours beer for both of them. Pause.)
BREWMASTER	Listen, I'm gonna tell you somethin'—strictly between you and me—if anybody else was sitting in my place here—you would not be working here today—I'll guarantee you that much—
VANĚK	Was there a lot of problems with this?
BREWMASTER	You can say that again!
VANĚK	I feel really obliged to you—
BREWMASTER	You understand I'm not out to make a big deal out of this—but when I see that I can help somebody, why wouldn't I help him? I just got this kind of a mentality even today still! In this situation—people should help each other in my opinion—today I scratch your back, the next time you scratch mine—ain't that so?
VANĚK	Yes—
	(Pause.)
BREWMASTER	D'you take your break yet?
VANĚK	Not yet—
BREWMASTER	Well, you can take it later. Just tell the guard that you been in my office—
VANĚK	Thank you—
BREWMASTER	And quit thanking me all the time, will ya!
	(Pause.)
	Lemme tell ya, these days everybody's afraid of gettin' their tits caught in the wringer—
VANĚK	I know—
	(Pause.)
BREWMASTER	The important thing is that we're all in the same damn boat

	here, so let's act like it—
VANĚK	Yes—
BREWMASTER	You know I don't know how you feel about it, but I've always said, you gotta have teamwork. A good team's the key to everything—
VANĚK	I agree—
BREWMASTER	So why ain't you drinkin'? You'd rather be sippin' a little wine, wouldn'tcha?
VANĚK	Well—
BREWMASTER	Here you're gonna get used to drinkin' beer. We all drink beer here, everybody—It's kind of like a tradition or something we got in this brewery—
VANĚK	I know—

(Pause.)

BREWMASTER	But Karel Gott's got it made these days, don't he?
VANĚK	I suppose so—

(Pause.)

BREWMASTER	You married?
VANĚK	Yes—
BREWMASTER	Any kids?
VANĚK	No—

(Pause.)

BREWMASTER	Like I said, you got my respect—
VANĚK	Oh, please—
BREWMASTER	No seriously! This's gotta be a bitch to get used to—

(Pause.)

Excuse me—

(Brewmaster gets up and leaves. Vaněk quickly pours his beer into Brewmaster's glass. A few moments later, Brewmaster returns, zipping up his fly. He sits back down.)

So how old is she?

VANĚK	Who?
BREWMASTER	Bohdalová—
VANĚK	About forty-three or so—
BREWMASTER	You serious? She sure don't look it on TV—

(Pause.)

No, but really: Everything will come out all right, so long we all hang in there together—so long we all act like we're all in the same boat—like I said: A good team's the key to everything—

(Brewmaster opens another bottle and pours himself more beer.)

Too bad you weren't here about five years ago. Then you would've seen some teamwork around here. Today, shit! Today I don't trust nobody here—

(Pause.)
So who the hell is this guy Kohout?

VANĚK   What Kohout?

BREWMASTER   Some Kohout was supposed to visit you—

VANĚK   That's one of my colleagues—

BREWMASTER   Some kind of a writer, too?

VANĚK   Yes. Why do you ask?

BREWMASTER   No reason.
(Pause.)
Don't get the wrong impression, Vaněk. I got my share of problems here, too—

VANĚK   Yes?

BREWMASTER   Why d'you think they stuck me in this dump? But I'm sure you're not interested in any of that—

VANĚK   I am interested as a matter of fact—

BREWMASTER   You know what I was supposed to be doin'?

VANĚK   What?

BREWMASTER   I was supposed to be running a brewery in Pardubice—

VANĚK   Seriously?

BREWMASTER   And look at me! I'm here—Them is the paradoxes, right?

VANĚK   Why didn't you go there?

BREWMASTER   Let's just drop it.
(Pause.)
You married?

VANĚK   Yes—

BREWMASTER   Any kids?

VANĚK   No—
(Pause.)

BREWMASTER   Listen, it ain't any of my business, but you should tell that Holub[4] guy not to come around—

VANĚK   You must mean my colleague Kohout—

BREWMASTER   And what did I say?

VANĚK   You said Holub—

BREWMASTER   Who cares! Look, it ain't none of my business—I don't even know that person—I don't know who he is or anything—I'm just tellin' you this, because it's in your own interest—

VANĚK   Well I'm sorry, boss, but I—

BREWMASTER   Man, you're suckin' on it like it was some French cognac, or somethin'!

VANĚK   I've told you I wasn't used to it—

BREWMASTER   Gimme a break!

VANĚK   No, seriously—

BREWMASTER   Or maybe it's that I just ain't good enough for you to drink with—

VANĚK   Oh no, not at all—

BREWMASTER	Well, you know I ain't no pop star like Gott or nothin'. I'm just your everyday brewery hick—
VANĔK	You're a professional at what you do just like Gott is at what he does. So what happened that you didn't go to Pardubice?
BREWMASTER	Let's just drop it—
	(Brewmaster opens another bottle and pours himself beer. Pause.)
	It'll all be okay, Vanĕk! Don't you worry, I won't let you down! You're a quiet, hardworking guy. You check in regular every day, you don't talk crap like all the others, you don't beef about the pay—and considerin' the shortage of man-power, eh?
VANĔK	I am very grateful to you—
BREWMASTER	Besides, you are a decent guy, I can tell, I got a nose for that. I can spot a ripoff artist from a mile off. That Mlynařik from upstairs—know which one I mean?
VANĔK	Yes—
BREWMASTER	I got his number the moment he turned up. Watch out for him—
	(Pause.)
VANĔK	So why didn't you go to Pardubice?
BREWMASTER	Let's just drop it—
	(Pause.)
	Anyway, Vanĕk, me you can count on! I'm standing by you—
VANĔK	Thank you—
BREWMASTER	All I need from you is to be sure I can count on you, too—that you ain't gonna pull the rug from under me—that I'm able to lean on you—
VANĔK	I'll do everything I can to make sure you're satisfied with my work.
BREWMASTER	Look, I didn't have to tell you a goddam thing! By rights, I shouldn't 've even mentioned anything to you! In my position, everbody else would've—
VANĔK	Excuse me, but what were you not supposed to tell me?
BREWMASTER	Well, the stuff about that Holub—
VANĔK	Kohout—
BREWMASTER	Lookit, I dunno what kind of a guy he is, and I don't even wanna know either. I don't care about him—fuck him, okay— you are what's at stake here, right? All in all, you ain't got it so bad here—you roll your empties—everybody's stayin' off your back—that Kohout guy ain't gonna give you a job now, is he, if I can't swing keepin' you here, right? Or is he?
VANĔK	It's not very likely—
BREWMASTER	So you see my point! So why the hell not be sensible about it, man!

	(Pause.)
VANĚK	Boss—
BREWMASTER	What?
VANĚK	I am sorry, but I—
BREWMASTER	You what?
VANĚK	I can see whomever I want to, after all—
BREWMASTER	And am I tellin' you any different? You see whoever you feel like! That's your constitutional right! Don't let nobody bullshit you about that! Don't let nobody take that away from you! Because you are a man and not some old sock or somethin'! This here is a matter of principle, damn it!
VANĚK	So you see yourself—
BREWMASTER	And he's gonna understand it that way, too, that Kohout guy. He's gotta understand that you're gonna see whoever you wanna see! Or won't he? *(Brewmaster opens another bottle and pours himself beer. Pause.)*
VANĚK	Boss—
BREWMASTER	What?
VANĚK	It's time for me to go—
BREWMASTER	What's the big hurry?
VANĚK	They'll be looking for me in the cellar—
BREWMASTER	Fuck 'em if they can't take a joke! They got Sherkezy down there, don't they? You sit here and drink! *(Pause.)* You don't care why I never made it to Pardubice?
VANĚK	I do.
BREWMASTER	For real?
VANĚK	Really! Why didn't you go there?
BREWMASTER	You know what they did to me? They accused me of splitting five hundred barrels of lager—this surplus we had here—with this one restaurant manager. Ain't that somethin'? The whole thing didn't happen that way at all of course, but this son of a bitch—this Mlynařik from fermenting upstairs—you know who I'm talkin' about?
VANĚK	Yes—
BREWMASTER	That's just to show you what kind of folks you're dealin' with here! Me, I don't trust nobody here! People are assholes, you know! Real assholes! You better believe me! Just do your job and don't get into no deep discussions here—that really ain't worth it—especially in your case—
VANĚK	I understand— *(Pause.)*
BREWMASTER	D'you take your break yet?
VANĚK	Not yet.

13

BREWMASTER	Well, you can take it later. Just tell the guard that you been in my office—
VANĚK	Thank you.
BREWMASTER	And quit thanking me all the time, will ya! *(Pause.)* Excuse me— *(Brewmaster gets up and leaves. Vaněk quickly pours his beer into the Brewmaster's glass. A few moments later, the Brewmaster returns, zipping up his fly. He sits back down.)* So when you gonna bring her over?
VANĚK	Who?
BREWMASTER	Bohdalová, fer Chrissake!
VANĚK	I'll ask her when I get a chance—
BREWMASTER	So how about inviting her for this Saturday?
VANĚK	This coming Saturday?
BREWMASTER	Why the hell not?
VANĚK	I don't know if she'd have the time—
BREWMASTER	For you, she'll make the time, right?
VANĚK	You know actors have all kinds of commitments—their time is booked up way in advance—they can't just start changing everything—
BREWMASTER	Well, of course if you don't think we're good enough for her here, then you don't have to invite her at all—
VANĚK	No, I don't think that at all—
BREWMASTER	I'm not gonna twist your arm about it—Seemed to me we could of had some fun here—
VANĚK	Well— *(Pause.)*
BREWMASTER	And don't you let it get you down!
VANĚK	I'm not down! *(Pause.)*
BREWMASTER	Listen, Ferdinand—you're Ferdinand, aren't you?
VANĚK	Yes—
BREWMASTER	Listen, Ferdinand, I wanted to have a word with you—
VANĚK	I know— *(Pause.)*
BREWMASTER	Why the hell aren't you drinkin'?
VANĚK	As I said before, I'm not much of a beer drinker—
BREWMASTER	Over here, everybody's a beer drinker—
VANĚK	I know— *(Pause.)*
BREWMASTER	Listen, Ferdinand—can I call you that?
VANĚK	Of course—
BREWMASTER	What would you say if we put you in charge of the warehouse here? That wouldn't be bad, would it? In any case, you are a

	pencil-pusher, you ain't no ripoff artist, so? You're not gonna keep on rollin'em ballbusters with the gypsies down there forever! The warehouse is warm—you'd close it up around lunchtime, tell 'em you're straightenin' stuff out—and you'd have a little time to dream up a few jokes for them plays of yours—hell, if you wanted to, you could even catch a nap in there—what do you say?
VANĚK	You think that it would be possible?
BREWMASTER	Why wouldn't it be possible?
VANĚK	Naturally, I am not in a situation where I can pick and choose—but if there really should be such a possibility, I'd really think that it would be just outstanding—I am pretty much organized—I can type—I get by in a few foreign languages— and you know that it can get really cold down in the cellar—particularly if one isn't used to it—
BREWMASTER	That's just it. You understand what evidencing is?
VANĚK	I'm sure that I can learn—I do have four semesters of economics—
BREWMASTER	Oh yeah? So you understand evidencing then?
VANĚK	I'm sure I can learn—
BREWMASTER	It's warm in there—you'd lock up at lunchtime—you're not gonna keep on rollin'em ballbusters with the gypsies forever!
VANĚK	Well, if there were to be an opening like that— *(Pause.)*
BREWMASTER	No, no, no Vaněk! I can spot a ripoff artist from a mile off! You're a straightshooter, I'm a straightshooter, so I don't see why we can't get together on this! What do you say?
VANĚK	Yes, of course—
BREWMASTER	So you're all for it?
VANĚK	Of course—
BREWMASTER	If you don't want to, then tell me! Maybe you don't care to form a team with me—maybe you got somethin' against me—maybe you just got some other plans—
VANĚK	I have nothing against you—on the contrary—you've done quite a lot for me—I feel obliged to you—particularly if the warehouse should work out—naturally, I'll do everything I can to make sure you're satisfied with my work— *(Brewmaster opens another bottle and pours beer into both glasses.)*
BREWMASTER	So we can drink to that?
VANĚK	Yes— *(They both drink.)*
BREWMASTER	Bottoms up! *(Vaněk struggles to empty his glass; Brewmaster immediately refills it. Pause.)*

	And don't you let it get you down!
VANĚK	I'm not down—
	(Pause.)
BREWMASTER	Listen, Ferdinand—
VANĚK	Yes—
BREWMASTER	We're buddies, right?
VANĚK	Yes—
BREWMASTER	You're not just sayin' that?
VANĚK	No—
BREWMASTER	So you trust me?
VANĚK	Of course I do—
BREWMASTER	Hold it: No bullshit now, you trust me?
VANĚK	I trust you—
BREWMASTER	All right then—I'm gonna tell you somethin'—but this is strictly between you and me, okay?
VANĚK	Okay—
BREWMASTER	I can depend on you now?
VANĚK	You can—
BREWMASTER	So listen— *(He lowers his voice.)* They come here to ask about you—
VANĚK	Who does?
BREWMASTER	*They* do, who else—
VANĚK	Really?
BREWMASTER	I swear—
VANĚK	And you get the feeling that—as far as my job here at the brewery—that it may be on the line? *(Pause.)* Are they putting pressure on you to fire me? *(Pause.)* Or are they holding it against you that you've hired me? *(Pause.)*
BREWMASTER	All right—I'm gonna tell you somethin'—but this is strictly between you and me, okay?
VANĚK	Okay—
BREWMASTER	I can depend on you now?
VANĚK	You can—
BREWMASTER	All right—If there was anybody else sittin' here in my place, you wouldn't be workin' here, I'll guarantee you that! Need I say more?
VANĚK	Yes, of course—I feel very obliged to you—
BREWMASTER	I'm not fishin' for no compliments here—
VANĚK	I know that—
BREWMASTER	It's just to let you know how things stand—
VANĚK	Thank you—
	(Pause.)

BREWMASTER	Excuse me—
	(Brewmaster struggles to get up and exits on unsteady feet. Vaněk quickly pours his beer into Brewmaster's glass. A few moments later, Brewmaster returns, zipping up his fly. He sits back down.)
	You ever got it on with her?
VANĚK	With whom?
BREWMASTER	Bohdalová, fer Chrissake—
VANĚK	Me? No—
BREWMASTER	You sure?
VANĚK	Yes—
BREWMASTER	Then you're just a wimp in my book!
	(Pause.)
VANĚK	Boss—
BREWMASTER	What?
VANĚK	It's time for me to go—
BREWMASTER	What's the big hurry?
VANĚK	They'll be looking for me in the cellar—
BREWMASTER	Fuck 'em if they can't take a joke! They got Sherkezy down there, don't they? You sit here and drink!
	(Pause.)
	Listen, Ferdinand—you're Ferdinand, aren't you?
VANĚK	Yes—
BREWMASTER	Listen Ferdinand—I can call you that, can't I?
VANĚK	Go ahead—
BREWMASTER	Hold it, I'm makin' sure I ask first, so you don't get pissed off at me, or somethin'.
VANĚK	Why would I get pissed off?
BREWMASTER	With you, I never know where the hell I'm at—you don't say shit—God only knows what the hell you're thinkin'—all you ever say is "yes, boss," "thank you, boss"—
VANĚK	I was brought up that way—
BREWMASTER	Whereas me, I'm just an ignorant brewery hick! That's what you meant, didn't you? Don't tell me you didn't—
VANĚK	I did not—
BREWMASTER	Right, let's cut out this bullshit—so at least I know where I'm at here—
VANĚK	I don't think badly of you, really I don't—on the contrary—
BREWMASTER	So we're buddies then, right?
VANĚK	Yes—
BREWMASTER	So you trust me?
VANĚK	I trust you—
BREWMASTER	All right then. Look, I happen to know one of them that come here on account of you—we went to school together—I know him pretty good—his name is Tonda Mašek—he's an

17

	all right guy, at least I get along with him okay—
VANĚK	Good for you—
BREWMASTER	It's not like he is a big shot over there—because that he ain't—but he did help me out a couple of times—and I don't know when I'm gonna need him again—besides which, like I said, he's an all right guy—so I just— well, to make a long story short—I just couldn't leave him hangin', you understand?
VANĚK	I understand—
	(Pause.)
BREWMASTER	Well—why the hell you starin'?
VANĚK	I'm not staring—
BREWMASTER	Well, say it then, what you're thinkin'! Go ahead and spell it out!
VANĚK	I'm not thinking anything.
BREWMASTER	Don't tell me! I know exactly what you're thinkin' right now! Except you probably don't realize that if I didn't promise to do it, they would've found somebody else, and that would've been even worse, because then it wouldn't've been nobody straight like me for sure! Because I'm always gonna level with you, unlike most other people, that's just the kind of mentality I got—even today still! And that's your only break, if you wanna know somethin'. Because people are real assholes! Real assholes! Or do you think you're gonna run into another dumb fucker like me, who's gonna spill the beans like this? You believe that and I'll give you a great deal on a bridge downtown! Where the hell do you think you live anyway?
VANĚK	I do value your honesty, of course—
BREWMASTER	D'you have any idea of the chances I'm takin' by levelling with you here? How am I ever gonna get even with you, if you doublecross me? I'm puttin' myself completely into your hands here, fer Chrissake!
VANĚK	I won't say anything to anybody—
BREWMASTER	Then you're gonna write it down somewhere! You're gonna put it in one of them plays—they'll confiscate it from you— and me, I'll be completely washed up!
VANĚK	I'll keep this to myself, you can depend on that—
BREWMASTER	For real?
VANĚK	For real—
	(Brewmaster opens another bottle and pours himself beer. Pause.)
	Boss—
BREWMASTER	Uh huh—
VANĚK	If it were to work out—I mean the warehouse business— what about old *Sustr*?
BREWMASTER	What about him?

(Pause.)
But anyway—Them's the paradoxes, right?

VANĚK   Well—

BREWMASTER   Boy, I'll tell you—
(Pause.)

VANĚK   Boss—

BREWMASTER   Uh huh.

VANĚK   Getting back to the warehouse—you think that they'd allow it? They must know that it's pretty warm in there—

BREWMASTER   They don't know shit!
(Pause.)
You married?

VANĚK   Yes—

BREWMASTER   Any kids?

VANĚK   No—

BREWMASTER   I got three myself. Just so you know—
(Pause.)

VANĚK   If it came to it, you could argue that I'll be more isolated from other people there—

BREWMASTER   Listen, Ferdinand—

VANĚK   That's what they're concerned about, isn't it, that I don't come into contact with people?

BREWMASTER   Listen, Ferdinand—

VANĚK   That could have the desired effect, right?

BREWMASTER   Listen, Ferdinand—

VANĚK   Yes?

BREWMASTER   Do you play poker?

VANĚK   No—

BREWMASTER   I do—we used to have this pretty good bunch of guys—we'd get together every Thursday, you know—and what do you think happened? I had to blow it off, too, on account of this Lojza Hlavatý—

VANĚK   Uh huh.

BREWMASTER   Just to show you that none of us got it easy—
(Pause.)
Listen, Ferdinand—

VANĚK   Yes?

BREWMASTER   You know my old lady?

VANĚK   No—
(Pause.)

BREWMASTER   Listen, Ferdinand—

VANĚK   Yes?

BREWMASTER   Everything's all fucked up—

VANĚK   I know—

BREWMASTER   You don't know shit! You've got it made! You write your damn plays—you roll your barrels—and they can all go to hell for all you care! What more do you want? The fact is, they're even afraid of you, man!

VANĚK That I would doubt—

BREWMASTER They sure are! But what about me? Nobody gives a damn about me! Nobody's sendin' no reports about me nowhere! They can squeeze me every time they feel like! They got me by the balls! They can squash me like a bug—whenever they decide! Like a goddam bug! You—you got it made!
(Pause.)
Listen, Ferdinand—

VANĚK Yes?

BREWMASTER But you're gonna bring that Bohdalová around, ain't you? You're not gonna just blow it off? Right? You're not just gonna forget about it?

VANĚK You can depend on that—I'm going to give her a call tonight and I'll set it up—

BREWMASTER You think she'll come?

VANĚK I'll do what I can—

BREWMASTER You two are buddies, ain't you?

VANĚK Yes, that's true—

BREWMASTER Hold it. You said you were buddies—

VANĚK We are—

BREWMASTER Hold it. So are you buddies or are you not buddies?

VANĚK I said we are—

BREWMASTER So what's the hitch?
(Pause.)
She can see whoever she wanna see, damn it!

VANĚK Of course—

BREWMASTER That's her constitutional goddam right!

VANĚK Of course—

BREWMASTER This is a matter of principle, goddam it!
(Pause.)
And anyhow—nobody ever needs to know who brought her here! We'll just turn it into a Friendship-with-the-workin'-masses kind of thing! They can't find anything wrong with that!

VANĚK I agree—

BREWMASTER So you gonna get her to come?

VANĚK I'll do whatever I can—I'll give her a call tonight—we are friends—there is nothing wrong with this—
(Pause.)

BREWMASTER Listen, Ferdinand—

VANĚK Yes?

BREWMASTER If you only knew how sick I am of all this shit!

VANĚK	I understand that—
BREWMASTER	You don't understand didley! You're just sayin' to yourself— He's stupid—let him talk it out of his system—
VANĚK	I'm not thinking that—
BREWMASTER	Why ain't you drinkin'?
VANĚK	I am drinking—
BREWMASTER	D'you take your break yet?
VANĚK	Not yet—
BREWMASTER	Fuck the break—
VANĚK	I don't feel like eating anyway—
BREWMASTER	I may be stupid, but I'm callin' it like it is—
VANĚK	I know that—
BREWMASTER	I wanted to have a talk with you—
VANĚK	I know—
BREWMASTER	People are assholes! Real assholes! Why ain't you drinkin'?
VANĚK	I am drinking—
BREWMASTER	D'you take your break yet?
VANĚK	Not yet—
BREWMASTER	Hell you—You got it made—
VANĚK	I feel obliged to you—
BREWMASTER	Everything's all fucked up—
	(Brewmaster opens another bottle and pours himself beer. Pause.)
	Listen, Ferdinand—
VANĚK	Yes—
BREWMASTER	You don't mind me callin' you Ferdinand and all?
VANĚK	No—
BREWMASTER	If you do, just lemme know—
VANĚK	I don't mind—
BREWMASTER	Well, at least you don't mind—
VANĚK	On the contrary. I'm glad we became acquainted—
BREWMASTER	"I'm glad we became acquainted"—"I do value your honesty"— why the hell do you talk so— so—
VANĚK	Bookishly?
BREWMASTER	Yeah—
VANĚK	Well, if it irritates you, then—
BREWMASTER	Nothing irritates me—I do value that we became acquainted —Shit!
VANĚK	Sorry?
BREWMASTER	Shit!
	(Pause.)
VANĚK	Excuse me—
BREWMASTER	What?
VANĚK	I have to go—
BREWMASTER	What's the big hurry?

VANĚK	They'll be looking for me in the cellar—
BREWMASTER	Fuck'em if they can't take a joke! They got Sherkezy down there, don't they? You sit here and drink!
VANĚK	Seriously—They'll be upset—
BREWMASTER	I get it, now I'm borin' you, huh? I know that with Karel Gott and Bohdalová, you used to have better parties!
VANĚK	I feel good here talking with you, I wouldn't want people to start commenting about this—that wouldn't make sense— particularly now that there is the prospect of a job in the warehouse—
BREWMASTER	You really feel good here?
VANĚK	Really—
BREWMASTER	You're not just sayin' that?
VANĚK	No—

(Brewmaster opens another bottle and pours himself beer. Pause.)

BREWMASTER	Ferdinand—
VANĚK	Yes?
BREWMASTER	You know the worst thing about it?
VANĚK	What?
BREWMASTER	That I'm runnin' outta ideas about what to keep on tellin'em every damn week—I really don't know the first thing about you—I hardly ever even run into you around here—and the little bullshit gossip I do catch up here—that you go hide out in the lab—that they saw you downtown a couple of times with Maruška from the bottling plant—that the maintenance guys did some work on your heating system at home—that ain't shit! You tell me— what the hell am I supposed to tell 'em all the time? What?
VANĚK	I'm sorry, but I can hardly help you in this—
BREWMASTER	Sure you can! If only you wanted to—
VANĚK	Me? How?
BREWMASTER	You're what they call an intellectual, right? You keep up with politics, don't you? You're writing stuff, ain't you? Who the hell should know whatever the fuck it is they wanna know if not you?
VANĚK	I'm sorry, but this would—
BREWMASTER	Look, in the warehouse, you'd have tons of time—so what's wrong with jottin' somethin' down on paper for me once a week? You could do that much for me, couldn't you? Look, I'm gonna take care of you! You'll be happier there than a pig in shit! You can even take beer back there—as much as you want, too! It would be child's play for you! You're a writer, damn it, right? This Tonda Mašek really is a decent guy and he really does need it, so we can't just leave him hangin'!

	Damn it, didn't we just finish sayin' that we're all in this together? That we gotta give each other a hand? That we're gonna be a team here? Didn't we just toast to that now? You tell me—did we or did we not just toast to that?
VANĚK	We did, but—
BREWMASTER	Right now it's all up to you, Ferdinand! If you take care of us, everything'll turn out great! You'll scratch my back, I'll scratch his, he mine and I'll scratch yours—so nobody's gonna get shortchanged in the deal. Let's not make life hell for each other!
	(Pause.)
	Well, why you starin'?
VANĚK	I'm not staring—
	(Pause.)
BREWMASTER	You'd have direct control over what they're gonna know about you—that ain't too damn shabby either—
VANĚK	I know—
	(Pause.)
BREWMASTER	And that warehouse would be pretty good for you, too, wouldn't it? It's warm—tons of time—
VANĚK	That would be excellent—
	(Pause.)
BREWMASTER	So—what the hell's the issue here?
	(Pause.)
VANĚK	Boss—
BREWMASTER	What?
VANĚK	I really am very grateful to you for everything you've done for me—I appreciate it, because I know better than anybody how rare this attitude is these days— you really gave me a lift, because I seriously don't know what I would have done without your help—that warehouse job would mean even more of a relief to me than you might think—but I just—don't be angry with me—I can't be snitching on myself—
BREWMASTER	What do you mean snitch? Who's talkin' about snitchin' here?
VANĚK	It isn't because of me—it couldn't hurt me any more—but it really is a matter of principle! I just cannot, as a matter of principle, become a part of—
BREWMASTER	A part of what? Go ahead and spell it out! You can't be a part of what?
VANĚK	A part of a way of doing things that I don't agree with—
	(A short, tense pause.)
BREWMASTER	Well. So you can't. You can't then. That's great! Now you're showin' your true colours! Now you've really said it all!

(Brewmaster gets up and begins pacing nervously around the room.)

And what about me? You're just gonna let me sink, right? You're just gonna say, fuck you! It's okay if I end up being an asshole! Me, I can wallow in this shit, because I don't count, I ain't nothin' but a regular brewery hick—but the VIP here can't have any part of this! It's okay if I get smeared with shit, so long the VIP here stays clean! The VIP is worried about the principle! But he don't bother thinkin' about other people! Just as long as he comes out smellin' like a rose! The principle is dearer to him than another human being! That's typical of all of you!

VANĚK   Who?

BREWMASTER   You, damn it! You intellectuals. VIP's! All that stuff's just smooth bullshit, except that you can afford it, because nothin' can ever happen to you, there's always somebody interested in how you doin', you always know how to fix that, you're still up there, even when you're down and out, whereas a regular guy like me is bustin' his ass and ain't got shit to show for it and nobody will stick up for him and everybody just fucks him and everybody blows him off and everybody feels free to yell at him and he ain't got no life at all and, in the end, the VIP's will say, hell, he ain't got no principles! A soft job in the warehouse, you'd take that from me—but to take a piece of that shit I gotta walk knee-deep in every damn day along with it, that you don't wanna! No way! You're all too goddam smart, you got everything worked out ahead of time, you know exactly how to look out for yourselves! Principles! Principles! Damn right you gonna fight for your damn principles—they're worth a fortune to you, you know just how to sell them principles, you're makin' a killin' on them, you're livin' off them—but what about me? I only get my ass busted for havin' principles! You always got a chance, but what kind of a chance have I got? Nobody's gonna take care of me, nobody's afraid of me, nobody's gonna write anything about me, nobody's gonna gimme a hand, nobody's interested in me, all I'm good for is to be the manure that your damn principles gonna grow out of, and to scare up heated rooms so you can play heroes! And lookin' like a damn fool gonna be all I'm gonna have to show for it! You're gonna go back to all your actresses one day—you gonna floor 'em with how you rolled barrels—you gonna be a hero—but what about me? What can I go back to? Who's ever gonna pay any attention to me? Who's ever gonna appreciate anything I did? What the hell do I ever get out of life? What's in store for me? What?

(Brewmaster is crushed. He drops back into his chair, puts his head on Vaněk's breast, and begins sobbing loudly. After a few moments, he calms down, looks up at Vaněk, and says quickly)

Ferdinand—

VANĚK Uh huh.

BREWMASTER You my buddy?

VANĚK I am—

BREWMASTER Please go and get her—bring her over right now—I beg you—

(Pause.)

Tell her "Jiřinka—I got this one buddy back there—he's a regular brewery hick—but he calls it the way it is"—

(Pause.)

I'm gonna fight like hell and get you the warehouse job—I'm not gonna ask you for no reports—just do this one thing for me, please—

(Pause.)

Are you gonna do that much for me? You are gonna do it for me, right? For one damn evening—I'll be okay after that— everything's gonna be different after that—I'm gonna know I didn't waste my life after that—that fucked-up life I got ain't been all the way fucked up—you gonna bring her?

(Pause; then Brewmaster grabs Vaněk's clothes and begins to scream desperately into his face.)

If you're not gonna bring her over here—I—I dunno—I might—I might—

(Brewmaster begins to sob again, quietly, and he puts his head on Vaněk's breast. Pause. After a while, Brewmaster's sobbing turns into loud snoring. Vaněk waits for a few moments, then gently lays Brewmaster's head on the desk of the table, gets up quietly, and heads for the door. He stops there, turns around, hesitates for a moment, and finally says to the sleeping Brewmaster)

VANĚK Don't let it get you down—

(Vaněk exits. Soon thereafter, there is a knock on the door. Brewmaster wakes up immediately, completely sobered up after his short sleep and behaving exactly the way he did in the opening scene of the play. He has evidently forgotten everything that has gone on.)

BREWMASTER Come in—

(Vaněk enters, zipping up his fly.)

Oh, Mr. Vaněk! Come on in! Have a seat—
(Vaněk sits down.)
How about a beer?
(Vaněk nods; Brewmaster pulls a bottle out of the case, opens it, pours beer into two glasses, one of which he pushes in front of Vaněk. Vaněk downs it quickly.)
Well? So how is it goin'?

VANĚK   Everything's all fucked up—
(Curtain falls.)

THE END

NOTES

1. Sherkezy, though he never actually appears on stage, is also mentioned in Dienstbier's *Reception*, where he is referred to as the prison's dope expert and expert tattooer.
2. Jiřiná Bohdalová is a popular stage and television actress in Czechoslovakia.
3. Karel Gott is a successful popular singer, one of the few who move relatively freely across the border to the West and back. He has made numerous recordings in Czechoslovakia, Germany, and Austria. It may be of interest that Milan Kundera calls Gott an exponent of "music minus memory, the music in which the bones of Beethoven and Ellington, the dust of Palestrina and Schönberg, lie buried" *(The Book of Laughter and Forgetting* [New York: Knopf, 1981], p. 181).
4. Miroslav Holub (born 1923), a distinguished Czech scientist, is also a well-known poet whose work is available in English. The confusion of the names of Kohout and Holub provides linguistic humour in Czech which gets lost in translation: the Brewmaster mixes up not only writers but also bird species (Kohout means rooster and Holub means pigeon in Czech).

VÁCLAV HAVEL

Unveiling

Translated by Jan Novak

CHARACTERS

Vera
Michael
Ferdinand Vaněk[1]

PLACE

Apartment of Vera and Michael

(On stage is the apartment of Vera and Michael. It consists of a large living room, extending into a step-up dining area upstage. A serving window connects the dining area with the kitchen behind the stage. Stage right, there is a door leading into a hallway; stage left, a large fireplace; at the centre of the stage stands an antique table, surrounded by soft, modern seats. A mass of sundry antiques and curious objects decorates the room—for example, there is an Art Nouveau marquee, a Chinese vase, a limestone Baroque angel, an inlaid chest, a folkloristic painting on a glass pane, a Russian icon, old handmortars and grinders, and so on; a niche in the wall houses a wooden Gothic madonna; a rococo musical clock adorns the fireplace, and a Turkish scimitar hangs above it. The dining area is furnished in a "rustic style," with a wooden farm-cart wheel on the wall; the floor is covered with a thick, shaggy carpet, on it lie several Persian mats and, near the fireplace, a bear hide with a stuffed head; downstage left stands a filigreed wooden confessional. The room also has a hi-fi stereo and a bar cart, standing near the fireplace and holding various bottles, glasses, ice cubes, as well as a bowl with stuffed oysters. As the curtain rises, Vaněk is standing at the door, evidently having just come in. Vera and Michael are facing him. Vaněk is holding a bouquet of flowers behind his back.)

VERA We're so glad that you've made it—
MICHAEL We were afraid that you might not make it any more—
VERA We've been looking forward to seeing you so much—
MICHAEL What can I get you? A whiskey?
VANĚK All right—
(Michael steps over to the bar cart and starts preparing three whiskeys; Vaněk is momentarily at a loss about what to do, then he hands the flowers to Vera.)
VERA Oh, they are lovely! *(She takes the bouquet and looks at it.)* And you never forget— *(She smells it.)* What a beautiful aroma! Thank you, Ferdinand—
(Vera walks upstage and puts the flowers into a vase; Vaněk looks around the apartment with curiosity. A short pause.)
VANĚK It looks different here somehow—
VERA I hope so! Michael has poured a lot of sweat into it! You know how he is when he gets involved in something: He won't let go till he has everything just the way he's planned it—
MICHAEL I only finished the thing the day before yesterday: we haven't had anybody over yet, so this actually is sort of an unveiling. Ice?

VANĚK	All right—

(Vera comes back downstage; the surprised Vaněk is still looking around.)

Where did you get all this?

MICHAEL It wasn't easy, as you can imagine. I did have a few contacts among the antique dealers and collectors. I had to establish a few more. The most important thing was not to give up when I wasn't able to get my hands on what I wanted the first time around—

VERA He did quite a job on this, didn't he?

VANĚK I guess so—

VERA I confess that even I didn't think it would come out this well! When you want to give your place some character, it's not enough merely to like old things—you have to know how to get them and how to present them and how to integrate them with your modern furnishings—but, it so happens that Michael is really good at that—that's why you won't find a single goof here—

(Michael hands the glasses to Vera and Vaněk, then he takes his glass, raises it, and turns to Vaněk.)

MICHAEL Welcome, Ferdinand—

VERA We've missed you—

MICHAEL As I was working on this, I thought about you often—what you were going to say when you saw it all.

VANĚK Well, cheers—

(They all drink; a short pause.)

MICHAEL Of course, if I didn't have Vera's full support, it would have never come out like this. And it wasn't just a matter of support and understanding either, she gave me direct assistance in this, too! Take that Turkish scimitar there—how do you like it?

VANĚK It's nice—

MICHAEL And how does it fit in with everything here?

VANĚK Very well—

MICHAEL You see, and it's something that Vera found on her very own, and she even put it up there, too—all the while not knowing that this was exactly the thing I had in mind for that spot over the fireplace! Isn't that awesome?

VANĚK That's great—

(A short, awkward pause.)

VERA Have a seat—

VANĚK Thank you—

(They all sit down in the soft seats. A short pause, Vaněk is looking around again; Vera and Michael watch him with satisfaction; Vaněk eventually notices the confessional.)

	What's that?
MICHAEL	It's what you see — a confessional —
VANĚK	Where did you get that?
MICHAEL	You won't believe how lucky I was. I heard that they were going to liquidate a church that'd been closed down, so I dropped everything and jumped in the car. And this is the result. I managed to get it out of the sexton for three hundred —
VANĚK	That's all?
MICHAEL	Not bad, is it? Pure Baroque!
VANĚK	What are you going to do with it?
MICHAEL	What do you mean, what are we going to do with it? You don't like it?
VANĚK	Well I do —
MICHAEL	Isn't that a fantastic object, we're really happy about it, aren't we, Vera?
VERA	It really is a superb piece of craftsmanship, I'd say that Michael really got another one of his steals there — *(A short pause.)* What do you think of the dining area?
VANĚK	*(Turns around)*: It's cozy —
VERA	Wasn't that a nice idea — to do it so simply — as if on a farm —
VANĚK	Mmn — *(A short pause.)*
MICHAEL	Do you know what I like best here?
VANĚK	What?
MICHAEL	This Gothic madonna! I needed one that would fit into that niche, and they were all either bigger or smaller —
VANĚK	And there was no way to enlarge the niche?
MICHAEL	But that's just what I didn't want to do. It strikes me that it's got the perfect dimensions the way it is —
VERA	See, that's Michael! He'd rather wear out his feet than simply enlarge the thing! *(Pause.)*
MICHAEL	And what about you? When are you going to get started?
VANĚK	On what?
MICHAEL	On your place —
VANĚK	I don't know —
MICHAEL	You should finally do something about it! You can't go on living out of boxes forever —
VANĚK	I don't even pay any attention to it anymore —
MICHAEL	If you don't feel like tackling it yourself, why doesn't Eva do something about it? She has plenty of time on her hands —
VERA	I think Eva actually needs to get involved in something like that — it would be a good way to get her back on her feet —
MICHAEL	We would gladly come to the rescue if she found she couldn't

	handle something—
VERA	Michael has tons of experience with this now—he'd tell her what to do—where to start—what she'd need—
MICHAEL	I'd tell her who's got what—where to go and who to see—
VERA	That's true, Ferdinand. Why don't you put Eva in charge of it anyway?
VANĚK	It's not really Eva's cup of tea—
VERA	We know that, but if you were to waken her interest somehow—
MICHAEL	Damn it, you have to do something about that home of yours—
VERA	You know, Michael and I think that a person lives the way a person lives. When you have what we call a place with character, your whole life suddenly—like it or not—acquires a certain face, too—a sort of new dimension—a different rhythm, a different content, a different order—isn't that so, Michael?
MICHAEL	She's right, Ferdinand! One really shouldn't be indifferent to what one eats, one shouldn't be indifferent to what one eats on, and what one eats with, what one dries oneself with, what one wears, what one takes a bath in, what one sleeps on. And once any of these things starts to matter, you'll find that something else suddenly matters, too, and then another thing gets you, and so a whole sort of a chain of things develops— and if you head down that road, what else can it mean but that you're upgrading your life to another, higher level of culture—and that you raise yourself to a kind of higher harmony—which then in effect translates itself into your relationships with other people! You tell him, Vera!
VERA	That is a fact, Ferdinand! If the two of you were to put a little more effort into the way you live, I'm sure that things would get smoother in your marriage, too—
VANĚK	But things are smooth—
VERA	Ferdinand!
VANĚK	But really—
VERA	You don't like to talk about it, I know. But you know, Michael and I have been talking about the two of you a lot lately; we've been thinking about you a lot—and we really care about how you two live!
MICHAEL	We're only trying to help, Ferdinand!
VERA	You're our best friend—we like you a lot—you have no idea how happy we'd be for you if your situation finally got resolved somehow!
VANĚK	What situation?
VERA	Let's just drop it. Shouldn't I light the fireplace?
VANĚK	Not for me—

MICHAEL	So I'll put on some music, all right?
VERA	Michael has just brought a ton of new records from Switzer-land—
VANĚK	Maybe later, perhaps?
	(Pause; then suddenly the musical clock on the mantlepiece breaks into a period tune, startling Vaněk. After a while, the clock falls silent. Pause.)
VERA	So tell us—how is everything with you?
VANĚK	Well, you know—nothing's changed—
VERA	Is it true that you've got a job in a brewery now?
VANĚK	Yes—
VERA	That's horrible!
	(Pause. Then Vera points at the bar cart.)
	Michael, would you—
MICHAEL	Oh yeah—
	(Michael takes the bowl with oysters off the bar and stands it in front of Vaněk.)
VERA	Help yourself—
VANĚK	What is it?
MICHAEL	That's Vera's specialty: sauteed groombles—
VANĚK	Groombles? I never heard of this—
VERA	We've really become very fond of them lately, Michael has just brought a whole box of them from Switzerland—
MICHAEL	Because Vera really knows how to make them—
VERA	What you have to do is to watch for the precise moment, when they've just stopped puffing up and before they start falling—
MICHAEL	Taste one!
	(Vaněk takes one oyster and, using a spoon, begins to scoop out its contents. He concentrates on the taste; Vera and Michael watch him tensely.)
	So what do you think?
VANĚK	It's good—
MICHAEL	Isn't it?
VANĚK	You went to all the trouble of making this just for me?
VERA	We're having our unveiling today, right?
VANĚK	It sort of reminds me of blackberries a little bit—
VERA	That may be because I put in a few drops of woodpeak to help the taste—
VANĚK	Drops of what?
MICHAEL	Woodpeak—
VERA	That's my original contribution—
VANĚK	Really?
MICHAEL	An excellent idea, isn't it? I can't help it, but Vera's really got a talent for cooking. A week doesn't go by without her

making some novelty—and she always uses her imagination to improve it. Take this Saturday for example—what was it that we had now? Oh yeah, the liver with walnuts! And it was such a delicacy; anyway, would you ever think of putting woodpeak on groombles?

VANĚK   Never—

MICHAEL   See what I mean!
(Vaněk puts away the empty oyster shell and wipes his mouth with a napkin.)

VERA   Well, it's a joy cooking for Michael! He knows how to appreciate and praise even the most modest idea, and when something turns out well, he really gets off on it. If he just stuffed everything in like a mechanical pie-eater, not even knowing what it is that he's swallowing, then I probably wouldn't have so much fun with it either—

VANĚK   I can understand that—

MICHAEL   But there's even more to it than that. When you know that an interesting dinner, some small gourmet surprise, is waiting for you at home, you look that much more forward to getting there and you have that much less reason to go bar-hopping with your buddies. Maybe it'll strike you as being petty, but I think that these things also represent a kind of cement that holds a family together and helps to create that important feeling that you've got something to back you up at home. Don't you think?

VANĚK   Yes, of course—
(Pause.)

VERA   How's Eva doing? Has she learned to cook anything yet?

VANĚK   She's always cooked—

VERA   Granted, but how!

VANĚK   I pretty much like her cooking—

VERA   Because you got used to it already. Don't get offended, but those pepper steaks she made when we were over that time before Christmas—it was before Christmas, wasn't it?

VANĚK   Yeah—

VERA   Don't get offended, but they were dreadful! Do you remember, Michael?

MICHAEL   How could I forget!

VANĚK   Eva was a little nervous that time—

VERA   I'm sorry, but something like that should never ever happen to a cook! What does she cook for you usually anyway?

VANĚK   We tend to have cold-plate dinners—

VERA   Even on Saturdays?

VANĚK   Sometimes we have something warm, too—breaded cutlets, for example—

MICHAEL	Listen, Ferdinand, it's none of my business, but why don't you send Eva to some of those courses? She has plenty of time on her hands—
VERA	Eva? Come on! You think Eva would take any courses?
MICHAEL	Well, that's true—
VERA	If she did learn how to cook though, it would immediately boost her self-confidence— but she won't see the connection. She's floating around somewhere, God knows where—
VANĚK	I think her cooking's fine—
VERA	Ferdinand!
VANĚK	Really, I—
MICHAEL	You don't like to talk about it, I know. But you know Michael and I have been talking about the two of you a lot lately, we've been thinking about you a lot—and we really care about how you two live!
VERA	We're only trying to help, Ferdinand!
MICHAEL	You're our best friend—we like you a lot—you have no idea how happy we'd be for you if your situation finally got resolved somehow!
VANĚK	What situation?
MICHAEL	Let's just drop it. Shouldn't I light the fireplace?
VANĚK	Not for me—
VERA	So I'll put on some music, all right? Michael has just brought a ton of new records from Switzerland—
VANĚK	Maybe later, okay?
(Pause. Then suddenly the musical clock on the mantlepiece breaks into a period tune, startling Ferdinand. After a while, the clock falls silent. Pause.)
MICHAEL	So what do you actually do there, in that brewery?
VANĚK	I draw beer—
MICHAEL	Into barrels?
VANĚK	Yes—
MICHAEL	That's got to be pretty rough, doesn't it?
VANĚK	It's not that bad—
(Pause.)
MICHAEL	Are we going to show Pete to Ferdinand?
VERA	A little later, Michael, he might still wake up right now—
VANĚK	How is Pete doing?
MICHAEL	He's fantastic! I'd only been gone to that Switzerland for ten days, but when I got back, I tell you I barely recognized him—that's how much of a jump he's made in that time!
VERA	He's extremely curious—
MICHAEL	Bright—
VERA	Perceptive—
MICHAEL	He has a superb memory—

VERA	And yet he's such a good-looking kid, too!
MICHAEL	Just to give you an example. Do you know what he asked me this morning? *(To Vera.)* I forgot to tell you about that! All of a sudden, he comes to me and says, "Daddy, can a frog drown?" What do you think about that? Isn't that awesome?
VERA	Did he really ask you that? If a frog can drown?
MICHAEL	Imagine that! He comes to me and says, "Daddy, can a frog drown?"
VERA	Outstanding! I don't even know if I could have thought of that. Can a frog drown! Outstanding! Outstanding!
MICHAEL	You know, Ferdinand, sometimes I say to myself that to have a child and to bring it up is the only thing that has any meaning in life! Because it is such an awesome encounter with the mystery of life—such a lesson in life appreciation! Unless you actually go through it, you can never even understand it—
VERA	Absolutely, Ferdinand, it's an awesomely strange and beautiful experience: One day this tiny being shows up here—and you know he is yours—that without you, he wouldn't even be here—that you've made him and now he's here—and he's living his own life—and is growing before your eyes—and then he starts to walk—and say things—and reason—and ask questions—now isn't that a miracle?
VANĚK	Certainly is—
MICHAEL	You know a child really changes you a lot—suddenly you begin to understand everything differently, more deeply—life—nature—people—and all of a sudden your own life—like it or not—acquires sort of a new dimension—a different rhythm, a different content, a different order—isn't that so, Vera?
VERA	Exactly! Just take the responsibility you suddenly have. It's up to you what kind of a person he will turn out to be—what he'll feel—think—how he'll live—
MICHAEL	But not only that: Because it was you who tossed him into this world, who offered it to him for his use and who provides him with some orientation in it, you suddenly start feeling a much greater responsibility for this world that now contains your child—do you know what I mean?
VANĚK	I guess so—
MICHAEL	I never believed this, but now I see how a child gives you a brand new point of view, a brand new set of values—and suddenly it begins to dawn on you that the most important thing now is what you do for that child, what sort of a home you create for him, what sort of a start you give him, what openings you provide—and in the light of this awesome responsibility you start seeing the utter insignificance of

	most of the things you had once thought world-shattering—
VERA	How did he put it? Can a frog drown? Do you see what that tiny head can give birth to? Isn't that fantastic?
VANĚK	Mmn—
	(Pause.)
MICHAEL	So what about you two?
VANĚK	What about us two?
MICHAEL	Why don't you have a child yet anyway?
VANĚK	I don't know—
VERA	Eva probably doesn't want one, does she?
VANĚK	Oh no—she does—
VERA	I really don't understand that girl! Is she so afraid of all the worries that go along with having a child? Because if she really wanted a baby, you would have had one ages ago!
MICHAEL	You are the ones who will lose out by not pursuing this— because for the two of you, a child would definitely be the best possible solution! It would help you, Ferdinand, to see many things far more sensibly, realistically, wisely—
VERA	It would straighten out your relationship, because it would give you a common purpose in life—
MICHAEL	And what a good thing it would be for Eva!
VERA	You'd see how it would change her!
MICHAEL	How it would suddenly bring out the woman in her again!
VERA	How it would teach her to pay attention to the house—
MICHAEL	To cleanliness—
VERA	To routine—
MICHAEL	To you—
VERA	To herself—
MICHAEL	Seriously, Ferdinand, you ought to have a child, believe us!
VERA	You have no idea how happy we'd be for you!
MICHAEL	We really would, Ferdinand—
VANĚK	I believe you—
	(Pause.)
VERA	Of course, there are women who don't respond even to that—and then you really feel for the children—
MICHAEL	Of course, just to rely on the kid as some sort of panacea that will solve all your problems, that wouldn't be right either—a certain aptitude probably already has to be there before anything else—
VERA	Absolutely! For example, Michael here makes an ideal father: He drives himself hard at the office, till I feel really sorry for him sometimes, just so that he brings home some money— and then he still devotes almost all his free time to the family and to the home! Just take this remodelling he did. He came from the office and instead of stretching out and relaxing, he

went right back to work—just so Pete can grow up in a nice environment from the very beginning, and learn to love nice things! And even while doing all that, he still found the time for Pete—

MICHAEL   Of course, Vera is awesome, too. Do you know what it is—to shop, take care of the kid, cook, clean up, do the laundry—while the apartment is a disaster area—despite all that to look just the way she looks right now? That really is no joke! I have to say I admire her more and more as time goes on—

VERA   A lot of that is because our marriage is working—

MICHAEL   Definitely! We get along just awesomely. I don't even remember us having any serious quarrels lately—

VERA   We are interested in one another, yet we don't limit or tie each other down—

MICHAEL   We are kind and attentive to one another without tiring each other with too much thoughtfulness—

VERA   And we always have things to say to each other, because we're fortunate enough to have exactly the same sense of humour—

MICHAEL   The same definition of happiness—

VERA   The same interests—

MICHAEL   The same taste—

VERA   The same views on family life—

MICHAEL   And what is extremely important: We also perfectly complement each other physically—

VERA   That's true, it is really extremely important! And Michael is awesome in that respect—he can be wild as well as tender—honestly selfish as well as awesomely attentive and giving—passionately spontaneous as well as inventively cunning—

MICHAEL   But Vera deserves all the credit for that, because she manages to excite and stimulate me again and again—

VERA   You'd be surprised, Ferdinand, how often we do it! And that's only possible because we always approach it as though it were our very first time, so that it becomes something new, something different for us every time. Something unique, unforgettable. In short, we really invest ourselves fully into it, and, consequently, for us it can never become just a matter of a stereotype or a boring routine—

MICHAEL   You see, Vera knows, too, that to be a good wife doesn't mean merely being a good homemaker and a good mother—she rightly feels that what it means more than anything else is to be a good lover! That's why she takes such wonderful care of herself. So that she keeps her sex appeal even while doing the heaviest chores—in fact, even more so then than at other times!

VERA Do you remember the day before yesterday, Michael—when you got home early just as I was scrubbing the floor?

MICHAEL It was beautiful, wasn't it?

VERA Why do you think Michael isn't drawn to other women? Because he knows that he doesn't have some mop-swinging wifey at home, but a real woman who knows how to take as well as give—

MICHAEL Of course, Vera is still just as attractive as always—I'd even say that now, after Pete, she has ripened even more—she has an astonishingly fresh and youthful body now—well, judge for yourself!
(Michael undoes Vera's clothes, uncovering her breasts.)
Not bad, right?

VANĚK Great—

MICHAEL Do you know what I will do, for example?

VANĚK No—

MICHAEL I'll kiss her, switching from her ear to her neck and back—which really turns her on and I like it, too—like this, look!
(Michael starts to kiss Vera, alternating between her ear and her neck; Vera groans excitedly.)

VERA Don't, darling, no—please—wait—a little later, okay—come on—
(Michael stops kissing Vera.)

MICHAEL We'll talk a little more first, then we'll show you more—to give you an idea of the range of our technique—

VANĚK Won't I make you nervous by being here?

VERA You silly boy! You're our best friend, right?

MICHAEL And we'll be happy to show you how far you can take these things!
(Pause.)

VERA So what about you two?

VANĚK How do you mean?

VERA Do you still sleep with each other at all?

VANĚK Oh yes—now and then—

VERA Not too often, right?

VANĚK That depends—

VERA And how is it?

VANĚK I don't know—it's normal—

MICHAEL I'm sure you don't put any effort into it—just go through the motions, so it's over and done with—

VANĚK We do our best—

VERA I don't understand that girl at all! Why wouldn't she try a little harder at least in this—

MICHAEL	Is it really impossible for you to get her involved in this a little more?
VANĚK	We really don't pay that much attention to it—
VERA	See? That's where you go wrong, ignoring such an important thing! That's why you're in the shape you're in! Yet it would require so little effort—and maybe it would pull your relationship back up on its feet again!
MICHAEL	And what a good thing it would be for Eva—you'd see how it would change her!
VERA	How it would bring out the woman in her again!
MICHAEL	How it would teach her to pay attention to the house—
VERA	To you—
MICHAEL	To herself—
VERA	And what a change it would effect in you! Just imagine, suddenly there are no more reasons to go bar-hopping with your cronies—
MICHAEL	Chase waitresses—
VERA	Drink—
VANĚK	I don't chase waitresses—
VERA	Ferdinand!
VANĚK	I don't—
VERA	You don't like to talk about it, I know. But you know Michael and I have been talking about the two of you a lot lately, we've been thinking about you a lot—and we really care about how you two live!
MICHAEL	We're only trying to help, Ferdinand!
VERA	You're our best friend—we like you a lot—you have no idea how happy we'd be for you if your situation finally got resolved somehow!
VANĚK	What situation?
VERA	Let's just drop it. Shouldn't I light the fireplace?
VANĚK	Not for me—
MICHAEL	So I'll put on some music, all right?
VERA	Michael has just brought a ton of new records from Switzerland—
VANĚK	Maybe later—okay?
	(Pause. Then suddenly the musical clock on the mantlepiece breaks into a period tune, startling Vaněk. After a while, the clock falls silent again. Pause.)
MICHAEL	But anyway—that's what I call art!
VANĚK	What is?
MICHAEL	That madonna—
VANĚK	Mmn—
MICHAEL	Do you realize the dramatic tension that arises between her and that scimitar?

VANĚK	Mmn—
	(Pause.)
VERA	You probably don't use much woodpeak, do you?
VANĚK	Not really—
VERA	If you'd like, Michael could bring you some from Switzerland—
VANĚK	Oh yeah?
MICHAEL	You know that'd be no trouble at all for me.
	(Pause.)
VERA	Have some more—
VANĚK	No, thank you—
	(Pause.)
MICHAEL	Why didn't you bring Eva with you?
VANĚK	She didn't feel well—
MICHAEL	It's not any of my business, of course, but you should take her out now and then—give her a reason to put some nice clothes on, put on some make-up, do her hair—
VANĚK	She does her hair—
MICHAEL	Ferdinand!
VANĚK	She does—
MICHAEL	You don't like to talk about it, I know. But we're only trying to help—
VERA	We like you a lot—
MICHAEL	You're our best friend—
VANĚK	I know—
	(Pause; the musical clock plays its tune.)
MICHAEL	Did you get my card from Switzerland?
VANĚK	That was from you?
MICHAEL	You didn't figure that out?
VANĚK	Should have thought of it—
	(Pause.)
VERA	*(To Michael)* What did Pete ask you now? Can a frog drown?
MICHAEL	Right, imagine that—
VERA	Outstanding! Outstanding!
	(Pause.)
MICHAEL	*(To Vaněk)* Have some more—
VANĚK	No, thank you—
	(Pause.)
VERA	Do you know what we started to do again?
VANĚK	What?
VERA	Going to the sauna!
VANĚK	Really?
VERA	We've been going every week now, and you wouldn't believe how good it is for us. For the nerves, you know—
MICHAEL	Do you want to start coming with us?
VANĚK	Not really—

VERA	Why not?
VANĚK	I wouldn't have the time—
MICHAEL	Don't get offended, Ferdinand, but you're making a mistake! It would really get you into a better shape spiritually, psychically, as well as physically, and it would definitely be better for you and cost you less time, too, than the endless tongue-thrashing in bars with all those wise-guy cronies of yours—
VANĚK	Whom do you mean by that?
MICHAEL	Well, all those various failures. Landovský and so on—
VANĚK	I wouldn't call them failures—
VERA	Ferdinand!
VANĚK	Not at all—
VERA	You don't like to talk about it, I know. But we're only trying to help you—
MICHAEL	We like you a lot—
VERA	You're our best friend—
VANĚK	I know—
	(Pause; the clock plays its tune.)
MICHAEL	Do you know what Vera promised me?
VANĚK	What's that?
MICHAEL	That she'll give me another child next year!
VANĚK	That's nice—
VERA	I think Michael deserves no less—
	(Pause.)
	Do you know what Michael brought me from Switzerland?
VANĚK	What's that?
VERA	An electric almond peeler—
MICHAEL	You'll have to take a look at it, it's a beautiful thing—
VERA	As well as practical—
MICHAEL	Because Vera does a lot with almonds, so it saves her tons of time—
VANĚK	I believe it—
	(Pause.)
VERA	Have some more—
VANĚK	No, thank you—
	(Pause.)
MICHAEL	Listen, Ferdinand—
VANĚK	Huh?
MICHAEL	Do you ever write anything anymore?
VANĚK	Not a whole lot—
MICHAEL	That's what we thought—
VANĚK	Now that I have that job, I don't have the time for it, nor the concentration—
MICHAEL	But from what I hear, you weren't doing much writing anyway, even before you got this job—

VANĚK	Not all that much—
VERA	Listen, didn't you maybe take that job because in your own mind it gave you an excuse for not writing?
VANĚK	Not that—
MICHAEL	So what is your real reason for not writing? Is it just that it's not pouring out? Or are you going through some kind of a crisis?
VANĚK	It's hard to say—the times, everything that is going on—you get this feeling of futility—
MICHAEL	Don't get offended, Ferdinand, but I think that the times are just another excuse for you, just like the job at the brewery, and that the real problem is inside of you and nowhere else! You're just all bent out of shape, you've given up on everything, you find it too tedious to strive for anything, to fight, to wrestle with problems—
VERA	Michael is right, Ferdinand. Somehow you should finally pull yourself together—
MICHAEL	Take care of problems at home—with Eva—
VERA	Start a family—
MICHAEL	Give your place some character—
VERA	Learn how to budget your time—
MICHAEL	Stop carousing—
VERA	Start going to the sauna again—
MICHAEL	Simply begin to live a decent, healthy, rational life—
VANĚK	I don't feel that I'm doing anything irrational—
MICHAEL	Ferdinand!
VANĚK	I don't—
MICHAEL	You don't like to talk about it, I know. But we're only trying to help you—
VERA	We like you a lot—
MICHAEL	You're our best friend—
VERA	You have no idea how happy we'd be for you if your situation finally got resolved somehow!
MICHAEL	Shouldn't I light the fireplace?
VANĚK	Not for me—
VERA	So I'll put some music on, all right? Michael has just brought a ton of new records from Switzerland—
VANĚK	Maybe later, okay?
	(Pause; the musical clock plays its tune.)
MICHAEL	Listen, Ferdinand—
VANĚK	Huh?
MICHAEL	Listen, honestly now. Are you serious with that brewery?
VANĚK	What do you mean?
MICHAEL	You know, don't get offended now, but we just don't understand what the purpose of the whole thing it—

VERA	To just throw yourself away like that— to bury yourself in a brewery somewhere—only to ruin your health—
MICHAEL	All these gestures are completely senseless! What are you trying to prove? It's been a long time since that kind of thing impressed anybody—
VANĚK	I'm sorry, but it was the only thing I could do in my situation—
MICHAEL	Ferdinand! Don't tell me that you couldn't do better than that—if only you really wanted to and tried a little harder— I'm convinced that with a little more effort and a little less ego on your part, you could've long been sitting in an editorial office somewhere—
VERA	You are, after all, basically an intelligent, hard-working person— you have talent—you have clearly proven that in the past with your writing—so why would you suddenly be afraid of confronting life?
MICHAEL	Life is rough and the world is divided. The world doesn't give a damn about us and nobody's coming to our rescue—we're in a nasty predicament, and it will get worse and worse—and you are not going to change any of it! So why beat your head against the wall and charge the bayonets?
VERA	What I can't understand is how could you have got mixed up with those Communists—
VANĚK	What Communists?
VERA	Well, that Kohout and his crowd—you don't have anything in common with them! Don't be silly, forget about them and go your own way—
MICHAEL	We're not saying that breaking out of that charmed circle is going to be easy, but it's your only chance and nobody's going to do it for you! In these things, it's every man for himself, but you're definitely strong enough to withstand that isolation!
VERA	Just take a look at us—you could be just as happy as we are—
MICHAEL	You could have a home with character of your own—
VERA	Full of nice things and good family vibrations—
MICHAEL	A well-coiffed and elegant wife—
VERA	A bright kid—
MICHAEL	You could have a more appropriate job—
VERA	Make a few crowns—
MICHAEL	Later they'd even let you go to Switzerland—
VERA	Eat decent food—
MICHAEL	Dress better—
VERA	Go to the sauna—
MICHAEL	Now and then you could have some friends over—
VERA	Show them your place—
MICHAEL	Your kid—
VERA	Put on some music for them—

MICHAEL	Make groombles—
VERA	In short, live a little more like humans!

(Vaněk has quietly got up and begun shyly to back up to the door. When Vera and Michael notice it, they stand up in surprise.)

MICHAEL	Ferdinand—
VANĚK	Mmn—
MICHAEL	What's the matter?
VANĚK	Nothing's the matter—
VERA	You're leaving?
VANĚK	I have to go now—
MICHAEL	Go where?
VANĚK	Home—
VERA	Home? How come? Why?
VANĚK	It's late—I get up early—
MICHAEL	But you can't do this—
VANĚK	I really have to go—
VERA	I don't understand! Here we are in the middle of our unveiling—
MICHAEL	We wanted to give you a tour of the place—
VERA	Show you everything we have here—
MICHAEL	We thought you'd finish that bottle—
VERA	Eat the rest of the groombles—
MICHAEL	Take a look at Pete—
VERA	Michael wanted to tell you about Switzerland—
MICHAEL	Vera wanted to light the fireplace—
VERA	Michael wanted to play those new records for you—
MICHAEL	We thought you'd stay the night—
VERA	See how we make love—
MICHAEL	That we'd share a little of that family warmth you don't have at home—
VERA	Get into a different frame of mind—
MICHAEL	Pull you out of that mess you're living in—
VERA	Get you back up on your feet—
MICHAEL	Suggest some ways of how you can resolve your situation—
VERA	Show you what happiness is—
MICHAEL	And love—
VERA	Family harmony—
MICHAEL	A life that has some meaning—
VERA	You know that we're only trying to help you—
MICHAEL	That we like you a lot—
VERA	That you are our best friend—
MICHAEL	You cannot be this ungrateful!
VERA	We don't deserve this—not while we're trying to do so much for you!
MICHAEL	Who did you think Vera has spent the whole afternoon

	baking the groombles for?
VERA	Who do you think Michael has bought that whiskey for?
MICHAEL	Who do you think we wanted to play those records for? Why do you think I wasted all that hard currency on them, and dragged them half way across Europe?
VERA	Why do you think I dressed up like this, put the make-up and the perfume on, got my hair done?
MICHAEL	Why do you think we fixed this place up like this anyway? Who do you think we're doing all this for? For ourselves? *(Vaněk is by the door now.)*
VANĚK	I'm sorry, but I'll be off now—
VERA	*(Agitated.)* Ferdinand! You can't just leave us here! You're not going to do that to us! You can't just pick up and go now; there's so much we still wanted to tell you! What are we going to do here without you? Don't you understand that? Stay, I beg you, will you stay here with us!
MICHAEL	You haven't even seen our electric almond peeler yet!
VANĚK	See you later! And thank you for the groombles— *(Vaněk is leaving, but before he closes the door behind him, Vera breaks into hysterical sobs. Vaněk stops and looks at her, not knowing what to do.)*
VERA	*(Crying.)* You're selfish! A disgusting, unfeeling, inhuman egotist! An ungrateful, ignorant traitor! I hate you—I hate you so much—go away! Go away! *(Vera runs to the bouquet that she got from Vaněk, tears it out of the vase, and throws it at Vaněk.)*
MICHAEL	*(To Vaněk)* See what you're doing? Aren't you ashamed? *(Vaněk is at loss about what to do for a moment, then picks up the bouquet, carries it hesitantly to the vase, puts it back in, slowly returns to his seat, and sits down with some embarassment. Vera and Michael watch tensely to see what he will do. As soon as they see that he has sat back down, they instantly return to their old selves, smiling as they sit down, too. A short pause.)*
VERA	Michael, won't we put some music on for Ferdinand?
MICHAEL	That a good idea— *(Michael walks over to the record-player and the instant he turns it on, music starts pouring forth out of all the speakers: preferably some international hit, such as Sugar Baby Love in the interpretation of Karel Gott.[2] The curtain falls; the music is booming on, the same tune over and over again, until the last spectator has left the theatre.)*

THE END

NOTES

1. In the original Czech version the Vaněk-figure here was called Bedřich (Frederick in Czech). At this stage, however, when Ferdinand Vaněk has become a well-known character, the editor feels free to rename Bedřich in accordance with his meaning in the play.
2. See note 3 to *Audience.*

VÁCLAV HAVEL

Protest

Translated by Vera Blackwell

CHARACTERS

Vaněk
Staněk

PLACE

Staněk's Study, Prague.

Staněk's study. On the left, a massive writing desk, on it a typewriter, a telephone, reading glasses, and many books and papers; behind it, a large window with a view into the garden. On the right, two comfortable arm chairs and between them a small table. The whole back wall is covered by bookcases, filled with books and with a built-in bar. In one of the niches there is a tape recorder. In the right back corner, a door; on the right wall, a large surrealist painting. When the curtain rises, Staněk and Vaněk are on stage: Staněk, standing behind his desk, is emotionally looking at Vaněk, who is standing at the door holding a briefcase and looking at Staněk with signs of embarrassment. A short, tense pause. Then Staněk suddenly walks excitedly over to Vaněk, takes him by the shoulders with both arms, shakes him in a friendly way, calling out.)

STANĚK   Vaněk!—Hello!

(Vaněk smiles timidly. Staněk lets go, trying to conceal his agitation.)

Did you have trouble finding it?

VANĚK   Not really—

STANĚK   Forgot to mention the flowering magnolias. That's how you know it's my house. Superb, aren't they?

VANĚK   Yes—

STANĚK   I managed to double their blossoms in less than three years, compared to the previous owner. Have you magnolias at your cottage?

VANĚK   No—

STANĚK   You must have them! I'm going to find you two quality saplings and I'll come and plant them for you personally. *(Crosses to the bar and opens it.)* How about some brandy?

VANĚK   I'd rather not—

STANĚK   Just a token one. Eh?

(He pours brandy into two glasses, hands one glass to Vaněk, and raises the other for a toast.)

Well—here's to our reunion!

VANĚK   Cheers—

(Both drink; Vaněk shudders slightly.)

STANĚK   I was afraid you weren't going to come.

VANĚK   Why?

STANĚK   Well, I mean, things got mixed up in an odd sort of way— What?— Won't you sit down?

VANĚK   *(Sits down in an armchair, placing his briefcase on the floor beside him.)*

Thanks—

STANĚK   *(Sinks into an armchair opposite Vaněk with a sigh.)* That's

	more like it! Peanuts?
VANĔK	No, thanks—
STANĔK	*(Helps himself. Munching.)* You haven't changed much in all these years, you know?
VANĔK	Neither have you—
STANĔK	Me? Come on! Getting on for fifty, going gray, aches and pains setting in—Not as we used to be, eh? And the present times don't make one feel any better either, what? When did we see each other last, actually?
VANĔK	I don't know—
STANĔK	Wasn't it at your last opening night?
VANĔK	Could be—
STANĔK	Seems like another age! We had a bit of an argument—
VANĔK	Did we?
STANĔK	You took me to task for my illusions and my over-optimism. Good Lord! How often since then I've had to admit to myself you were right! Of course, in those days I still believed that in spite of everything some of the ideals of my youth could be salvaged and I took you for an incorrigible pessimist.
VANĔK	But I'm not a pessimist—
STANĔK	You see, everything's turned around! *(Short pause.)* Are you—alone?
VANĔK	How do you mean, alone?
STANĔK	Well, isn't there somebody—you know—
VANĔK	Following me?
STANĔK	Not that I care! After all, it was me who called you up, right?
VANĔK	I haven't noticed anybody—
STANĔK	By the way, suppose you want to shake them off one of these days, you know the best place to do it?
VANĔK	No—
STANĔK	A department store. You mingle with the crowd, then at a moment when they aren't looking you sneak into the wash-room and wait there for about two hours. They become convinced you managed to slip out through a side entrance and they give up. You must try it out sometime! *(Pause.)*
VANĔK	Seems very peaceful here—
STANĔK	That's why we moved here. It was simply impossible to go on writing near that railway station! We've been here three years, you know. Of course, my greatest joy is the garden. I'll show you around later—I'm afraid I'm going to boast a little—
VANĔK	You do the gardening yourself?
STANĔK	It's become my greatest private passion these days. Keep puttering about out there almost every day. Just now I've

been rejuvenating the apricots. Developed my own method, you see, based on a mixture of natural and artificial fertilizers plus a special way of waxless grafting. You won't believe the results I get! I'll find some cuttings for you later on—
(Staněk walks over to the desk, takes a package of foreign cigarettes out of a drawer, brings matches and an ashtray, and puts it all on the table in front of Vaněk.)
Ferdinand, do have a cigarette.

VANĚK Thanks—
(Vaněk takes a cigarette and lights it; Staněk sits in the other chair; both drink.)

STANĚK Well now, Ferdinand, tell me—How are you?

VANĚK All right, thanks—

STANĚK Do they leave you alone—at least now and then?

VANĚK It depends—
(Short pause.)

STANĚK And how was it in there?

VANĚK Where?

STANĚK Can our sort bear it at all?

VANĚK You mean prison? What else can one do?

STANĚK As far as I recall, you used to be bothered by hemorrhoids. Must have been terrible, considering the hygiene in there.

VANĚK They gave me suppositories—

STANĚK You ought to have them operated on, you know. It so happens a friend of mine is our greatest hemorrhoid specialist. Works real miracles. I'll arrange it for you.

VANĚK Thanks—
(Short pause.)

STANĚK You know, sometimes it all seems like a beautiful dream—all the exciting opening nights, private views, lectures, meetings—the endless discussions about literature and art! All the energy, the hopes, plans, activities, ideas—the wine-bars crowded with friends, the wild booze-ups, the madcap affrays in the small hours, the jolly girls dancing attendance on us! And the mountains of work we managed to get done, regardless! —That's all over now. It'll never come back!

VANĚK Mmn—
(Pause. Both drink.)

STANĚK Did they beat you?

VANĚK No—

STANĚK Do they beat people up in there?

VANĚK Sometimes. But not the politicals—

STANĚK I thought about you a great deal!

VANĚK Thank you—
(Short pause.)

THE VANĚK PLAYS

STANĚK	I bet in those days it never even occurred to you—
VANĚK	What?
STANĚK	How it'll all end up! I bet not even you had guessed that!
VANĚK	Mmn—
STANĚK	It's disgusting, Ferdinand, disgusting! The nation is governed by scum! And the people? Can this really be the same nation which not very long ago behaved so magnificently? All that horrible cringing, bowing and scraping! The selfishness, corruption and fear wherever you turn! What have they made of us, old pal? Can this really be us?
VANĚK	I don't believe things are as black as all that—
STANĚK	Forgive me, Ferdinand, but you don't happen to live in a normal environment. All you know are people who manage to resist this rot. You just keep on supporting and encouraging each other. You've no idea the sort of environment I've got to put up with! You're lucky you no longer have anything to do with it. Makes you sick at your stomach! *(Pause. Both drink.)*
VANĚK	You mean television?
STANĚK	In television, in the film studios—you name it.
VANĚK	There was a piece by you on the T.V. the other day—
STANĚK	You can't imagine what an ordeal that was! First they kept blocking it for over a year, then they started changing it around—changed my whole opening and the entire closing sequence! You wouldn't believe the trifles they find objectionable these days! Nothing but sterility and intrigues, intrigues and sterility! How often I tell myself—wrap it up, chum, forget it, go hide somewhere—grow apricots—
VANĚK	I know what you mean—
STANĚK	The thing is though, one can't help wondering whether one's got the right to this sort of escape. Supposing even the little one might be able to accomplish today can, in spite of everything, help someone in some way, at least give him a bit of encouragement, uplift him a little.—Let me bring you a pair of slippers.
VANĚK	Slippers? Why?
STANĚK	You can't be comfortable in those boots.
VANĚK	I'm all right—
STANĚK	Are you sure?
VANĚK	Yes. Really— *(Both drink.)*
STANĚK	*(Pause.)* How about drugs? Did they give you any?
VANĚK	No—
STANĚK	No dubious injections?
VANĚK	Only some vitamin ones—

58

STANĚK	I bet there's some funny stuff in the food!
VANĚK	Just bromine against sex—
STANĚK	But surely they tried to break you down somehow!
VANĚK	Well—
STANĚK	If you'd rather not talk about it, it's all right with me.
VANĚK	Well, in a way, that's the whole point of pre-trial interrogations, isn't it? To take one down a peg or two—
STANĚK	And to make one talk!
VANĚK	Mmn—
STANĚK	If they should haul me in for questioning—which sooner or later is bound to happen—you know what I'm going to do?
VANĚK	What?
STANĚK	Simply not answer any of their questions! Refuse to talk to them at all! That's by far the best way. Least one can be quite sure one didn't say anything one ought not to have said!
VANĚK	Mmn—
STANĚK	Anyway, you must have steel nerves to be able to bear it all and in addition to keep doing the things you do.
VANĚK	Like what?
STANĚK	Well, I mean all the protests, petitions, letters—the whole fight for human rights! I mean the things you and your friends keep on doing—
VANĚK	I'm not doing so much—
STANĚK	Now don't be too modest, Ferdinand! I follow everything that's going on! I know! If everybody did what you do, the situation would be quite different! And that's a fact. It's extremely important there should be at least a few people here who aren't afraid to speak the truth aloud, to defend others, to call a spade a spade! What I'm going to say might sound a bit solemn perhaps, but frankly, the way I see it, you and your friends have taken on an almost superhuman task: to preserve and to carry the remains, the remnant of moral conscience through the present quagmire! The thread you're spinning may be thin, but—who knows—perhaps the hope of a moral rebirth of the nation hangs on it.
VANĚK	You exaggerate—
STANĚK	Well, that's how I see it, anyway.
VANĚK	Surely our hope lies in all the decent people—
STANĚK	But how many are there still around? How many?
VANĚK	Enough—
STANĚK	Are there? Even so, it's you and your friends who are the most exposed to view.
VANĚK	And isn't that precisely what makes it easier for us?
STANĚK	I wouldn't say so. The more you're exposed, the more responsibility you have towards all those who know about you, trust

	you, rely on you and look up to you, because to some extent you keep upholding their honour, too! *(Gets up.)* I'll get you those slippers!
VANĚK	Please don't bother—
STANĚK	I insist. I feel uncomfortable just looking at your boots. *(Pause. Staněk returns with slippers.)*
VANĚK	*(Sighs.)*
STANĚK	Here you are. Do take those ugly things off, I beg you. Let me— *(Tries to take off Vaněk's boots.)* Won't you let me—Hold still—
VANĚK	*(Embarrassed.)* No—please don't—no—I'll do it— *(Struggles out of his boots, slips on slippers.)* There—Nice, aren't they? Thank you very much.
STANĚK	Good gracious, Ferdinand, what for?—*(Hovering over Vaněk.)* Some more brandy?
VANĚK	No more for me, thanks—
STANĚK	Oh, come on. Give me your glass!
VANĚK	I'm sorry, I'm not feeling too well—
STANĚK	Lost the habit inside, is that it?
VANĚK	Could be—But the point is—last night, you see—
STANĚK	Ah, that's what it is. Had a drop too many, eh?
VANĚK	Mmn—
STANĚK	I understand. *(Returns to his chair.)* By the way, you know the new wine-bar, "The Shaggy Dog"?
VANĚK	No—
STANĚK	You don't? Listen, the wine there comes straight from the cask, it's not expensive and usually it isn't crowded. Really charming spot, you know, thanks to a handful of fairly good artists who were permitted—believe it or not—to do the interior decoration. I can warmly recommend it to you. Lovely place. Where did you go, then?
VANĚK	Well, we did a little pub-crawling, my friend Landovský and I—
STANĚK	Oh, I see! You were with Landovský, were you? Well! In that case, I'm not at all surprised you came to a sticky end! He's a first class actor, but once he starts drinking—that's it! Surely you can take one more brandy! Right?
VANĚK	*(Sighs.)* *(Drinks are poured. They both drink. Vaněk shudders.)*
STANĚK	*(Back in his armchair. Short pause.)* Well, how are things otherwise? You do any writing?
VANĚK	Trying to—
STANĚK	A play?
VANĚK	A one-act play—

STANĚK	Another autobiographical one?
VANĚK	More or less—
STANĚK	My wife and I read the one about the brewery[1] the other day. We thought it was very amusing.
VANĚK	I'm glad—
STANĚK	Unfortunately we were given a rather bad copy.[2] Very hard to read.
VANĚK	I'm sorry—
STANĚK	It's a really brilliant little piece! I mean it! Only the ending seemed to me a bit muddy. The whole thing wants to be brought to a more straightforward conclusion, that's all. No problem. You can do it. *(Pause. Both drink. Vaněk shudders.)*
STANĚK	Well, how are things? How about Pavel?[3] Do you see him?
VANĚK	Yes—
STANĚK	Does he do any writing?
VANĚK	Just now he's finishing a one-act, as well. It's supposed to be performed together with mine—
STANĚK	Wait a minute. You don't mean to tell me you two have teamed up also as authors!
VANĚK	More or less—
STANĚK	Well, well!—Frankly, Ferdinand, try as I may, I don't get it. I don't. I simply can't understand this alliance of yours. Is it quite genuine on your part? Is it?—Good heavens! Pavel! I don't know! Just remember the way he started! We both belong to the same generation, Pavel and I, we've both—so to speak—spanned a similar arc of development, but I don't mind telling you that what he did in those days—Well! It was a bit too strong even for me!—Still, I suppose it's your business. You know best what you're doing.
VANĚK	That's right— *(Pause. Both drink.)*
STANĚK	Is your wife fond of gladioli?
VANĚK	I don't know. I think so—
STANĚK	You won't find many places with such a large selection as mine. I've got thirty-two shades, whereas at a common or garden nursery you'll be lucky to find six. Do you think your wife would like me to send her some bulbs?
VANĚK	I'm sure she would—
STANĚK	There's still time to plant them you know. *(Pause.)* Ferdinand—
VANĚK	Yes?
STANĚK	Weren't you surprised when I suddenly called you up?
VANĚK	A bit—
STANĚK	I thought so. After all, I happen to be among those who've still managed to keep their heads above water and I quite

	understand that—because of this—you might want to keep a certain distance from me.
VANĚK	No, not I—
STANĚK	Perhaps not you yourself, but I realize that some of your friends believe that anyone who's still got some chance today has either abdicated morally, or is unforgivably fooling himself.
VANĚK	I don't think so—
STANĚK	I wouldn't blame you if you did, because I know only too well the grounds from which such prejudice could grow. *(An embarrassed pause.)* Ferdinand—
VANĚK	Yes?
STANĚK	I realize what a high price you have to pay for what you're doing. But please don't think it's all that easy for a man who's either so lucky, or so unfortunate as to be still tolerated by the official apparatus, and who—at the same time—wishes to live at peace with his conscience.
VANĚK	I know what you mean—
STANĚK	In some respects it may be even harder for him.
VANĚK	I understand.
STANĚK	Naturally, I didn't call you in order to justify myself! I don't really think there's any need. I called you because I like you and I'd be sorry to see you sharing the prejudice which I assume exists among your friends.
VANĚK	As far as I know nobody has ever said a bad word about you—
STANĚK	Not even Pavel?
VANĚK	No—
STANĚK	*(Embarrassed pause.)* Ferdinand—
VANĚK	Yes?
STANĚK	Excuse me— *(Gets up. Crosses to the tape recorder. Switches it on: Soft, nondescript background music. Staněk returns to his chair.)* Ferdinand, does the name Javurek mean anything to you?
VANĚK	The pop singer? I know him very well—
STANĚK	So I expect you know what happened to him.
VANĚK	Of course. They locked him up for telling a story during one of his performances. The story about the cop who meets a penguin in the street—
STANĚK	Of course. It was just an excuse. The fact is, they hate his guts because he sings the way he does. The whole thing is so cruel, so ludicrous, so base!
VANĚK	And cowardly—
STANĚK	Right! And cowardly! Look, I've been trying to do something for the boy. I mean, I know a few guys at the town council and at the prosecutor's office, but you know how it is. Prom-

ises, promises! They all say they're going to look into it, but the moment your back is turned they drop it like a hot potato, so they don't get their fingers burnt! Sickening, the way everybody looks out for number one!

VANĚK   Still, I think it's nice of you to have tried to do something—

STANĚK   My dear Ferdinand, I'm really not the sort of man your friends obviously take me for! Peanuts?

VANĚK   No, thanks—

STANĚK   *(Short pause.)* About Javurek—

VANĚK   Yes?

STANĚK   Since I didn't manage to accomplish anything through private intervention, it occurred to me perhaps it ought to be handled in a somewhat different way. You know what I mean. Simply write something—a protest or a petition? In fact, this is the main thing I wanted to discuss with you. Naturally, you're far more experienced in these matters than I. If this document contains a few fairly well-known signatures— like yours, for example—it's bound to be published somewhere abroad which might create some political pressure. Right? I mean, these things don't seem to impress them all that much, actually—but honestly, I don't see any other way to help the boy. Not to mention Annie—

VANĚK   Annie?

STANĚK   My daughter.

VANĚK   Oh? Is that your daughter?

STANĚK   That's right.

VANĚK   Well, what about her?

STANĚK   I thought you knew.

VANĚK   Knew what?

STANĚK   She's expecting. By Javurek—

VANĚK   Oh, I see. That's why—

STANĚK   Wait a minute! If you mean the case interests me merely because of family matters—

VANĚK   I didn't mean that—

STANĚK   But you just said—

VANĚK   I only wanted to say, that's how you know about the case at all; you were explaining to me how you got to know about it. Frankly, I wouldn't have expected you to be familiar with the present pop scene. I'm sorry if it sounded as though I meant—

STANĚK   I'd get involved in this case even if it was someone else expecting his child! No matter who—

VANĚK   I know—

(Embarrassed pause.)

STANĚK   Well, what do you think about my idea of writing some sort of protest?

(Vaněk begins to look for something in his briefcase, finally finds a paper, and hands it to Staněk.)

VANĚK   I guess this is the sort of thing you had in mind—

STANĚK   What?

VANĚK   Here—

STANĚK   *(Grabs the document.)* What is it?

VANĚK   Have a look—

(Staněk takes the paper from Vaněk, goes quickly to the writing desk, picks up his glasses, puts them on, and begins to read attentively. Lengthy pause. Staněk shows signs of surprise. When he finishes reading, he puts aside his glasses and begins to pace around in agitation.)

STANĚK   Now isn't it fantastic! That's a laugh, isn't it? Eh? Here I was cudgeling my brains how to go about it, finally I take the plunge and consult you—and all this time you've had the whole thing wrapped up and ready! Isn't it marvellous? I knew I was doing the right thing when I turned to you! *(Staněk returns to the table, sits down, puts on his glasses again, and rereads the text.)* There! Precisely what I had in mind! Brief, to the point, fair, and yet emphatic. Manifestly the work of a professional! I'd be sweating over it for a whole day and I'd never come up with anything remotely like this!

VANĚK   *(Embarrassed.)*

STANĚK   Listen, just a small point—here at the end—do you think "wilfulness" is the right word to use? Couldn't one find a milder synonym, perhaps? Somehow seems a bit misplaced, you know. I mean, the whole text is composed in very measured, factual terms—and this word here suddenly sticks out, sounds much too emotional, wouldn't you agree? Otherwise it's absolutely perfect. Maybe the second paragraph is somewhat superfluous; in fact, it's just a rehash of the first one. Except for the reference here to Javurek's impact on nonconformist youth. This is excellent and must stay in! How about putting it at the end instead of your "wilfulness"? Wouldn't that do the trick?—But these are just my personal impressions. Good heavens! Why should you listen to what I have to say! On the whole the text is excellent, and no doubt it's going to hit the mark. Let me say again, Ferdinand, how much I admire you. Your knack for expressing the fundamental points of an issue, while avoiding all needless abuse, is indeed rare among our kind!

VANĚK   Come on—you don't really mean that—

(Staněk takes off his glasses, goes over to Vaněk, puts the paper in front of him, sits again in the easy chair, and sips his drink. Short pause.)

STANĚK	Anyway, it's good to know there's somebody around whom one can always turn to and rely on in a case like this.
VANĚK	But it's only natural, isn't it?
STANĚK	It may seem so to you. But in the circles where I've to move such things aren't in the least natural! The natural response is much more likely to be the exact opposite. When a man gets into trouble everybody drops him as soon as possible, the lot of them. And out of fear for their own positions they try to convince all and sundry they've never had anything to do with him; on the contrary, they sized him up right away, they had his number! But why am I telling you all this, you know best the sort of thing that happens! Right? When you were in prison your long-time theatre pals held forth against you on television. It was revolting—
VANĚK	I'm not angry with them—
STANĚK	But I am! And what's more I told them so. In no uncertain terms! You know, a man in my position learns to put up with a lot of things, but—if you'll forgive me—there are limits! I appreciate it might be awkward for you to blame them, as you happen to be the injured party. But listen to me, you've got to distance yourself from the affair! Just think: Once we, too, begin to tolerate this sort of muck—we're *de facto* assuming co-responsibility for the entire moral morass and indirectly contributing to its deeper penetration. Am I right?
VANĚK	Mmn—
STANĚK	*(Short pause.)* Have you sent it off yet?
VANĚK	We're still collecting signatures—
STANĚK	How many have you got so far?
VANĚK	About fifty—
STANĚK	Fifty? Not bad! *(Short pause.)* Well, never mind, I've just missed the boat, that's all.
VANĚK	You haven't—
STANĚK	But the thing's already in hand, isn't it?
VANĚK	Yes, but it's still open—I mean—
STANĚK	All right, but now it's sure to be sent off and published, right? By the way, I wouldn't give it to any of the agencies, if I were you. They'll only print a measly little news item which is bound to be overlooked. Better hand it over directly to one of the big European papers, so the whole text gets published, including all the signatures!
VANĚK	I know—
STANĚK	*(Short pause.)* Do they already know about it?
VANĚK	You mean the police?
STANĚK	Yes.
VANĚK	I don't think so. I suppose not—

STANĔK   Look here, I don't want to give you any advice, but it seems to me you ought to wrap it up as soon as possible, else they'll get wind of what's going on and they'll find a way to stop it. Fifty signatures should be enough! Besides, what counts is not the number of signatures, but their significance.

VANĔK   Each signature has its own significance!

STANĔK   Absolutely, but as far as publicity abroad is concerned, it is essential that some well-known names are represented, right? Has Pavel signed?

VANĔK   Yes—

STANĔK   Good. His name—no matter what one may think of him personally—does mean something in the world today!

VANĔK   No question—

STANĔK   *(Short pause.)* Listen, Ferdinand—

VANĔK   Yes?

STANĔK   There's one more thing I wanted to discuss with you. It's a bit delicate, though—

VANĔK   Oh?

STANĔK   Look here, I'm no millionaire, you know, but so far I've been able to manage—

VANĔK   Good for you—

STANĔK   Well, I was thinking—I mean—I'd like to—Look, a lot of your friends have lost their jobs. I was thinking—would you be prepared to accept from me a certain sum of money?

VANĔK   That's very nice of you! Some of my friends indeed find themselves in a bit of a spot. But there are problems, you know. I mean, one is never quite sure how to go about it. Those who most need help are often the most reluctant to accept—

STANĔK   You won't be able to work miracles with what I can afford, but I expect there are situations when every penny counts. *(Takes out his wallet, removes two banknotes, hesitates, adds a third, hands them to Vanĕk.)* Here—please—a small offering.

VANĔK   Thank you very much. Let me thank you for all my friends—

STANĔK   Gracious, we've got to help each other out, don't we? *(Pause.)* Incidentally, there's no need for you to mention this little contribution comes from me. I don't wish to erect a monument to myself. I'm sure you've gathered that much by now, eh?

VANĔK   Yes. Again many thanks—

STANĔK   Well now, how about having a look at the garden?

VANĔK   Mr. Stanĕk—

STANĔK   Yes?

VANĔK   We'd like to send it off tomorrow—

STANĚK	What?
VANĚK	The protest—
STANĚK	Excellent! The sooner the better!
VANĚK	So that today there's still—
STANĚK	Today you should think about getting some sleep! That's the main thing! Don't forget you've a bit of a hangover after last night and tomorrow is going to be a hard day for you!
VANĚK	I know. All I was going to say—
STANĚK	Better go straight home and unplug the phone. Else Ladovský rings you up again and heaven knows how you'll end up!
VANĚK	Yes, I know. There're only a few signatures I've still got to collect—it won't take long. All I was going to say—I mean, don't you think it would be helpful—as a matter of fact, it would, of course, be sensational! After all, practically everybody's read your *Crash*!
STANĚK	Oh, come on, Ferdinand! That was fifteen years ago!
VANĚK	But it's never been forgotten!
STANĚK	What do you mean—sensational?
VANĚK	I'm sorry, I had the impression you'd actually like to—
STANĚK	What?
VANĚK	Participate—
STANĚK	Participate? Wait a minute. Are you talking about *(points to the paper)* this? Is that what you're talking about?
VANĚK	Yes—
STANĚK	You mean I—
VANĚK	I'm sorry, but I had the impression—
	(Staněk finishes his drink, crosses to the bar, pours himself a drink, walks over to the window, looks out for a while, whereupon he suddenly turns to Vaněk with a smile.)
STANĚK	Now that's a laugh, isn't it?
VANĚK	What's a laugh?
STANĚK	Come on, can't you see how absurd it is? Eh? I ask you over hoping you might write something about Javurek's case—you produce a finished text and what's more, one furnished with fifty signatures! I'm bowled over like a little child, can't believe my eyes and ears, I worry about ways to stop them from ruining your project—and all this time it hasn't occurred to me to do the one simple, natural thing which I should have done in the first place! I mean, at once sign the document myself! Well, you must admit it's absurd, isn't it?
VANĚK	Mmn—
STANĚK	Now, listen Ferdinand, isn't this a really terrifying testimony to the situation into which we've been brought? Isn't it? Just think: even I, though I know it's rubbish, even I've got used to the idea that the signing of protests is the business of local

specialists, professionals in solidarity, dissidents! While the rest of us—when we want to do something for the sake of ordinary human decency—automatically turn to you, as though you were a sort of service establishment for moral matters. In other words, we're here simply to keep our mouths shut and to be rewarded by relative peace and quiet, whereas you're here to speak up for us and to be rewarded by blows on earth and glory in the heavens! Perverse, isn't it?

VANĚK   Mmn—

STANĚK   Of course it is! And they've managed to bring things to such a point that even a fairly intelligent and decent fellow—which, with your permission, I still think I am—is more or less ready to take this situation for granted! As though it was quite normal, perfectly natural! Sickening, isn't it? Sickening the depths we've reached! What do you say? Makes one puke, eh?

VANĚK   Well—

STANĚK   You think the nation can ever recover from all this?

VANĚK   Hard to say—

STANĚK   What can one do? What can one do? Well, seems clear, doesn't it? In theory, that is. Everybody should start with himself. What? However! Is this country inhabited only by Vaněks? It really doesn't seem that everybody can become a fighter for human rights.

VANĚK   Not everybody, no—

STANĚK   Where is it?

VANĚK   What?

STANĚK   The list of signatures, of course.

VANĚK   *(Embarrassed pause.)* Mr. Staněk—

STANĚK   Yes?

VANĚK   Forgive me, but—I'm sorry, I've suddenly a funny feeling that perhaps—

STANĚK   What funny feeling?

VANĚK   I don't know—I feel very embarrassed—Well, it seems to me perhaps I wasn't being quite fair—

STANĚK   In what way?

VANĚK   Well, what I did—was a bit of a con trick—in a way—

STANĚK   What are you talking about?

VANĚK   I mean, first I let you talk, and only then I ask for your signature—I mean, after you're already sort of committed by what you've said before, you see—

STANĚK   Are you suggesting that if I'd known you were collecting signatures for Javurek, I would never have started talking about him?

VANĚK   No, that's not what I mean—

PROTEST

STANĚK	Well, what do you mean?
VANĚK	How shall I put it—
STANĚK	Oh, come on! You mind I didn't organize the whole thing myself, is that it?
VANĚK	No, that's not it—
STANĚK	What is it then?
VANĚK	Well, it seems to me it would've been a quite different matter if I'd come to you right away and asked for your signature. That way you would've had an option—
STANĚK	And why didn't you come to me right away, actually? Was it because you'd simply written me off in advance?
VANĚK	Well, I was thinking that in your position—
STANĚK	Ah! There you are! You see? Now it's becoming clear what you really think of me, isn't it? You think that because now and then one of my pieces happens to be shown on television, I'm no longer capable of the simplest act of solidarity!
VANĚK	You misunderstand me.—What I meant was—
STANĚK	Let me tell you something, Ferdinand. *(Drinks. Short pause.)* Look here, if I've—willy-nilly—got used to the perverse idea that common decency and morality are the exclusive domain of the dissidents—then you've—willy-nilly—got used to the idea as well! That's why it never crossed your mind that certain values might be more important to me than my present position. But suppose even I wanted to be finally a free man, suppose even I wished to renew my inner integrity and shake off the yoke of humiliation and shame? It never entered your head that I might've been actually waiting for this very moment for years, what? You simply placed me once and for all among those hopeless cases, among those whom it would be pointless to count on in any way. Right? And now that you found I'm not entirely indifferent to the fate of others—you made that slip about my signature! But you saw at once what happened, and so you began to apologize to me. Good God! Don't you realize how you humiliate me? What if all this time I'd been hoping for an opportunity to act, to do something that would again make a man of me, help me to be once more at peace with myself, help me to find again the free play of my imagination and my lost sense of humour, rid me of the need to escape my traumas by minding the apricots and the blooming magnolias! Suppose even I prefer to live in truth! What if I want to return from the world of custom-made literature and the proto-culture of television to the world of art which isn't geared to serve anyone at all?
VANĚK	I'm sorry—forgive me! I didn't mean to hurt your feelings—.

69

Wait a minute, I'll—just a moment—

(Vanĕk opens his briefcase, rummages in it for a while, finally extracts the sheets with the signatures and hands them to Stanĕk. Stanĕk gets up slowly and crosses with the papers to the desk, where he sits down, puts on his glasses, and carefully studies the sheets nodding his head here and there. After a lengthy while, he takes off his glasses, slowly rises, thoughtfully paces around, finally turning to Vanĕk.)

STANĔK   Let me think aloud. May I?

VANĔK   By all means—

STANĔK   *(Halts, drinks, begins to pace again as he talks.)* I believe I've already covered the main points concerning the subjective side of the matter. If I sign the document, I'm going to regain—after years of being continually sick to my stomach —my self-esteem, my lost freedom, my honour, and perhaps even some regard among those close to me. I'll leave behind the insoluble dilemmas, forced on me by the conflict between my concern for my position and my conscience. I'll be able to face with equanimity Annie, myself, and even that young man when he comes back. It'll cost me my job, though my job brings me no satisfaction—on the contrary, it brings me shame—nevertheless, it does support me and my family a great deal better than if I were to become a night watchman. It's more than likely that my son won't be permitted to continue his studies. On the other hand, I'm sure he's going to have more respect for me that way, than if his permission to study was bought by my refusal to sign the protest for Javurek, whom he happens to worship.—Well then. This is the subjective side of the matter. Now how about the objective side? What happens when—among the signatures of a few well-known dissidents and a handful of Javurek's teenage friends— there suddenly crops up—to everybody's surprise and against all expectation—my signature? The signature of a man who hasn't been heard from regarding civic affairs for years! Well? My co-signatories—as well as many of those who don't sign documents of this sort, but who nonetheless deep down side with those who do—are naturally going to welcome my signature with pleasure. The closed circle of habitual signers— whose signatures, by the way, are already beginning to lose their clout, because they cost practically nothing. I mean, the people in question have long since lost all ways and means by which they could actually pay for their signatures. Right? Well, this circle will be broken. A new name will appear, a name the value of which depends precisely on its previous absence. And of course, I may add, on the high price paid for its appearance! So much for the objective "plus" of my prospective signature. Now what about the authorities? My signature is going to surprise, annoy, and upset them for the very reasons which will bring joy to the other signatories. I mean, because it'll make a breach in the barrier the authorities have been building around your lot for so long and with such effort. All right. Let's see about Javurek. Concerning his case, I very much doubt my participation would significantly influence its outcome. And if so, I'm afraid it's more than likely going to have a negative effect. The authorities will be anxious to prove they haven't been panicked. They'll want to show that a surprise of this sort can't make them lose their cool. Which brings us to the consideration of what they're going to do to me. Surely, my signature is bound to have a much more significant influence on what happens in my case. No doubt, they're going to punish me far more cruelly than you'd expect. The point being that my punishment will serve them as a warning signal to all those who might be tempted to follow my example in the future, choose freedom, and thus swell the ranks of the dissidents. You may be sure they'll want to show them what the score is! Right? The thing is—well, let's face it—they're no longer worried all that much about dissident activities within the confines of the established ghetto. In some respects they even seem to prod them on here and there. But! What they're really afraid of is any semblance of a crack in the fence around the ghetto! So they'll want to exorcize the bogey of a prospective epidemic of dissent by an exemplary punishment of myself. They'll want to nip it in the bud, that's all. *(Drinks. Pause.)* The last question I've got to ask myself is this: what sort of reaction to my signature can one expect among those who, in one way or another, have followed what you might call "the path of accommodation." I mean people who are, or ought to be, our main concern, because—I'm sure you'll agree—our hope for the future depends above all on whether or not it will be possible to awake them from their slumbers and to enlist them to take an active part in civic affairs. Well, I'm afraid that my signature is going to be received with absolute resentment by this crucial section of the populace. You know why? Because, as a matter of fact, these people secretly hate the dissidents. They've become their bad conscience, their living reproach! That's how they see the dissidents. And at the same time, they envy them their honour and their inner freedom, values which they themselves were denied by fate. This is why they never miss an opportunity to smear the dissidents. And precisely this opportunity is going to be offered to them by my signature. They're going to spread nasty rumours about you and your friends. They're going to say that you who have nothing more to lose—you who have long since landed at the bottom of the heap and, what's more, managed to make yourselves quite at home in there—are now trying to drag down to your own level an unfortunate man, a man who's so far been able to stay above the salt line. You're dragging him down—irresponsible as you are—without the slightest compunction, just for your own whim, just because you wish to irritate the authorities by creating a false impression that your ranks are being swelled! What do you care about losing him his job! Doesn't matter, does it? Or do you mean to suggest you'll find him a job down in the dump in which you yourselves exist? What? No—Ferdinand! I'm sorry. I'm afraid I'm much too familiar with the way these people think! After all, I've got to live among them, day in day out. I know precisely what they're going to say. They'll say I'm your victim, shamelessly abused, misguided, led astray by your cynical appeal to my humanity! They'll say that in your ruthlessness you didn't shrink even from making use of my personal relationship to Javurek! And you know what? They're going to say that all the humane ideals you're constantly proclaiming have been tarnished by your treatment of me. That's the sort of reasoning one can expect from them! And I'm sure I don't have to tell you that the authorities are bound to support this interpretation, and to fan the coals as hard as they can! There are others, of course, somewhat more intelligent perhaps. These people might say that the extraordinary appearance of my signature among yours is actually counterproductive, in that it concentrates everybody's attention on my signature and away from the main issue concerning Javurek. They'll say it puts the whole protest in jeopardy, because one can't help asking oneself what was the purpose of the exercise: was it to help Javurek, or to parade a newborn dissident? I wouldn't be at all surprised if someone were to say that, as a matter of fact, Javurek was victimized by you and your friends. It might be suggested his personal tragedy only served you to further your ends—which are far removed from the fate of the unfortunate man. Furthermore, it'll be pointed out that by getting my signature you managed to dislodge me from the one area of operation—namely, backstage diplomacy, private intervention—where I've been so far able to manoeuvre and where I might have proved infinitely more helpful to Javurek in the end! I do hope you understand me, Ferdinand. I don't wish to exaggerate the importance of these opinions, nor am I prepared to become their slave. On the other hand, it seems to be in the interests of our case for me to take them into account. After all, it's a matter of a political decision and a good politician must consider all the issues which are likely to influence the end result of his action. Right? In these circumstances the question one must resolve is as follows: what do I prefer? Do I prefer the inner liberation which my signature is going to bring me, a liberation paid for—as it now turns out—by a basically negative objective impact—or do I choose the other alternative. I mean, the more beneficial effect which the protest would have without my signature, yet paid for by my bitter awareness that I've again—who knows, perhaps for the last time—missed a chance to shake off the bonds of shameful compromises in which I've been choking for years? In other words, if I'm to act indeed ethically—and I hope by now you've no doubt I want to do just that—which course should I take? Should I be guided by ruthless objective considerations, or by subjective inner feelings?

VANĚK   Seems perfectly clear to me—
STANĚK   And to me—
VANĚK   So that you're going to—
STANĚK   Unfortunately—
VANĚK   Unfortunately?
STANĚK   You thought I was—
VANĚK   Forgive me, perhaps I didn't quite understand—
STANĚK   I'm sorry if I've—
VANĚK   Never mind—
STANĚK   But I really believe—
VANĚK   I know—

(Both drink. Vaněk shudders. Lengthy embarrassed pause. Staněk takes the sheets and hands them with a smile to Vaněk who puts them, together with the text of the letter of protest, into his briefcase. He shows signs of embarrassment. Staněk crosses to the tape recorder, unplugs it, comes back and sits down.)

STANĚK   Are you angry?
VANĚK   No—
STANĚK   You don't agree, though—
VANĚK   I respect your reasoning—
STANĚK   But what do you think?
VANĚK   What should I think?
STANĚK   That's obvious, isn't it?

VANĚK	Is it?
STANĚK	You think that when I saw all the signatures, I did, after all, get the wind up!
VANĚK	I don't—
STANĚK	I can see you do!
VANĚK	I assure you—
STANĚK	Why don't you level with me?! Don't you realize that your benevolent hypocrisy is actually far more insulting than if you gave it to me straight?! Or do you mean I'm not even worthy of your comment?!
VANĚK	But I told you, didn't I, I respect your reasoning—
STANĚK	I'm not an idiot, Vaněk!
VANĚK	Of course not—
STANĚK	I know precisely what's behind your "respect"!
VANĚK	What is?
STANĚK	A feeling of moral superiority!
VANĚK	You're wrong—
STANĚK	Only, I'm not quite sure if you—you of all people—have any right to feel so superior!
VANĚK	What do you mean?
STANĚK	You know very well what I mean!
VANĚK	I don't—
STANĚK	Shall I tell you?
VANĚK	Please do—
STANĚK	Well! As far as I know, in prison you talked more than you should have! *(Vaněk jumps up, wildly staring at Staněk, who smiles triumphantly. Short tense pause. The phone rings. Vaněk, broken, sinks back into his chair. Staněk crosses to the telephone and lifts the receiver.)*
STANĚK	Hello—yes—what? You mean—Wait a minute—I see—I see—Where are you? Yes, yes, of course—absolutely! —good— You bet!—Sure—I'll be here waiting for you! Bye bye. *(Staněk puts the receiver down and absent-mindedly stares into space. Lengthy pause. Vaněk gets up in embarrassment. Only now Staněk seems to realize that Vaněk is still there. He turns to him abruptly.)* You can go and burn it downstairs in the furnace!
VANĚK	What?
STANĚK	He's just walked into the canteen! To see Annie.
VANĚK	Who did?
STANĚK	Javurek! Who else?
VANĚK	*(Jumps up.)* Javurek? You mean he was released? But that's wonderful! So your private intervention did work, after all! Just as well we didn't send off the protest a few days earlier!

I'm sure they would've got their backs up and kept him inside!

(Staněk searchingly stares at Vaněk, then suddenly smiles, decisively steps up to him, and with both hands takes him by the shoulders.)

STANĚK My dear fellow, you mustn't fret! There's always the risk that you can do more harm than good by your activities! Right? Heavens, if you should worry about this sort of thing, you'd never be able to do anything at all! Come, let me get you those saplings—

THE END

NOTES

1. Staněk is of course referring to *Audience*.
2. Literary works circulating as *samizdat* texts in typescript are understandably often of poor quality. If one gets to read the, say, sixth carbon copy on onion skin, the readability of the script leaves much to be desired.
3. Staněk means Pavel Kohout.

PAVEL KOHOUT

Permit

Translated by Jan Drabek

in collaboration with the Kitsilano Theatre Company
under the direction of Kico Gonzalez-Risso

Pavel Kohout, *Permit*

CHARACTERS

Ferdinand Vaněk, a writer
Ivanka (sixteen years old)
Mrs. Blažová (middle-aged)
Madame Supervisor, also Comrade Trubačová (middle-aged)
Engineer Čech (a vigorous seventy-year-old)

PLACE

A Government Office

(An office divided by a high partition. Built into the partition is a part that can be raised with a gate underneath. In front of the partition are two desks facing each other, having a telephone on a movable arm. There are files and lockers; to the right is a door to the Supervisor's office. Behind the partition there is a coat hanger and a bench, at the moment invisible. On the left is a door leading to the corridor and on the back wall there are posters: LOVE YOUR COUNTRY, LOVE YOUR DOG and DOGBREEDERS FOR PEACE. Seated at the desk on the right, with her back to the Supervisor's office and to the partition, is Ivanka. She is about sixteen, but already quite developed with elaborate hairdo and make-up. Her breasts lie in an inventive brassiere as if on a plate. With every nerve straining, her index finger keeps wandering over the keyboard of her typewriter. After a few moments, she strikes a key and at that moment there is a knock on the door. There is fleeting satisfaction on her face which, however, quickly gives way to new anxiety. Again her index finger wanders and again there is a knock on the door. After a while the door to the corridor slowly opens and Vaněk peeks in.)

VANĚK   Hello—

IVANKA   *(Is neither interested in nor aware of his presence.)*

VANĚK   *(Enters, but only after he has brought something with him—something that is invisible behind the partition and something he urges to enter with a hissing sound. There is also a jingling sound.)* Hello—

IVANKA   I can't believe it!

VANĚK   *(Confused.)* Excuse me, but what is it you can't—?

IVANKA   There's no "zh".

VANĚK   Is that a Czech typewriter?

IVANKA   I don't know.

VANĚK   Well—are there the little hooks and accents?

IVANKA   *(Studying her typewriter.)* Yeah.

VANĚK   If you'll allow me, I'll—Just a moment—*(searching through his pockets.)* Gee—my glasses.

IVANKA   You can borrow mine. *(Hands him gigantic-sized dark glasses from her wild handbag.)*

VANĚK   Are they prescription?

IVANKA   Sure—What else? They're Italian, you know.

VANĚK   *(Trying them on.)* But—You see, I need normal ones.

IVANKA   What did you come in here for—to borrow glasses?

VANĚK   *(Confused.)* Sorry—but you wanted me to—

IVANKA   Oh sure.

VANĚK   Just a moment. *(He is typing on an imaginary typewriter with*

81

	the leash still around his thumb.) First row — sixth key — what's on it?
IVANKA	*(Counts the keys with newly acquired respect for him.)* Number six!
VANĚK	And underneath?
IVANKA	*(With respect.)* How did you guess?
VANĚK	*(With a modest smile.)* Occasionally I do a thing or two on a typewriter.
IVANKA	I'll never get it — not in a million years. *(She concentrates, then hits another key.)*
VANĚK	How long have you been trying to learn?
IVANKA	Since this morning. *(New anxiety follows her fleeting moment of satisfaction.)*
VANĚK	I'm sure you'll master it.
IVANKA	I dunno. It's hard. Look at that: Now I can't find the "i" with an accent and see? A while ago I already had it. *(Studying the machine.)*
VANĚK	I don't want to take up your time. I only wanted to ask—
IVANKA	Oh yeah, the glasses.
VANĚK	No, no. I got this — well, actually my wife got this dog, you see.
IVANKA	Not too well so far.
VANĚK	I beg your — Oh — of course, how could you—
IVANKA	But don't worry about it. — There's lots of stuff I don't get.
VANĚK	You see he's a purebred and they told my wife that we need a permit.
IVANKA	So?
VANĚK	Well, I thought there were special tests—
IVANKA	*(Chuckles.)* A little nipper like that taking tests!
VANĚK	He doesn't have to?
IVANKA	I dunno.
VANĚK	You see I thought that someone here could—
IVANKA	Sure someone here could. But I only started here yesterday.
VANĚK	Well then who could—
IVANKA	*(Gets up, walks through the partition, then jumps.)* Son of a bitch — he scared me!
VANĚK	That's the one.
IVANKA	*(Looking in the direction of the jingling.)* Is it a German shepherd?
VANĚK	*(Confused.)* A German shepherd?
IVANKA	A German shepherd — that's a dog too, isn't it?
VANĚK	Yes — yes, it is.
IVANKA	All dogs look the same to me.
VANĚK	But this is — at least so we've been told — a rare breed: He's a Czech Grabber.

IVANKA	*(Giggles.)* Grabber? That's a hoot. Is there something wrong with him?
VANĚK	*(Looking in the direction of the jingling.)* What makes you think —
IVANKA	Well, he isn't grabbin' anything. Look, he's under the bench — a big guy like that.
VANĚK	You see grabbers are actually well known for their shyness — When he's not afraid, he's grabbing all the time, but he never means it — We were told that he's even friendly with cats — That's why he's called the *Czech* grabber.
IVANKA	*(Has other thoughts already.)* Do you know why I came over here?
VANĚK	No, I don't.
IVANKA	Oh yeah. *(Opens the door and yells into the corridor.)* Mrs. Blaaaažovááá! *(Closes the door and bends down.)* Is he cold?
VANĚK	He shivers like that whenever he doesn't know someone.
IVANKA	Then he's the perfect kind of dog for our Supervisor.
VANĚK	Why?
IVANKA	All dogs want to — at least that's what they say — rip her to pieces.
VANĚK	But why?
IVANKA	I heard that all dogs are like that when someone's afraid of them.
VANĚK	And she's —
IVANKA	Well, they say when she sees a dog she's supposed to absolutely sh — — —. Well, you know.
VANĚK	So, why is she the Supervisor here?
IVANKA	She's supposed to have been everywhere else.
Mrs. BLAŽOVÁ	*(Enters from the corridor. She is a baroque woman of middle age, the type the British call full-bodied, full of humour and energy but tough when necessary. She is the classic motivating force of Czech offices and households, brilliantly performing each task she choses and vice versa.)* Ivanka, dear, let me give you some advice. If I'm not here then it's because I either have to be somewhere else or because I do not wish to be here. At such times, therefore, you are searching for me either in vain or inopportunely.
IVANKA	*(Nodding toward Vaněk.)* He wants something.
Mrs. BLAŽOVÁ	Well, taking into account the fact that we're not exactly an emergency service, a few minutes here or there hardly make a — *(Hears the jingling and looks underneath the bench.)* And who have we here? *(She disappears behind the partition.)* Now don't be afraid — such a big boy! *(Appears again.)* He's not a purebred, is he?
VANĚK	Yes — well actually we were —

Mrs. BLAŽOVÁ	Does he have papers?
VANĚK	Yes, he does. *(Searching through his pockets.)* He's a—
Mrs. BLAŽOVÁ	Wait a minute, let me guess. I got it. *(Staring down.)* The head looks like—but he couldn't be a St. Bernard!
VANĚK	No, he isn't—
Mrs. BLAŽOVÁ	Of course not, of course not. From the back he's—*(Thinking hard.)* I've got it! *(She gives up.)* Come on, help me out!
VANĚK	That third part I can never rem—*(Taking a paper from his wallet.)* I have it written down. *(Looks for his glasses.)* Unfortunately I don't have my—
Mrs. BLAŽOVÁ	Let me see. *(Takes his paper.)* Of course, one of Horak's laboratory dogs, those poor things— *(Looking down again.)* But what exactly is he?
IVANKA	*(Who has seated herself back behind her typewriter long ago, searching for yet another letter.)* A Czech grubber.
VANĚK	Grabber.
Mrs. BLAŽOVÁ	*(Claps her hands together.)* So this is the big wonder dog. Come here, come here baby. *(Disappears behind the partition.)* What do they call you?
VANĚK	Adi—actually Adam.
Mrs. BLAŽOVÁ	Come here, Adi baby, come on. *(Jingling.)* So we're that famous grabber, are we? *(Appears again.)* And why are we hiding behind our master? Are they really such good dogs?
VANĚK	Yes—That's why my wife—you see I used to dislike dogs in the city because they don't have any freedom really to run around, but I have a feeling that without me Adi couldn't possibly—well, he may look like he's made of steel but he's really such a tame little—
Mrs. BLAŽOVÁ	Exactly what that engineer Mr. Čech says. He's been raving about them for years now. They're included in the *Book of Purebreds*, of course, but this is the first time I've actually seen one.
VANĚK	Well, they're supposed to have won all sorts of prizes at dog shows. At least that's what we've been—
Mrs. BLAŽOVÁ	My dear man! I see nothing but dogs all week long, surely you don't expect me to go looking for them on weekends as well? *(While she talks, she walks through the partition to her desk.)* Dogs are something for people with time and money. I'm just your ordinary working woman. I have my hubby, the kids, grandchildren—and they mean a lot more to me than all the grabbers of this world put together—even the Slovak ones. *(Over the partition.)* But we're not upset, are we, Adi baby? Let's just go get us a little something— *(Takes an old-fashioned metal box out of her desk, places it atop some files, and takes some pieces of sugar from it.)*

IVANKA	*(Happily calling to Vaněk.)* Got it!
VANĚK	I beg your—
IVANKA	The "i" with an accent. *(Concentrates for a moment, then hits the key.)*
VANĚK	*(To Mrs. Blažová.)* Excuse me, but I don't think you should—
Mrs. BLAŽOVÁ	Why not?
VANĚK	We were told they were supposed to be kept thin—because of their delicate greyhound spine.
Mrs. BLAŽOVÁ	My dear sir, every living thing on this earth knows what's good and what's bad for it. If I paid attention to such talk, I'd have picked up TB a long time ago, the same way Ivanka here's soon going to have it. Not to mention the fact that my husband would never have paid any attention to me, let alone married me. As it is he had to make an exception in my case—since for him a woman isn't a real woman unless she weighs at least 200 pounds. *(Over the partition.)* So our nasty master won't give us any sugar-wooger? That's bad. But we'll get some from nice Mrs. Blažová, it's all the same to us, isn't it?
IVANKA	*(Concentrates and then strikes a key, full of happiness.)* This time I found the "zh" right away!
VANĚK	They say the spine could crack.
Mrs. BLAŽOVÁ	*(Handing over the partition another lump of sugar. There is jingling on the other side while she is exhibiting her considerable behind to the audience.)* But what's our master-waster saying—that we could crack in the middle? Such nonsense, when we're such a famous doggie-woggie!
IVANKA	*(Gets up, throws her handbag over her shoulder, puts on her glasses, and walks through the partition. To Mrs. Blažová.)* If someone heats up my wire, tell him I went to—you know.
Mrs. BLAŽOVÁ	If somebody what?
IVANKA	Calls.
Mrs. BLAŽOVÁ	Oh.
IVANKA	*(To Vaněk.)* You don't happen to know how to say it in Italian?
VANĚK	What?
IVANKA	To take a piss.
VANĚK	Sorry.
IVANKA	*(To Mrs. Blažová.)* So say boo into the phone, all right? *(Exits to the corridor.)*
Mrs. BLAŽOVÁ	Our shining star! Every time I see her father on T.V. I am dumbstruck.
VANĚK	*(Not understanding, but still courteous.)* You are?
Mrs. BLAŽOVÁ	*(Not content with his reaction.)* You do know who her father is? *(Stops feeding the dog, gestures to Vaněk with her finger,*

	then leans over the partition to be closer to his ear. While whispering, she points upwards, finally leans away from him triumphantly.) Would you have believed it? He's a widower, really sees himself in her.
VANĚK	What a coincidence!
Mrs. BLAŽOVÁ	Coincidence, my eye. It's your typical Czech backscratching. Her old man created the job just for her, and she'll hang around here until she gets married. But when she leaves we'll still have her spot. It's worth it.
VANĚK	Well—
Mrs. BLAŽOVÁ	Jesus, you're not some sort of inspector, are you?
VANĚK	Definitely not. I—
Mrs. BLAŽOVÁ	Because you're so reserved.
VANĚK	I was just surprised you'd be telling me all that.
Mrs. BLAŽOVÁ	Well, we're all Czech, so let's call a spade a spade. But bastards like that I can smell miles away. My hubby always says to me, "You should've been a policewoman," but what the hell— I'd feel happier being a deaf mute than a— *(Grabs hold of her mouth.)* You aren't one of those either, are you?
VANĚK	What?
Mrs. BLAŽOVÁ	You know. *(Shows him her palm as if she had an i.d. card or badge in it.)*
VANĚK	Absolutely not.
Mrs. BLAŽOVÁ	Well don't you go thinking that I'd pass out if you were. I have no secrets from anybody. What I want to say I say because if he has to, my hubby will take care of me, and everyone at home will be very happy that grandma's around the house to take care of the kids.
VANĚK	I was just surprised to hear all this from a woman who—
Mrs. BLAŽOVÁ	You'll hear it from every single one of us except for the odd cow who still wants to get from politics what she didn't get in bed.
VANĚK	—who's afraid of dogs—and is still a Supervisor?
Mrs. BLAŽOVÁ	Now wait a minute! This is an error. I—
SUPERVISOR	*(Enters from the corridor. She is a dried-up fiftyish matron wearing glasses and the unhappy yet perennially provoked face of those women who since youth have had bad luck in love and who also fear all kinds of accidents. She glances below the partition, and, thanks to her agility, the next moment it is as if she flew to the top of the hidden bench.)* Help! Keep that beast back. Get him out! *(As if near death.)* Mrs. Blažová, please!
Mrs. BLAŽOVÁ	*(Happily.)* Don't be afraid, he's only a grabber.
SUPERVISOR	*(Flailing her arms silently.)*
Mrs. BLAŽOVÁ	It's that good little dog Mr. Čech spoke about. The one that's

	afraid of those who show fear. *(Walks through the partition, bends down.)* Look, we're actually trembling. Now Adi baby, tell our Supervisor that we do like her.
VANĚK	He's never hurt a fly.
SUPERVISOR	And I don't want him to start here.
VANĚK	He doesn't even bark.
Mrs. BLAŽOVÁ	That's right. All other dogs bare their fangs at you, and this one—not a sound. See how he's looking at you?
SUPERVISOR	I know, I know. Everyone of them looks like a saint and then they strike. Would you please take him away?
VANĚK	Yes, certainly. Except that, you see, I'm actually here because of him.
SUPERVISOR	I'll go mad, completely mad—At least hold him until I'm on the other side.
VANĚK	But I'm sure he won't—
SUPERVISOR	Go tell that to someone else. I'm already marked for life. I have never hurt anyone, but for some reason animals viciously attack the moment they see me. The number of times I've been scratched by cats, bitten, poked—Even chickens charge me.
VANĚK	But why? I—
SUPERVISOR	All those sleepless nights I've spent on account of it! As a child I couldn't even go to summer camp because right away there'd be bees, snakes, and whatnots all around me, and before you knew it I was on my way to the hospital. I can't even go to the zoo. The beasts start to rattle their cages and roar so terribly that the guards have to escort me out. The number of doctors I've seen—specialists too! The only thing they could tell me was to try and not be afraid because it seems I have this acid in my perspiration and the animals can smell it.
VANĚK	And did you try?
SUPERVISOR	Do you think I'm bent on suicide? I can't even go swimming because fish attack me too.
Mrs. BLAŽOVÁ	But we don't give a hoot about any old acid in her perspiration, do we, Adi baby? *(Jingling.)* No we don't. We don't have to be afraid of Madame Supervisor, do we? Don't worry, you can get down.
SUPERVISOR	Are you holding him?
Mrs. BLAŽOVÁ	Sure.
SUPERVISOR	*(To Vaněk.)* You grab hold of him too.
VANĚK	Certainly. *(Disappears behind the partition.)* Adi! Down!
SUPERVISOR	*(Quickly jumps from the bench, runs through the partition, closes the gate behind her, and with one hand over her heart slowly starts to revive.)*

Mrs. BLAŽOVÁ	*(Looking over the partition.)* Well, for goodness sake, we've gone and—
VANĚK	*(Reappears, looks down embarrassed.)* I'm sorry, that's terrible. And we've just been for a walk too.
SUPERVISOR	*(Belatedly alarmed.)* What's happ—
Mrs. BLAŽOVÁ	The poor little thing was so scared he got the shits. *(Walks through the partition to a file cabinet.)*
VANĚK	If you have something—I'll clean—
Mrs. BLAŽOVÁ	*(Taking a small chamber pot, a shovel, and a rag from the file cabinet.)* Don't worry, we're properly equipped. But Madame Supervisor should buy us all a drink. It's the first time I've ever seen that. *(Returns behind the partition and bends down.)* Come on, Adi baby, let's not be afraid. We'll clean it up and no one will ever know that anything like that happened here.
SUPERVISOR	*(Looking behind the partition, full of disbelief.)* What sort of a dog is it again?
VANĚK	A grabber.
Mrs. BLAŽOVÁ	*(Gets up, covers the pot with a lid, and places it on top of the partition.)* You know—Mr. Cech swears by them.
SUPERVISOR	I don't remember.
Mrs. BLAŽOVÁ	Sure you do. He tells you all the time: "Comrade Trubačová, you should try it with a grabber."
SUPERVISOR	I get scared to death when someone just talks about dogs.
Mrs. BLAŽOVÁ	Come on, give him a pat. Once you do it, you'll never have to worry again. You'll start to perspire normally and no animal will ever bother you.
SUPERVISOR	Oh no. It had already started the first time my parents took me to a circus. In the opening act these trained monkeys jumped right into our box and almost tickled me to death. We got some compensation for it, but since then I've been a marked woman and no one has any idea what I have to go through. You'd think they'd at least raise my salary on account of it.
Mrs. BLAŽOVÁ	Come on, we'll hold him down. You'll never get a chance like this again.
SUPERVISOR	Never!
Mrs. BLAŽOVÁ	Or else you'll be miserable for the rest of your life.
SUPERVISOR	Not really. I've asked the Chairman to declare this a dog-free area.
Mrs. BLAŽOVÁ	But people come here only because of their dogs—
SUPERVISOR	That's a bit of a myth, isn't it? We don't actually deal with dogs. We just file the papers. Dogs are meant to be shown to the judges, not to us.
Mrs. BLAŽOVÁ	But what if people bring their dogs from somewhere out in

	the country?
SUPERVISOR	The dog will just have to wait outside, in front of the building. A dog is supposed to be able to wait for his master, isn't he?
Mrs. BLAŽOVÁ	Some do. But let a dachshund pick up a scent and who knows when he'll be back. That is, if he doesn't get run over first.
SUPERVISOR	So we'll put up little cubbyholes for them downstairs in the courtyard—Actually we shouldn't be discussing this here in front of the comrade—My telephone is ringing. *(She goes to her office.)*
Mrs. BLAŽOVÁ	Have you ever in your life— *(Talking downwards.)* She really would want to put us in a cubbyhole. Did you hear that, Adi baby?
IVANKA	*(Entering and asking Vaněk right by the door.)* And why aren't they all in order—like in the alphabet, you know?
VANĚK	*(Confused.)* I beg your pardon?
IVANKA	The letters.
VANĚK	I don't know what—
IVANKA	The letters on the typewriter—why aren't they put one after another like in the alphabet. You know—a, b, c and so on?
VANĚK	Oh yes—As far as I know those that are needed the most are closest to the middle, closest to the index fingers.
IVANKA	*(Reaches her typewriter and studies it.)* That's weird.
SUPERVISOR	*(Quickly coming out from her office.)* Where is Iv— *(Sees her.)* Ivanka, someone wants to speak with you.
IVANKA	Then why is he calling *you*?
SUPERVISOR	Well you see, private conversations aren't encouraged—so every call must go through me.
IVANKA	Then hang up. I don't give a shit.
SUPERVISOR	But it's some foreigner. I tried speaking Russian with him, but he didn't understand.
IVANKA	Oh yeah? Then it must be Umberto.
SUPERVISOR	Why don't you go and talk to him? Maybe he wants something important.
IVANKA	He always wants the same thing. *(She picks up her things and goes next door, still trying out her mating walk.)*
SUPERVISOR	*(Feeling guilty.)* You're not angry, are you? I mean normally I don't allow anyone and now she—
Mrs. BLAŽOVÁ	*(Passing through the partition to her desk, talking with distinct lack of sincerity.)* Why shouldn't she get her wires heated up if it's good for her?
SUPERVISOR	*(With meaning.)* It's good for all of us.
Mrs. BLAŽOVÁ	As long as I can occasionally heat up my wire too.
SUPERVISOR	There is no problem—as long as it's within limits.
VANĚK	If you ladies would allow me—
Mrs. BLAŽOVÁ	*(Winking at him.)* Of course. Go on, heat up your wire

	too—it's all right with you, isn't it?
SUPERVISOR	Of course. As long as it's within—
VANĚK	Oh no, you see, I only want to take care of this little matter.
Mrs. BLAŽOVÁ	Just leave it to us! Here we are washing our dirty laundry in front of you without even asking what you'd like.
VANĚK	You see I—my wife has—actually I got this dog.
Mrs. BLAŽOVÁ	*(Throws a piece of sugar over the partition.)* Sure. We know, don't we, Adi baby?
VANĚK	And she was told—actually my wife—she was told by the dog breeder, that he needs to—in order to be allowed to— *(Searches through his pockets.)* I have it written down somewhere— *(Finds the paper but not his glasses.)* You see I don't have my—
Mrs. BLAŽOVÁ	He probably needs to be registered for a breeding permit. Let me see. *(Takes his paper.)*
VANĚK	Yes, yes, he has to be registered so that he can—
Mrs. BLAŽOVÁ	Breed. Naturally. *(Throwing another piece over the partition.)* Such nice little doggie-woggies like us have to breed, don't they?
SUPERVISOR	*(Not quite convinced, she lifts the lid to the chamberpot and looks inside once more.)* I have never seen anything like it—
Mrs. BLAŽOVÁ	What about the permit?
VANĚK	Well, you see this is why—My wife and I have no idea—
Mrs. BLAŽOVÁ	And he already has been tested?
VANĚK	No, that's just it. He hasn't.
Mrs. BLAŽOVÁ	*(Over the partition.)* So we haven't had any testy-westys? But we have to have them, otherwise we couldn't get any fun out of life, could we.? We are in the association, aren't we?
VANĚK	No, he isn't and without it it's—
Mrs. BLAŽOVÁ	*(Throws another piece of sugar.)* Not to worry. We'll fill out an application for Adi baby, and Madame Supervisor will see if Comrade Chairman will approve it without it having to go to the Central Committee, won't we? Seeing as how the dog lets got the moment he sees you—
SUPERVISOR	*(Puts the lid back on and stares first at Vaněk then behind the partition.)* I still don't believe it. Ever since I've been this high every goose for miles around has been after me. Once I went to a fair with my fiancé and there was a little donkey— one of those that kids ride on. It jumped right over the railing and chased me among all the stands. My whole spring suit was covered in mud. My fiancé eventually got hold of him, but that same evening he and that girl from the hippodrome— *(Suddenly she becomes silent.)*
IVANKA	*(Comes out of the office, sits down at her desk, and studies the typewriter.)*

SUPERVISOR	Are you finished, Ivanka? Can I go back?
IVANKA	What? Oh, yeah. Sure.
SUPERVISOR	Was it a good friend? I just want to—so that next time—
IVANKA	Filthy old man.
SUPERVISOR	*(Alarmed.)* Perhaps I shouldn't have—If you had only told me, Ivanka, I could have said you weren't here. I know what you mean: I live next to the Esplanade. They arrive in their gas guzzlers, get their money changed, and then they glue themselves onto the nearest skirt, as if our girls were for sale! That they even let them into the country!
IVANKA	He's a delegate.
SUPERVISOR	Oh they're the worst—A delegate?
IVANKA	A friend of my dad. *(Studies the typewriter.)*
SUPERVISOR	*(Swallows a few times.)*
IVANKA	*(To Vaněk.)* According to that the A should be in the middle.
VANĚK	*(Confused.)* According to what?
IVANKA	Would you say that you need an A a lot less then say a G?
VANĚK	Maybe not.
IVANKA	See? And G is right here in the middle while A is all the way over on the other side.
VANĚK	*(Helpless.)* Then I really don't know.
IVANKA	Don't worry about it. The main thing is that I found the A. Just when I need it too.
Mrs. BLAŽOVÁ	*(Pulls out a form from a drawer, rolls it into the typewriter and winks at Vaněk.)* So why don't you dictate it all to me, and perhaps Madame Supervisor will be so nice as to run it over to the Comrade Chairman? And maybe on the way she'll even pat Adi, won't she?
IVANKA	*(Lifts her head from the machine.)* Jesus—that's right! He's not even barking!
Mrs. BLAŽOVÁ	*(With warning in her voice.)* And why should he, dear?
SUPERVISOR	*(Forces herself to laugh.)* Ah, so someone has been spreading rumours a bit, has she? You mustn't take everything so seriously, Ivanka. We like to have a bit of fun now and then—And Comrade Blažová, I could also come out with a few things—
Mrs. BLAŽOVÁ	You know that I would never—
SUPERVISOR	If I worried that every now and then some poor little creature isn't going to feel at ease around me, well, it would be like— *(To Ivanka.)* your father worrying that here and there someone doesn't love him. That—in any case— *(She decides suddenly to lean over the partition.)* I'm certainly not afraid— *(There is a jingle and she pulls back as if he had bitten her.)*
Mrs. BLAŽOVÁ	*(Astonished.)* He licked your hand.
SUPERVISOR	*(Gazes at her hand as if looking for the wound.)* He actually—
Mrs. BLAŽOVÁ	*(Strikes while the iron's hot.)* Come on, come on, let's not

	keep the lady waiting. How old are we?
VANĚK	Fifty—I'll soon—
Mrs. BLAŽOVÁ	No. I meant Adi.
VANĚK	Sorry—A year ago—it was—
Mrs. BLAŽOVÁ	*(Typing like a machine gun.)* Dog?
VANĚK	*(Confused.)* I think so—A Czech Grabber is actually— At least we were told—
Mrs. BLAŽOVÁ	Dog is a sex: a dog or a bitch.
VANĚK	Oh—and both are called—
Mrs. BLAŽOVÁ	Dogs.
VANĚK	Oh—So—dog. Dog!
Mrs. BLAŽOVÁ	*(Typing like a machine gun.)* Name?
VANĚK	Adi—Adam, really—
Mrs. BLAŽOVÁ	I mean yours now.
VANĚK	Of course. Excuse me. Vaněk. Ferdinand—
Mrs. BLAŽOVÁ	*(Typing like a machine gun.)* Occupation?
VANĚK	*(After a moment's thought.)* Freelancer.
Mrs. BLAŽOVÁ	*(Typing like a machine gun.)* Employer?
VANĚK	*(After a moment's thought.)* I don't have one.
Mrs. BLAŽOVÁ	An artist?
VANĚK	*(Nods shyly.)*
Mrs. BLAŽOVÁ	So the name of the artist's association—whoever it is that signs your papers.
VANĚK	I'm sorry to be awkward, but is the membership absolutely necessary?
Mrs. BLAŽOVÁ	Well, as long as you want to have your dog bred—Wait a minute—did you take your hunting exams?
VANĚK	Do I have to?
Mrs. BLAŽOVÁ	Well, no. Except that if you had passed those he would automatically get the permit. But it doesn't matter; when it's only a question of breeding, you'll get temporary membership, but the Comrade Chairman still likes to have a ram's head on the papers.
VANĚK	A what?
Mrs. BLAŽOVÁ	A ram's head—a rubber stamp.
VANĚK	You see, I'm not—in any artists' association.
Mrs. BLAŽOVÁ	And at which office are you registered—re employment, I mean?
VANĚK	None. No office.
Mrs. BLAŽOVÁ	And what do you do actually?
VANĚK	*(Smiling as if excusing himself.)* I'm a playwright.
Mrs. BLAŽOVÁ	*(Stunned.)* You are—
SUPERVISOR	*The* Vaněk?
IVANKA	So, then, why should a G be more important than an A, pray tell? I don't know a single word with a G—Except maybe

	gum.
VANĚK	*(Now gratefully.)* You see, I think that the order was thought up by the English and they use lots of Gs. Great Britain for example needs one right at the beginning—
ČECH	*(Enters from the corridor, seventyish with a powerful mane and a thunderous voice. He is wearing a worn-out loden coat, holding a cane. He tips his greasy hunter's hat with a brush.)* Good hunting, everybody.
VANĚK	Hello.
ČECH	*(Looking down.)* I don't believe it, am I seeing right? A Czech grabber in all his glory. *(He bends down and there is jingling.)* A beautiful specimen. Where are you from, eh?
VANĚK	We got him at—
ČECH	Just a moment! A dog has more traits than wine. And if a wine connoisseur is able to distinguish fine wine by taste, the connoisseur of fine dogs should be able to pick at least the kennel. *(Bends down.)* Judging by the undercarriage he could be from Krispin in Pilsen except that—let's see your teeth boy. *(Gets up.)* He's from Novotný, isn't he?
VANĚK	*(Surprised.)* How did you know?
ČECH	Well now, you see, I've been around dogs for quite a few years. You weren't even a gleam in your father's eye when I started, and Comrade Trubačová here must have been seducing that cute baker at the time. *(He laughs alone. Both women are gazing at the depressed Vaněk.)* It's like this. Krispin and Novotný did the main work on the grabber. Except that they came up with the basic mix of St. Bernard and Horák, so they also decided to breed in their greyhound. Then Novotný, in order to get a decent topside, let his bitch have some fun in London. The greyhound was a champion CACIB but only because its owner had connections—CACIB, that's "Championat International de Beauté," you know? But the greyhound had a weak muzzle—something Novotný didn't know. That's why the incisors aren't quite up to snuff, but I wouldn't worry about it. With Krispin you would've had a stiff whip.
VANĚK	A what?
ČECH	An upright tail, sir. But otherwise you've got a top-notch grabber. *(Remembers something and turns to the Supervisor.)* Did he give tongue, Comrade Trubačová?
SUPERVISOR	*(Absentmindedly.)* What?
ČECH	Did he bark at you?
Mrs. BLAŽOVÁ	*(Behind her back giving Čech a sign not to go into it; at the same time she is shaking her head in negation.)*
ČECH	What did I tell you? They're great dogs, you wouldn't believe

	it. You could split wood on top of them and they wouldn't mind.
Mrs. BLAŽOVÁ	*(Happily uncovering the lid on the chamberpot.)* Look what he did when he saw Madame Supervisor!
SUPERVISOR	It was an accident.
ČECH	*(Looking into the chamberpot, also happy.)* No accident. They are the real dogs of our times. Also in that they don't have the slightest sense of humour, am I right?
VANĚK	We weren't t—
ČECH	Let me ask you, sir. Do you have lots of big laughs around the house? You don't, do you?
VANĚK	Well lately we've—
ČECH	See? It's because all the breeds that went into him are basically very serious. Horak's dog is actually melancholy. Actually you can't blame the Horaks; they don't have much to be happy about in that laboratory of his. And all of that inbreeding would have magnified that trait. The one thing that will upset a grabber is loud laughter—watch out for that. But then, who laughs loudly nowadays, am I right? Like I say, he is certainly the dog for our times. Are you trying to sell him?
VANĚK	No, I'm not.
ČECH	I'd have a buyer for you in a jiffy. Grabbers are very fashionable nowadays.
Mrs. BLAŽOVÁ	Mr. Vaněk would like to breed him—
ČECH	And you're absolutely right! A good grabber is still a rarity. They haven't managed to hit it right yet. You'll get one or two out of each litter and among the rest some true grandfather will make his appearance, and so they'll look like St. Bernards, Greyhounds or Horaks. But only on the surface. Deep inside they're real subversives—without any character at all. Listen, with this stud and a bit of luck you could even come up with a CACIB.
SUPERVISOR	Mr. Vaněk lacks membership.
ČECH	All right, let's quickly fill out an application and be off to see the Chairman—this is really an event. And while we're waiting, the gentleman can go and pick up a bottle of the bubbly.
SUPERVISOR	*(Almost tragically.)* This is Mr. Ferdinand Vaněk.
ČECH	My pleasure. The name's Čech, I'm an engineer. I'm also listed as no. 1 in their purebred stock books here. I come every day around this hour to let them know what's on this old man's mind. And they in return very kindly provide coffee so that I won't have to spend my hard-earned pension on it.
SUPERVISOR	This is Mr. Ferdinand Vaněk, the playwright.
ČECH	*(End of all fun.)* I'll be damned!

IVANKA	So why do we have to have it in the English order? It's the first English thing I've come across that's totally stupid!
VANĚK	It's probably a universal agreement so that every typist in the world can use any— *(Searches the others with his eyes.)* Well, how could it—
ČECH	Well so what? So we go on as if nothing's happened. As far as I know, a Czech grabber officially enjoys the green light.
SUPERVISOR	Except that you could say exactly the opposite about Mr. Vaněk.
ČECH	Are we breeding Mr. Vaněk or his dog?
SUPERVISOR	That's not the way the application for the breeding permit reads.
ČECH	So how does it read? We aren't breeding Mr. Vaněk, and his dog hasn't signed the Charter![1]
SUPERVISOR	Psst! *(Almost whispering.)* Do you remember how it was with Havel?
ČECH	So what's the problem? He had a schnauzer and got to pay lower taxes on account of it.
SUPERVISOR	And I almost got a reprimand.
ČECH	Only almost, Comrade Trubačová. Because they asked you, you asked me, and that was that. They accepted the fact that schnauzers are reservists for the Ministry of Defence and that can't be changed whether it's Mr. Havel or Schmavel.
SUPERVISOR	And what about Pavel? Kohout, I mean.
ČECH	What about Kohout? He transferred his champion dachshund Eda to his wife, and you accepted her when she used her maiden name. Who could have caught it?
SUPERVISOR	They nearly fired me.
ČECH	But only nearly. They were surprised, you cried right on cue, and that was the end of it. And Eda went off to breed—lucky dog.
VANĚK	Excuse me, but I heard the name of one of my colleagues— Is there some problem in my—with my—
SUPERVISOR	Unfortunately there is, Mr. Vaněk. We can't give you a permit.
VANĚK	But without it the dog cannot, if I understand correctly—
SUPERVISOR	Unfortunately, you understand only too well. I'm sorry.
Mrs. BLAŽOVÁ	I wouldn't see it all as darkly as Madame Supervisor here.
SUPERVISOR	*(Making sure that she is heard, especially by Ivanka, who is studying her typewriter once more.)* It's nice that someone can see it through rose-coloured glasses, but I'm the one responsible.
Mrs. BLAŽOVÁ	But you're also responsible for all the Czech grabbers. Especially for them. Mr. Čech was quite right about us taking responsibility for breeding Adi, right Adi? Would you like

	another one? *(She takes the box and bends over the partition. Čech watches her behind with delight; Vaněk, with trepidation, his dog.)*
SUPERVISOR	*(Nervously.)* I know all about my responsibilities. And I know the priorities as well—there they are! (Points to the poster LOVE YOUR COUNTRY, LOVE YOUR DOG!)
ČECH	And what if we had a cup of coffee along with the famous Mr. Vaněk here, ladies? Caffeine soothes the nerves and sharpens the brain. What do you say, Comrade Trubačová?
SUPERVISOR	You know I don't drink coffee.
Mrs. BLAŽOVÁ	Well you do drink the odd weak cup once in a while. I'll make it for you with the breath of a single bean. *(While she talks, she pulls out a hot plate and a coffee pot, which she shakes so she can hear if there's water inside. She takes out some cups from her desk drawer, from another a coffee grinder, and from yet another a bag with coffee.)* Everything can be nicely solved with a bit of thinking after all. It's not a big deal, just—if you'll excuse me—one little dog!
SUPERVISOR	*(Addressing Ivanka primarily.)* But yours is, Comrade Blažová, a very narrow point of view. Because already the first law of dialectics says that everything relates to everything else. And there are other, equally important laws. When you say that the problem only concerns one dog, it doesn't mean that we should stop looking at the whole thing from the point of view of class struggle. And there are other points of view as well. According to the facts provided by the regional office, Mr. Vaněk here has been unanimously classified as—well actually there were other things—and I personally have seen our comrades on T.V. last year who were—those comrades were offering him tickets and a whole train so that he could go to Austria since he didn't like it here so much. And all our greatest artists signed the resolution in the National Theatre— even Comrade Staněk,[2] comrades! Comrade, I mean *Mr.* Vaněk should have thought about all that before he went out to buy a dog. Because a dog in our governmental system— well a dog has many diverse functions aside from simply providing happiness after a good day's work. Sometimes a dog can bring—and Comrade, I mean, *Mr.* Vaněk, remained rather silent about this—lots of money. We all know comrades, that some breeders make thirty, fifty—even a hundred thousand a year. Therefore, our society has a justifiable interest in seeing that the benefits go to the working class—especially to the farm workers and industrial workers and the progressive intelligentsia. But never, never, Comrade Blažová, to enemies of our system!

IVANKA	*(After much concentration, she strikes a key, then raises her head to speak to Vaněk.)* I just typed an L and it was right after K, the way it should be. So why is it N and then M right underneath? Instead of M and N, I mean?
VANĚK	Well, I really don't know— *(He's interrupted by the ringing of the phone on the movable arm which Mrs. Blažová, who needed space for coffee-making, pushed toward Ivanka.)*
IVANKA	*(Lifts the receiver.)* Yeah?—What?—O.K. *(Hands it over to the Supervisor.)*
SUPERVISOR	*(Automatically accepting it.)* Yes—Hello? *(Looks at Ivanka, confused.)* There's no one—*(Someone just made a sound at the other end.)* What do you want?—Well, maybe *you* should introduce yourself first! *(Horrified.)* Oh God! I am—this is Trubačová—you see, I—Ivanka didn't—Ivanka it's your comrade father—I—I—Just a moment *(Thrusting the phone at her.)*
IVANKA	*(Lackadaisically accepts it.)* Yeah?—What?—O.K. Oh that! It had to do with your secretary, old lady Kadlecová—all right—*Mrs.* Kadlecová—all right, then, Comrade Kadlecová. Maybe I should call her mommie.
SUPERVISOR	*(Desperately.)* Ivanka—*(Pointing to the door of her office.)*
IVANKA	Yeah, yeah, yes I'm joking—What?—Sure—He was trying to get me inside the Cont—the Intercontinental—the hotel—No, I'm meeting the gang—Hey, listen, I just typed a whole sentence—wanna hear it? *(Reads from her typewriter.)* Daddy is a dodo.
SUPERVISOR	Why don't you use my off—
IVANKA	Dodo, Yeah, I'm gonna type it up real neat before I go— So why don't you lend Kadlec—O.K., Comrade Kadlecová— Sure I know she's married, but I didn't think you knew— Can't you take a joke?—No, I'm alone; they all went to some meeting—O.K. Ciao. *(Hangs up.)* Well hasn't anybody figured out yet that it should be just the alphabet?
VANĚK	I don't think so.
ČECH	I agree with you, Comrade Trubačová, one hundred percent and I am sure that everyone else will. Even Mr. Vaněk here. But we are concerned specifically with this particular grabber. And all those artists who signed that thing in the National Theatre, well, I wouldn't take the whole thing too seriously, all sorts of things have been signed there already. You see, I heard that the only reason they got Staněk to come was to tell him that Dubček[3] would speak there. And when he discovered that he wouldn't, all the exits were already locked.
SUPERVISOR	Comrade Čech!
VANĚK	I think that he went there voluntarily. Otherwise, he would

	have said something afterwards.
SUPERVISOR	*(With relief.)* See? Even Mr. Vaněk admits it.
ČECH	And as we all can see, Mr. Vaněk didn't make use of that railway ticket anyway, and, after all, Czech grabbers are as rare as palm trees in Siberia. The idea, Comrade Trubačová, is not to help out dissident writers but Adi. Because if he's allowed to breed, then the puppies will go to the working class. There aren't that many class enemies!
Mrs. BLAŽOVÁ	*(Handing a coffee cup to the Supervisor.)* The coffee is as light as a cloud. *(Shaking the metal box.)* How many lumps would you like?
SUPERVISOR	I don't take sugar.
Mrs. BLAŽOVÁ	Well, you should. Without something sweet, the nerves become raw. Two lumps for you and we'll see how it works. *(Puts them in and at the same time turns to Vaněk.)* How many for you?
VANĚK	It doesn't matter.
Mrs. BLAŽOVÁ	Then, two for you too, all right?
ČECH	Of course, the easiest way out would be for Mr. Vaněk here to sell his dog. But you wouldn't want to do that, would you?
VANĚK	No, I really—
ČECH	You certainly wouldn't lose money on the transaction. Novotný asked fifteen hundred for him, didn't he? *(To Mrs. Blažová.)* Four for me, I like to sweeten the old tooth.
Mrs. BLAŽOVÁ	Don't I know it!
VANĚK	*(Astonished.)* How did you—
ČECH	I know Novotný. He started off by asking two thousand for him because you're in the doghouse—no pun intended—and went down another five hundred because he's a patriot. But Adi is worth it. I could get you two thousand for him without any trouble.
VANĚK	Please don't be angry with me but I—
ČECH	*(Patting him on the back.)* I'd be angry with you if you'd said yes. One doesn't sell either one's dog or one's wife. But what if we only made it seem as if?
SUPERVISOR	Seem as if what?
ČECH	Seem as if it seemed.
SUPERVISOR	What do you mean seem as if it seemed?
ČECH	Listen, they're putting on some play of yours in Vienna, aren't they?
VANĚK	Yes, they are.
ČECH	My wife heard about it at the hairdresser's. She used to work in the theatre when she was young—boy, the things I know about actors! For example, does Kubišová[4]—the singer—does she still have the two poodles?

1

A rare private performance of *Audience* in the mid-seventies: Václav Havel playing Vaněk and Pavel Landovský the Brewmaster.

Photo: Ivan Kyncl. Reprinted from *Index on Censorship* (83/12:2).

2

Václav Havel (born 1936 in Prague) was stage technician and later dramaturge at the famous Theatre on the Balustrade in Prague. Forbidden to hold a professional position after 1969, he worked as labourer in a brewery at Trutnov (an experience which is reflected in *Audience*). In 1977 he was among the first three spokesmen of Charter 77. His four-and-a-half year prison sentence was slightly shortened as a result of international intervention when he became seriously ill. He is the recipient of several international literary prizes. He lives in Prague.

Photo courtesy of The Charter 77 Foundation. Stockholm.

3

Pavel Landovský (born 1936 in Havlíčkův Brod) performed in various theatres in smaller Bohemian towns during 1960-65. Then he joined the well-known theatre company Činoherní Klub in Prague, distinguishing himself particularly in plays by Chekhov and Gogol. He also acted in about thirty films, as well as radio and television plays. In 1976 he lost his position with the theatre. Having been arrested several times in connection with his signing of Charter 77, he was allowed to leave the country in 1978. He now lives in Vienna.

4

Jiří Dienstbier (born 1937 in Prague) was Far Eastern Correspondent for Czechoslovak radio during 1964-67; in those days he travelled widely. From 1968 to 1969 he was correspondent in the United States. In 1970 he lost his position with the Czechoslovak radio. In 1979 he became one of the spokesmen for Charter 77. From 1979 to 1982 he served a three year prison sentence. He lives in Prague.

7

Václav Havel's *Audience* (translation into Swedish by Eva Lindekrants and Kent Andersson) at the Gothenburg Stadstheater in 1979.

Ferdinand Vaněk (Ernst Günther)
Brewmaster (Eje Wall)

Director: Måns Westfelt
Stage set design: Olle Langert
Music: Sven-Eric Johanson

Photo Credit: Christer Hallgren

6

Pavel Kohout (born 1928 in Prague) was active in several Prague theatres from the fifties to the seventies. Having been persecuted in connection with Charter 77, he received permission in 1978 to spend a year in Vienna as visiting director to the Burgtheater. After the year's stay, however, he was barred from re-entering his home country and was deprived of Czechoslovak citizenship. His "apartment productions" of Shakespeare's *Macbeth*, when he was still in Prague, became famous and inspired Tom Stoppard's *Cahoots Macbeth*. Kohout now lives in Vienna.
(Behind Kohout is a poster by the Czech artist Karel Trinkewitz, entitled "Hommage to the Imprisoned Václav Havel.)

5

The première of Václav Havel's *Audience* (translation into German by Gabriel Laub) at the Akademietheater, Vienna, in 1976.

Ferdinand Vaněk
    (Joachim Bissmeier)
Brewmaster (Johannes Schauer)

Director: Vojtěch Jasný
Stage set design: Karl Schneider

Photo Credit: Elisabeth Hausmann

8

Pavel Landovský's *Arrest* at the
Akademietheater, Vienna, in 1981.

Fragrance (Michael Janisch)
Hořňak (Rudolf Jusits)
Matte (Thomas Kamper)
Soumar (Alexander Trojan)
Vaněk (Karlheinz Hackl)
Pejchl (Jaromir Borek)

Director: Rudolf Jusits

Photo Credit: Elisabeth Hausmann

9

Václav Havel's *Unveiling* (translation into German by Gabriel Laub) at the Akademietheater, Vienna, in 1976.

Ferdinand Vaněk
    (Joachim Bissmeier)
Michael (Sebastian Fischer)
Vera (Sonja Sutter)

Director: Vojtěch Jasný
Stage set design: Karl Schneider

10

Pavel Kohout's *Permit* (translation into English by Peter Tegal performed under the title of *The License*) at the Orange Tree Theatre, London, England, in 1980.

Ferdinand Vaněk (Frank Moorey)
Supervisor Trubačová
(Ann Windsor)
Ivanka (Camille Davis)
Mrs. Blažová (Auriol Smith)

Director: Geoffrey Beevers

Photo Credit: Sarah Saunders

11

Václav Havel's *Protest* (translation into English by Vera Blackwell). Performed by the Kitsilano Theatre Company, Vancouver, Canada in 1984.

Ferdinand Vaněk (Josef Skála)
Staněk (John Destry Adams)

Director: Kico Gonzalez-Risso
Stage set design: Deryk Houston

Photo Credit: Bruce Law

12

Pavel Kohout's *Permit* (translated into English by Jan Drabek) workshopped and performed by the Kitsilano Theatre Company, Vancouver, Canada in 1984.

Supervisor Trubačová
(Patricia Helgason)
Mrs. Blažová (Lorraine Butler)

Director: Kico Gonzalez-Risso
Stage set design: Deryk Houston

Photo Credit: Bruce Law

14

Václav Havel's *Protest* (translation into Polish by Mata Scena) at the Teatr Powszechny, Warsaw, in 1981.

Ferdinand Vaněk (Mariusz Benoit)
Staněk (Władysław Kowalski)

Director: Feliks Falk
Stage set design: Ryszard Winiarski

Photo Credit: Renata Pajchel

13

Václav Havel's *Protest* (translated into Swedish by Eva Lindekrantz and Kent Andersson) at the Dramaten-Målarsalen, in 1980.

Ferdinand Vaněk (Per Mattson)
Staněk (Palle Granditsky)

Director: Olof Willgren
Stage set design: Agneta Pauli

Photo Credit: Beata Bergström

15

The cast of the BBC (Radio 3) production of *Audience* and *Unveiling* (translation into English by Vera Blackwell, performed under the title of *Private View*), in 1977; with Harold Pinter (fourth from left) performing the role of Ferdinand Vaněk.

Photo courtesy of BBC Enterprises.

16

Pavel Landovský in a "double role."

17

This picture is a detail from a remarkable coloured woodcut represent-
ing the oldest map of Bohemia, dated
1518, which is associated with the
name of Nikolaus Klaudian (Claud-
ian). The coach is a symbol of trou-
bled Bohemia which is tragically
suspended amidst a struggle of opposite forces. Today, when the country is again pulled to the East as
well as the West, the picture seems
as topical as it was more than four
and a half centuries ago.

The caption reads:
"Truth begets enemies." Terence
"But under a righteous judge it is
victorious." Ezdrase
(The original is in the Státni archív,
Litoměřice, Czechoslovakia.)

18

Ferdinand Vaněk's hometown
Prague, the "city of a hundred spires,"
built, like Rome, on seven hills, at a
turn of the Vltava River, which it
spans with a succession of bridges;
an ancient city at the cross-roads of
East and West, North and South,
which saw the première of Mozart's
Don Giovanni, and formed the
background to Kafka's mysterious
writings.

VANĚK	Yes, she does.
ČECH	That black one must be pretty old. About ninety. Am I right?
VANĚK	I thought about thirteen.
ČECH	That's right. With dogs you multiply by seven. She used to have a donkey too.
VANĚK	That was quite some time ago—
ČECH	It's with Havel and Kohout, right?
VANĚK	*(Confused.)* The donkey?
ČECH	No no, the three of you are having plays put on. In Vienna, right?
VANĚK	Yes, that's right.
ČECH	But I'd say that most of you write under a different name. Am I right?
VANĚK	*(Embarrassed.)* I don't really now.
ČECH	Listen, I'm not an informer or anything. I'm just trying to put the whole thing into perspective for you. *L'art pour l'art*—a way is always found, right? So why not with the grabber? The main thing for him is to get his registration and be exhibited at a prestigious dog show. All he needs for that is a nice solid—if you know what I mean, sir—name. That's all. Once he's bred he'd be your dog again. Litter reports go through Mrs. Blažová here and what does she know about which Vaněk she's dealing with, am I right?
Mrs. BLAŽOVÁ	Absolutely. *(Over the partition.)* For us one owner is the same as another. All we know is Adi baby here, don't we? *(Throws him a piece of sugar.)*
SUPERVISOR	But that would be fraud!
ČECH	Since the beginning of time the only fraud in breeding comes about when you don't have the proper dog. As far as the owner is concerned, it could just as well be Count Dracula for all we care.
SUPERVISOR	Count Dracula maybe, but not— *(To Vaněk.)* You writers are all alike. When he was drafted, my fiancé used to send me poems by Kohout. And both of them were liars!
ČECH	But Mr. Vaněk here didn't have anything to do with that, or did you?
VANĚK	No, no I didn't.
ČECH	And so, he can actually sell his Adi.
SUPERVISOR	But only to—make it seem as if— *(Speaking to Ivanka.)*
IVANKA	*(Now speaking to the Supervisor.)* If it went like the alphabet, every kid could do it.
SUPERVISOR	Of course—Do what?
IVANKA	Maybe I should let daddy handle it?
SUPERVISOR	*(Alarmed.)* It never entered my mind, Ivanka—But seeing as how I myself am strongly opposed to the whole idea—

IVANKA	*(With unusual interest.)* I didn't know you were such a fan of the British.
SUPERVISOR	Briti—
Mrs. BLAŽOVÁ	Ivanka's talking about the typewriter.
SUPERVISOR	*(Astonished.)* And what does—
ČECH	Maybe you're a little bit confused by the construction "seem as if," Comrade Trubačová. So forget it. Mr. Vaněk will simply sell Adi to me with everything properly taken care of. Only there'll be an agreement that Adi will stay with him for the present time and that sometime in the future he'll buy him back. But that won't be anybody's business. The papers will be in order and that's that.
Mrs. BLAŽOVÁ	And that's the truth and nothing but—
SUPERVISOR	*(Uncertain.)* How do you see it, Ivanka?
IVANKA	You could actually take out a patent on a system like that.
SUPERVISOR	Patent?
Mrs. BLAŽOVÁ	Ivanka, my dear child, would you take your machine and stuff it—Otherwise, we'll never get anywhere with all this.
SUPERVISOR	Which machine?
Mrs. BLAŽOVÁ	You can make a mockery out of your Mrs. Kadlecová, but don't fool around with us!
SUPERVISOR	*(Shocked.)* Now wait a minute Mrs. Blažová—*(To Ivanka.)* She didn't mean it—
Mrs. BLAŽOVÁ	Oh yes she did. You just let me take care of it and we'll straighten it all out, won't we Ivanka? Wouldn't you like a lollipop?
IVANKA	*(With interest.)* Have you got—
Mrs. BLAŽOVÁ	*(Opening yet another drawer.)* I have everything, but most of all I have two darlings at home just like you. Here, get your teeth into this and leave us alone until we're finished with Mr. Vaněk here. *(Points to Ivanka's breasts.)* And as for those big treasures of yours, you can just put them away tomorrow or I'll come out with mine and there'll be a total eclipse— *(She notices the terrified look of the Supervisor and begins to explain somewhat inconsequentially.)* I am only interested in seeing that Adi has some puppies, that's all.
ČECH	*(Winking at Vaněk.)* Of course, this has nothing to do with Mr. Vaněk here. I'm certainly not a big fan of Kohout, Comrade Supervisor; I had to go dig ditches when he was a big star. But I get mad when I hear on the radio another breeder—actually a veterinarian—shoving dirt all over him. I don't know about Kohout's writing, but I certainly know about the quality of his dog—
VANĚK	Eda.[5]
ČECH	Eda, sure. I judged him once and I can tell you that except for

being a little thin on the undercoat, he is a king among dachshunds. And that veterinarian is able to breed them only because he's practising the right kind of politics. He calls his breed the Ruggers, but they're all hairy like sheep— But Eda, now there's purebred for you. Krispin crossed four bitches with him annually. In '76 they all whelped at the same time, and I took my wife over so she could see something that she'll never see again as long as she lives. Twenty-seven little dachshunds all together. That's Eda for you.

VANĚK Eda, he—

ČECH Yeah, Eda. He's a bit of a primadonna. Of course, show me a champion that isn't. But he is a primadonna's primadonna. At Budějovice he was so good, he got 220 out of 220 possible points. So I said to myself, wait a minute, wait a minute. A lot of fixing goes on at these things—especially at the obedience trials. The master is supposed to hide in the landscape, then whistle. Except that your everyday dachshund sniffs a rabbit and tends to arrive at the destination in half an hour. So that's why some masters wrap their hips in some stinking hide and the dog arrives as if there were rails leading there. So I said to Mr. Kohout—when it was already all over with the judging—I said to him, let me borrow that whistle of yours, I'll check him out. I scratched him behind his ears for a while, so he'd get the scent and then his master held him while I hid inside some high grass about a hundred metres away. So I give him a whistle and I wait. Nothing's happening, so I wait some more, nothing again. Aha, I said to myself, that's the way it is. And as I'm getting ready to get up, I suddenly feel this strange warm moisture on my left leg and guess what? He outflanked me and with his back to me peed on my leg, making out as if he didn't see me, that son of a bitch! *(Laughing. From behind the partition comes a terrible growl and Čech is suddenly alarmed. Talking to the dog behind the partition.)* No one is laughing at you. *(With a note of warning to Vaněk.)* See?

VANĚK About Eda—

ČECH Of course, Eda is an aristocrat, that's what he is. I deserved everything I got for my lack of faith, but normally he's a very wise dog—so wise you sometimes wonder how's he really different from a human—just like you wonder when you get a real bastard how's he different from an animal. But, of course, then you're not being fair to the animal because the animal is always true to what's natural for it. If it needs killing it kills, but never tortures. Can you say that about people? One look at Eda and you see harmony—outdoors he's a hard worker, at home a cuddly dog, a charmer. But deep down he's a loner because he's inherited the instinct for it—knowing that when it's a matter of life and death, he'll have to handle himself in the dark and without his master. I'm not saying all that because of Mr. Kohout, no sir. I'm trying to show how an accident as well as damn hard work can combine to produce a perfect specimen like that. But the glory, the glory of it all, Comrade Trubačová—well there simply wouldn't be any without you. And the entire working class which will enjoy Eda's children—it has only you to thank for it because it was you who so bravely started to cry at the right moment when permission was needed to breed him.

SUPERVISOR *(Despite herself feeling flattered.)* Well, you know—if it's at all possible, one is able to—

ČECH See? And what if we have a new Eda in Adi here?

VANĚK Yes but Eda—

ČECH I know, I know: There's only one Eda, isn't there?

VANĚK *(Finally able to finish.)* You see Eda—Kohout doesn't have his Eda anymore.

ČECH What? They sold him when he was this old? That's terrible.

VANĚK He is dead!

ČECH *(Explodes.)* Damn! And I told him—watch out for those trains!

VANĚK He was poisoned.

ČECH Poisoned? Some idiot of a neighbour trying to get rid of his rats, eh? God, what a way to bow out for the greatest world class in Bohemia!

VANĚK Well, not exactly. You see, one morning he ran out, found himself a piece of sausage underneath this apple tree. And he hardly bit into it when he got these cramps. He couldn't even bark. He just kept looking at them with those sad eyes. There was Kohout's wife, mother-in-law, his niece, and his aunt. They all just kept looking at Eda until—

Mrs. BLAŽOVÁ Jesus!

ČECH *(Quite agitated.)* Was there an autopsy?

VANĚK Yes—apparently a high concentration—I have it here somewh— *(Searching through his pockets.)* Here. *(Pulls out another piece of paper from his breast pocket, then remembers his lack of glasses.)* Unfortunately, I don't have my—

ČECH Let me see it. *(Displays eyes like an eagle.)* Strychnine chloride—Do you know that that's kept in vaults because this much of it can take care of a whole army?

VANĚK I know.

ČECH What about the police?

VANĚK They were right there.

ČECH How do you mean right there?

VANĚK   Well, you see, Kohout got an anonymous letter. In it someone demanded a half a million to be placed in a toilet on the freeway; otherwise, he and his family would pay the price. And because he didn't have half a million and also because Sakharov[6] had been asked for the same amount—except in rubles, of course—he didn't like it. So he went to the police, and they wanted to know if he was demanding protection. He wasn't, but since it was just before the tenth anniversary of the Soviet inv— of the brotherly help, they provided it anyway. Three of them went right along with him and three more came around to his backyard. But someone still managed to get into that backyard and leave the sausage.

ČECH   And what about the police?

VANĚK   So Kohout caught the first train, but when he got to Krispin, Krispin had only one puppy left. And it had already been promised to someone. But Kohout pleaded with him, saying that Eda used to mount there all the time. Finally, he brought Eda's granddaughter back home with him. It was just like an automobile accident. After you have one, you should get behind the wheel right away again. And the bitch, Fina, when they took her for a walk the next day found another sausage. Fortunately she picked it up by the wrong end.

ČECH   And what about the police?

VANĚK   A week after that, he got another letter saying that he was sure to come to a sad end, but he was mainly concerned with the pup because he found two more—

ČECH   And the po— *(Exhausted, he sits down.)*

Mrs. BLAŽOVÁ   But that's monstrous. If they got rid of Kohout, O.K., it's terrible, but when you come right down to it, he could have apologized and would have had his peace and quiet, except that— *(Looks over the partition.)* I've never been particularly crazy about dogs; they're all right for people who are rich and lazy. *(Catches a glare from Čech.)* And of course for gamekeepers and hunters— *(Catches Vaněk's glare.)* And maybe for artists too—But I've got my hubby, the kids, grandchildren. I've certainly got enough on my plate to keep me hopping, but when one works here and gets to know those dumb faces—the dogs' I mean—and then you hear a story like this—it's just dirty, that's what it is—plain dirty. *(Resolutely pulls out the form she has already started working on from her typewriter. She crumples it, puts in another, and like a machine gun begins to fill in the empty spaces. Then suddenly she stops.)* So who is the owner? Is it you Mr. Čech?

ČECH   *(Awakened from his thoughts.)* Wha—what?

Mrs. BLAŽOVÁ   Can I put you down as Adi's owner? But only if it's all right

	with Mr. Vanĕk, of course—
VANĔK	Yes, certainly—I'd be very grateful if—And if there's some way I could repay—
ČECH	No, I'm sorry, but really—
Mrs. BLAŽOVÁ	I think that after all we've heard we don't have to hide anything, Mr. Čech. Madame Supervisor knows that we all mean well and that the work around here isn't always easy. Ivanka is our colleague now and we have no need to play games, do we dear?
IVANKA	Sure.
Mrs. BLAŽOVÁ	There's no reason why everybody around here shouldn't know that you've helped dogs to breed, Mr. Čech. They should in fact erect a monument to you so that all the dogs could come every day and pee on its corner.
ČECH	(Flailing his hands in protest.)
Mrs. BLAŽOVÁ	You don't have any problems with the authorities, do you?
ČECH	Not really.
Mrs. BLAŽOVÁ	So where is the problem?
ČECH	(Depressed.) I know what you will think, Mr. Vanĕk—But you see my wife and I finally got permission for a trip to Yugoslavia and she'd never been outside the country. You understand, don't you? You see, it took this long because during the unfortunate events of the fifties I used to own a riding horse—
VANĔK	I fully understand, Mr. Čech.
ČECH	But you can't possibly imagine how I feel—
VANĔK	I think I can.
ČECH	But you see I'd rather—
VANĔK	Come on, don't worry about it anymore. I under—
ČECH	I'm sorry that I've—
VANĔK	And I'm sorry that it had to—
ČECH	But I was thinking that if maybe you could, Mrs. Blažo—
Mrs. BLAŽOVÁ	(Who had just been trying to attract the dog's attention is alarmed.) Me?
ČECH	Well, just this once—
Mrs. BLAŽOVÁ	(Forces a laugh.) I realize it would be just this once, but couldn't it wait a little while longer? You see my hubby also has a bit of a past. Ten years ago he signed a petition for them to get out. (To Ivanka.) Your father probably did too, except in my husband's case someone noticed and they demoted him; he came very close to getting fired. (To Vanĕk.) It's easier for you because you're already not allowed anything. But when you want the smallest thing you have to learn a self-criticism for every occasion. There are meetings to attend and demonstrations to march in, even if you're the only one

	who is marching. You have to put up posters too. And now, after so many years, they want to promote him to a shift technician. I just don't have it in my conscience to keep him from getting it—
VANĚK	And you're absolutely right. You mustn't!
Mrs. BLAŽOVÁ	Look, if it were just me I'd say to hell with it.
VANĚK	I know, I know. Don't worry.
Mrs. BLAŽOVÁ	My hubby'll take care of me and the kids will be overjoyed to have grandma at home—
VANĚK	Don't think about it anymore. Don't worry.
Mrs. BLAŽOVÁ	But I thought since Adi here is such a rare breed and such a good dog— *(To Supervisor)* maybe you would like to—
SUPERVISOR	What?
Mrs. BLAŽOVÁ	Well, you're a Party Member. If you were the owner, no one would dare open his mouth.
SUPERVISOR	But you've gone absolutely—All right, I am not entirely against it since you've convinced me that it is in the interest of the working class to breed him, but for me personally to cover up for Mr. Vaněk? So that he can go and write those pamphlets of his? Yes, yes, Comrade Blažová, Comrade Ivanka here is our colleague, you're absolutely right there, but that doesn't mean we have the right to get her involved in all sorts of intrigues. Quite the opposite is true. We have the daughter of a highly placed comrade among us and that should make us even more responsible: we must search out deeper principles, more pronounced—wider—
IVANKA	*(While Supervisor is talking, she pulls the telephone to her and dials a number.)*
SUPERVISOR	*(Grows quiet.)*
IVANKA	*(Sweetly.)* Comrade Kadlecová. Greetings, Comrade Kadlecová, Ivanka speaking. Would you be so kind and let me speak to my comrade father?—Yes, quite important: You see, I've got such a cute date for him—Oh, you're really very kind, comrade, I'm sure he'll find a way to express his gratitude to you. Thank you. *(To the Supervisor.)* You don't have to stop talking on account of me.
SUPERVISOR	*(Unable to say a word.)*
IVANKA	Yeah—What?—O.K. But I thought I was being really nice. Again? Listen: doesn't she have some sort of a nervous disorder or something? Look, daddy, I wanted to tell you somethin'. Sure I'll be quick. I got you a dog. What—Sure—No, it's not a joke. It's a grubber. A Czech grubber.
ČECH	*(First one to catch it.)* A grabber.
IVANKA	A grabber—Why're you breathing so hard? Very funny. Listen, aren't you happy? Why not? Oh. And what about

Comrade Kadlecová, she could take care of him for you—or Comrade Kadlecová's husband? You know him, don't you? He could do it, since he's alone so much—No, a joke. A JOKE!—Me? I just don't have the time—You know what? Until we figure all this out I'll just lend him to someone— Yes.—O.K., go back to your meeting. And if someone wants to know you can tell him that you've got a dog—a grabber. Oh yeah—his name's Adi. Ciao. *(She hangs up and everyone is quiet for a moment.)*

Mrs. BLAŽOVÁ   *(Finally speaks up.)* Ivanka, you're a dear! *(She walks up to her, pulls the lollipop from her mouth, kisses her and then shoves it back in.)* Welcome to the club. *(She returns to her machine and begins to type like a machine gun, finishing a line. Then she takes out the form and hands it to the Supervisor.)* When we file this one, you'll be made Vice-Chairman. *(To Vaněk.)* And Adi-baby will be admitted to graduate obedience school.

ČECH   *(Strokes Ivanka's cheek, obviously moved.)* My dear girl, you've taken the weight of cowardice from my shoulders and at the same time provided a cup full of hope which was so needed by my parched lips.

IVANKA   The main thing is that Kadlecová'll be mad as hell.

SUPERVISOR   *(Looking at her, still undecided.)* You really think I should—

ČECH   Go on. The juniors have a show in Písek the day after tomorrow, and it could mean a prize for comrade father.

VANĚK   Do you think that—

ČECH   Normally, there'd be no question he'd get it. But this way he'll get it, and maybe her father will face a bit of music as well. *(To Supervisor.)* Hurry, so he doesn't leave and maybe you could— *(To Vaněk.)* go and get some of that champagne. What do you say?

VANĚK   I'd be delighted.

IVANKA   I'm off. I love bubbles. *(She grabs her purse and extends her hand to Vaněk.)*

VANĚK   Thank you so much. Just a moment— *(He looks for his wallet, then for his glasses.)* I don't have my glasses—If you'd take what you need—

Mrs. BLAŽOVÁ   *(Searches through her desk and finds a big beef bone.)* Adi-baby will get something too, won't he? *(She passes through the partition after the Supervisor so that now everyone is behind it.)*

IVANKA   *(To Vaněk.)* That would really be something, wouldn't it?

VANĚK   What?

IVANKA   You know— with the letters.

VANĚK   Oh yes—no doubt. *(To Mrs. Blažová.)* Er—maybe he

	shouldn't—that bone—
Mrs. BLAŽOVÁ	Just this once—look how he's licking it just like he was licking your hand before. *(To Supervisor.)* Look, look! Here's your chance. Give him a pat and you won't ever have to worry again.
SUPERVISOR	No, no!
ČECH	Comrade Trubačová!
SUPERVISOR	Never!
ČECH	Fifty years I've been working with dogs. Would I tell you to do it if I didn't think—
SUPERVISOR	I know, I believe you, but—
Mrs. BLAŽOVÁ	*(Reproachfully.)* But now he's the dog of her father.
ČECH	Come on, let's get it over with. Bend down and a nice pat right here—
SUPERVISOR	*(As if under a spell of some sort she bends down. In everyone's face there is suspense, then relief. Finally comes applause.)*
Mrs. BLAŽOVÁ	Hooray!
SUPERVISOR	*(Appearing with a glow in her eyes.)* He let me. *(Screams.)* Help, he's coming at me. *(About to run away.)*
ČECH	*(Steps in her way.)* Not at you, after you. He's just following you, and when you want to stop him you just stamp your foot like this and say: Adi! Down!
SUPERVISOR	But he'll bite me.
ČECH	He won't.
VANĚK	Really. He won't.
ČECH	Try it. Adi! Down! And stamp your foot.
SUPERVISOR	*(Stamps her foot full of uncertainty and in a shaky voice.)* Adi, down.
ČECH	See there's nothing to— *(Bends down.)* What's he doing—
Mrs. BLAŽOVÁ	*(Laughing.)* He's got the shits again.
ČECH	*(Joins in with his hearty laugh and the others, including the Supervisor. The old man, suddenly alarmed, calls out.)* Don't laugh! DON'T LAUGH!

(But we already hear wild barking and desperate wails. The Supervisor falls down behind the partition, Ivanka jumps on top of the bench, and Mrs. Blažová saves herself by a courageous dive over the partition. Vaněk and Mr. Čech alternately call "Adi! Down!" and also fight with the enraged beast, which topples the hanger and finally pushes ahead of itself the entire partition including Mrs. Blažová behind it. Perhaps even the ceiling falls, but the curtain definitely does.)

THE END

Sázava, Sept. 4, 1978.

NOTES

1. We know of Staněk's efforts to remain in official good graces. See *Protest*.
2. Alexander Dubček (born 1921), First Secretary of the Communist Party of Czechoslovakia, whose reform programme led to the "Prague Spring" and ended with the Soviet invasion of Czechoslovakia in August 1968.
3. Marta Kubišová, Czech popular singer during the 1960's and 1970's. Since she became a signatory of Charter 77, she has been prohibited from performing in Czechoslovakia.
4. Andrei Dmitriyevich Sakharov (born 1921), leading Russian theoretical physicist, Nobel Peace Prize Winner (1975), and noted dissident, sentenced to internal exile in Gorky where he lived under police surveillance from 1980 to 1987.

PAVEL KOHOUT

Morass

Translated by Vera Pech
with the assistance of Kevin M. Grace

Dedicated to the convicted
VÁCLAV HAVEL
writer
recipient of the Austrian State Prize for European Literature
currently inmate of Correctional Institution Heřmanice
PS 2 Ostrava 13 71302

CHARACTERS

Ferdinand Vaněk
First Interrogator, 40
Second Interrogator, 50
Third Interrogator, 60
Mary, 25
George, 20
Ensign (Fourth Interrogator), 30
can be played by the First Interrogator with a different wig

PLACE

An office of the Administration of State Security
Prague—Ruzyně

TIME

Monday, 11 January 1977

(The room is furnished with sectional furniture. A writing desk, goose-neck lamp, telephone. Behind the desk, three wooden armchairs; in front of the desk, one chair. On one side a secretary's desk and chair. A metal cabinet, padlocked, serves as a safe. A coat rack. Bright green sofa. Through the dusty curtains on a metal barred window is visible the prison complex opposite. A picture of the President. A worn-out propaganda poster depicting the building of the state. A dirty washbasin with a cracked mirror, but with running water. The only door leading to the hall opens. Accompanied by staff employee George, Vaněk enters, a short fur sports jacket draped over his shoulders. In his right hand he carries a small bag which can also be worn as a shoulder bag. George wears a very colourful modern ski-jacket—an import; he closes the door. Distant sounds. In the yard, somebody is keeping time, one-two-three-four, hundreds of boots stamping; distant commands and sounds of shuffling feet come through even more frequently.

A short, though colourful study of waiting. At first, Vaněk is trying to calm down after the previous excitement; then he begins to notice the room, the sounds. Eventually, his acclimatization nearly complete, he starts to function almost normally.)

VANĚK Maybe we could sit down—

GEORGE *(Shrugs his shoulders.)*

VANĚK *(Looks at his watch, realizes it has stopped, takes it off unhappily, shakes it and gives up.)* Do you have the time?

GEORGE *(Shrugs his shoulders.)*

VANĚK Is it a state secret?

GEORGE *(Points to his wrist without a watch.)*

VANĚK Excuse me—

(The uneasy feeling of a well-brought-up man that he was rude, takes the wind out of his sails. Sounds of steps and whistling echoes through the hall. Enter a friendly looking man, not yet forty, dressed in a leather jacket, a long rolled-up object under his arm; he is eating an apple. Surprised, he returns to the hall to check the number on the door, then re-enters.)

1st INTERROG. I see, there are not too many of you here. Well, never mind. Sit down.

(Neither moves, surprised.)

1st INTERROG. *(To Vaněk.)* Take a seat, comrade! *(To the young one.)* No need for stage fright; we'll be okay! Everything nice and easy!

(They both sit down.)

1st INTERROG.	(Unrolls a wall poster with a picture of a car engine and after a slight hesitation hangs it on an electric switch under the portrait of the President.) So, let's get going. Engines in cars are usually, well? (Points to Vaněk.)
VANĚK	(Is perplexed.)
1st INTERROG.	(Points to George.) Well?
GEORGE	(Rises.) Combustion engines. (Sits down.)
1st INTERROG.	Correct, and they are divided into? (Points to Vaněk.)
VANĚK	(Is perplexed.)
1st INTERROG.	(Points to George.) Well?
GEORGE	(Rises.) Two-cylinder and four-cylinder models. (Sits down.)
1st INTERROG.	Good. And their performance is determined by what? (Points to Vaněk.)
VANĚK	(Recovers his senses and gets up.) Excuse me, but—
1st INTERROG.	First, try to answer me.
VANĚK	By gasoline—
1st INTERROG.	(Points to George.)
GEORGE	(Rises.) The engine's size. (Sits down.)
1st INTERROG.	Obviously. (He reprimands Vaněk.) My, my my! Now, you'll have to really get with it, comrade, if you ever want to get a driver's licence.
VANĚK	I have a driver's licence.
1st INTERROG.	You do?—Could I see it?
VANĚK	(Puts his bag on the table and with one hand tries to retrieve the licence.)
1st INTERROG.	(Opens it hastily while looking at Vaněk at the same time.) Then, what are you doing here?
VANĚK	(Pointing to George.)
GEORGE	(Standing at attention, hands a piece of folded paper to the First Interrogator.)
1st INTERROG.	Did you make a mistake, comrades? There is supposed to be a car club meeting here—!
GEORGE	(Shakes his head.)
1st INTERROG.	(Shakes his head.) Well, I'll be— (Goes to the phone, dials three numbers while at the same time examining Vaněk very carefully.) Where do we know each other from, comrade? The Legion?
VANĚK	No—
1st INTERROG.	(Extends to him his free hand.) My name is Vltavský.
VANĚK	(Embarrassed.) Vaněk—
1st INTERROG.	(Looking at the driver's licence.) Ah, you are that famous Frank Vaněk from the fingerprint division?
VANĚK	No, I am—
1st INTERROG.	Ferdinand, I see, I beg your pardon! (He finally makes the telephone connection.) Vltavský—Where are you hiding,

	Mary? You should carry your knitting with you—Where do you say the car club is? What an ass I am. Well, ciao. *(Puts down the receiver and smiles at Vaněk.)* Did you hear that joke about the man with sclerosis, how he comes to the doctor and asks him if he knows why he is there?
VANĚK	No—
1st INTERROG.	*(Takes off the screen and rolls it up.)* Well, the man comes to the doctor and asks him, "Doctor, do you know why I am here?" *(Laughs.)* I am one floor up! *(He looks at Vaněk even more carefully.)* But we know each other!
VANĚK	I really don't know—
1st INTERROG.	Didn't you spend your recreation time in Romania last year, comrade?
VANĚK	I don't have a passport.
1st INTERROG.	You don't have—just a moment—may I ask about your profession?
VANĚK	I'm a writer.
1st INTERROG.	*(Sits down behind the desk overcome by surprise.)* Ferdinand Va—my goodness! *(Starts reciting.)*

Excuse my answering just with a card
and lest I forget: stay well—

Do you know it still?

VANĚK   No—

1st INTERROG.   "A Letter from the Front" it was called, wasn't it?
(Continues his recitation.)

I'm not about to open my heart
and don't know what to tell!

That's a long time ago—I was not drafted until after I finished Engineering, in '67, and I found it pasted on the door of my locker. I must confess, at that time, I just laughed, in those days, other things were in vogue; this seemed, don't be offended, like from the horse and buggy days. But then, Vera, my girlfriend, wrote to me that she had another guy, and I decided to do myself in. A young kid *(Pointing to George.)* feels no other one will do, and, well, when I went to the munition depot where I was supposed to get my ammo, I took a last peek in the locker with the picture of Vera pasted there and all of a sudden one line of that poem bowled me over—

You write of crushing fear about me—!
Don't worry, no bullet for your mate!
I got the gun just to protect me
And not to compete with Fate!

After my guard duty I got drunk, and that was that. In a month's time, I met Gerry and today, I have three kids. And

	for all this, I am indebted to you. That's a fact. Gerry and I, we often think of you.
VANĚK	But that's—
1st INTERROG.	I know, all done with. Are you penning anything new? When can we look forward to something?
VANĚK	I? I have been forbidden to publish since 1968.
1st INTERROG.	All the time? I thought all that had been straightened out a long time ago—and what then—Aren't you in charge of some literary circle? Me, I'm nuts about cars, but if you organized some sort of a literary circle—
VANĚK	I've been arrested.
1st INTERROG.	No way! *(To George.)* Isn't this some sort of a mistake?
GEORGE	I took him over at the gate from the police.
1st INTERROG.	They could have made some sort of a mistake. Show it to me again!
VANĚK	I don't think they made a mistake—
1st INTERROG.	*(Studies the paper.)* But you are not under arrest! You have been called as a witness only.
VANĚK	Then, why did they break down our door?
1st INTERROG.	They did—did they think, maybe, your place was on fire—?
VANĚK	Our place was not on fire.
1st INTERROG.	Maybe they received a message of that sort. Or maybe, that there were burglars in the place. You wouldn't believe, how many hooligans do idiotic things like that.
VANĚK	I think they arrested me— *(Corrects himself.)* or called me as a witness in connection with the Charter.[1]
1st INTERROG.	Which Marta?
VANĚK	Not Marta—! Charter.
1st INTERROG.	What's that?
VANĚK	Sort of—Citizens' initiative.
1st INTERROG.	And what's punishable about that?
VANĚK	Nothing. The right to petition—
1st INTERROG.	So, why would they want to arrest you because of that?
VANĚK	The fact is, they arrested me— *(Corrects himself when he realizes the First Interrogator is ready to object.)* or in any case, called me as a witness.
1st INTERROG.	*(Studies the paper.)* That doesn't mean anything. *(To George.)* Who is waiting for Mister Vaněk?
GEORGE	I don't know.
1st INTERROG.	Well, what did they tell you at the gate?
GEORGE	That I should take him here and keep an eye on him.
1st INTERROG.	Hey, run along and ask the Chief.
GEORGE	The Chief—?
1st INTERROG.	If he is not there, ask the secretary.
GEORGE	Ask her what?—

1st INTERROG.	Tell her that somebody from the Police broke down Mr. Vaněk's door. And she should give them a buzz to get their act together!
GEORGE	Will do. *(Opens the door.)*
1st INTERROG.	Hold it! Tell them, I am taking care of Mr. Vaněk.
GEORGE	Will do. *(Opens the door.)*
1st INTERROG.	Hold it! Tell them to bring the car around!
GEORGE	Will do. *(Waits a while, then departs; diminishing sound of his steps in the hall.)*
VANĚK	Thank you—
1st INTERROG.	Don't mention it. As soon as he returns, I'll drive you home. If the door is not fixed, I'll slap it together myself.
VANĚK	You are very kind.
1st INTERROG.	That's my duty. I didn't want to mention it in front of the kid—he is just a trainee—but between the two of us—those gorillas here were slightly overdoing it. When you are associated with this outfit, you like the Security to look good.
VANĚK	Mainly here, yes—Well, there were proceedings conducted here in the '50's—
1st INTERROG.	What proceedings?
VANĚK	Slánský[2]—don't you know they put to death dozens of innocent—
1st INTERROG.	Yeah, now I remember, but, Mr. Vaněk, I have nothing to do with that, that's a fact, in those days, I had barely stopped peeing in my pants!
VANĚK	All I wanted to say, was, that whoever works here should always keep this in mind.
1st INTERROG.	I don't want to examine your conscience, Mr. Vaněk, but that's your problem, isn't it?
VANĚK	Mine?
1st INTERROG.	*(Recites with passion.)*

Let our hearts be full of watchful fires
As we were taught so nobly through the years
We answer every blow, nobody tires
Gottwald and Stalin—ever without peers!

	Do you like it still?
VANĚK	No.
1st INTERROG.	But in those days you liked it!
VANĚK	No.
1st INTERROG.	Then, why did you write it, Mr. Vaněk?
VANĚK	I didn't.
1st INTERROG.	What—?
VANĚK	Not the first one either—the one you—
1st INTERROG.	Who wrote it then?

VANĔK	*(Opens his mouth and closes it again.)* I don't wish to name anyone here.
1st INTERROG.	Dammit, Mr. Vanĕk, we are only talking poetry!
VANĔK	Well, here—
1st INTERROG.	It's not this place's fault, that the law sometimes got a little bit bent around here. It's the same with the Prague Castle. Hitler stayed there. Today, Comrade Husák[3] lives there— *(He doesn't elaborate any further.)* My hands are clean!
VANĔK	Your predecessors weren't born with bloody hands either—
1st INTERROG.	*(Sighs.)* No, yeah—Did you hear the joke about the bride who asked her mother before the wedding night, what she should do so her husband wouldn't find out that she wasn't a virgin, and her mother told her to put a razor blade there?
VANĔK	*(Bewildered.)* No—
1st INTERROG.	So, before the wedding night, the new bride asks her mother, "Mum, what should I do so that my husband won't find out that I am not a virgin," and her mother tells her, "Put a razor blade there." *(He laughs, then gets serious.)* It's really not yours? Wait a minute, didn't Kohout write that? I'll bet!
VANĔK	*(Shrugs his shoulders.)*
1st INTERROG.	For heaven's sake; I can look it up at home! It's tough luck for you scribblers, all you leave is black on white. It was him, wasn't it?
VANĔK	*(Shrugs his shoulders.)*
1st INTERROG.	I'm surprised, you being in the same boat with him these days. You never cared for him! He really is the prototype of an opportunist.
VANĔK	So, why is he banned?
1st INTERROG.	Go on. Nobody gives a hoot about him.
VANĔK	You yourself are here reciting his poe—*(Does not finish.)*
1st INTERROG.	So, you've remembered? It's nothing—! For Christ's sake, Mr. Vanĕk, take off your coat!
VANĔK	Well, it isn't worth it—you said yourself—
1st INTERROG.	Well, you know, we are an official authority, and what's more, an official authority in prison matters; every scrap of paper has to be under lock and key. I'll hang this up for you, so you won't catch a— *(When he takes Vanĕk's jacket off, he sees his left arm in a sling.)* Christ, what happened? I hope they didn't—
VANĔK	No, it's only an inflamed tendon—
1st INTERROG.	I am relieved—And how did you get an inflamed tendon; were you perhaps digging around at your cottage?
VANĔK	If I write for a long time, I get cramps. And from these cramps—
1st INTERROG.	And lots of people think writing is just a piece of cake. Have a

VANĚK	seat! *(Motions to a chair in front of the table.)* Cigarette?
1st INTERROG.	No, thanks—not now—
1st INTERROG.	*(Lights up and pushes the package of cigarettes and the lighter toward Vaněk.)* In case you change your mind. You'll have a coffee, won't you? *(He dials a number.)* Mary? Vltavský. Send over two coffees.
VANĚK	No, thanks not for me.
1st INTERROG.	Oh, sure, coffee always hits the spot. Yeah, Mary, O.K.? *(Hangs up.)* Do you know the one about the bridegroom who is having breakfast after the wedding night and says to his bride—"And you don't know how to make coffee either—"?
VANĚK	*(Embarrassed.)* No—
1st INTERROG.	Well, the bridegroom is having breakfast after the wedding night and he says to his bride—"So, you don't know how to make coffee either!" *(He laughs, then gets serious.)* When you were talking about that—you know, when I thought it was a woman—!
VANĚK	*(Instinctively.)* Charter—
1st INTERROG.	Yeah, Charter, Marta! I bet Kohout thought that one up, am I right?
VANĚK	*(Shrugs his shoulders.)*
1st INTERROG.	He's kind of a loudmouth. That's the way he advertises for himself when he can't succeed with his writing. Then he always gets sore when he lands in here.
VANĚK	I am here too.
1st INTERROG.	You are a different case altogether!
VANĚK	How?
1st INTERROG.	Look here; it's true you were never a Communist, but you are still a decent fellow.
VANĚK	So, why am I here?
1st INTERROG.	I am sure that will be explained. As far as I'm concerned, I find you ten times more appealing than that— *(Points somewhere Kohout is supposed to be.)* precisely because you never beat your own drum. That's why you are writing even now, while he has to think up all these Charters, isn't it so?
VANĚK	I don't know if the Charter was his idea.
1st INTERROG.	While you're sitting home working. Now, you've even got these inflamed tendons.
VANĚK	And you also broke down my door.
1st INTERROG.	Mister Vaněk, that's not fair. I am going to have it repaired.
VANĚK	I know, forgive me.
	(Steps approaching, George enters.)
1st INTERROG.	So? What?
GEORGE	I am supposed to let you know that the Chief is not around.
1st INTERROG.	Dammit. Are you in a hurry, Mister Vaněk?

VANĚK	Well—I try to write—
1st INTERROG.	Dammit. *(Looks at his watch.)*
VANĚK	*(He too looks at his watch.)* Do you have the time? My watch has stopped—
1st INTERROG.	Blame it on us—
VANĚK	Well, let's not—
1st INTERROG.	That's a relief!
VANĚK	I dropped it when they were pounding on our—
1st INTERROG.	It's almost three. Are you in a hurry, Mister Vaněk?
VANĚK	Well—I try to write—
1st INTERROG.	Does it get published abroad, at least?
	(Sound of woman's heels coming closer; door opens; enter a bosomy, fashionably dressed black-haired girl; she carries a record on which sit two plastic cups, steam rising from both.)
1st INTERROG.	*(Absentmindedly puts Vaněk's driver's licence in his pocket.)* Ah, thanks, Mary, that's nice—Goodness, what are you using for a tray?
MARY	*(Answers icily without looking at him.)* You should've ordered it in the cafeteria. George, take it from me!
GEORGE	*(Helps to put the cups on the table.)*
1st INTERROG.	*(Wipes the record with his sleeve.)* That's a piece of evidence— *(Since Mary ignores him, he talks to Vaněk.)* Are you familiar with this? Strauss's waltzes. Do you have this?
VANĚK	That's not my kind of music—
1st INTERROG.	It's no music at all, but various provocative themes. Swan songs of the *emigrés.*
MARY	*(She stands at the door now, looking at him meaningfully.)*
1st INTERROG.	Thanks, Mary. It has sugar in it— *(To Vaněk.)* I didn't ask if you take sugar!
VANĚK	Thanks, I really don't want any.
1st INTERROG.	You don't drink coffee?
VANĚK	Not here—
1st INTERROG.	Do you think we have poisoned it? Or maybe we spat in it? Do you know the joke about the guest asking the waiter who is bringing him his soup, why is he holding his thumb in it, and the waiter says that he has rheumatism in his thumb and has to keep it warm, and the guest is incensed and asks why not stick it up his rear and the waiter replies that's where he's had it until now? *(He laughs.)* Did you know that one, Mary? No? Well, the guest asks the waiter—
MARY	*(Looks at him icily.)*
1st INTERROG.	*(As casually as possible.)* Do you want anything?
MARY	My little boy is in kindergarten.
1st INTERROG.	Don't worry, Mary, you will make it in time! Just imagine, this is the writer Ferdinand Vaněk! You should ask him for an

	autograph— *(When he notices her icy stare.)*—for the boy, when he grows up!
MARY	I'll ask. *(With an ultimatum.)* Till four, at the latest! *(Leaves, the sound of her steps withdrawing.)*
1st INTERROG.	Here, help yourself.
VANĚK	*(Shakes his head.)*
1st INTERROG.	Why not—?
VANĚK	How did she find us here?
1st INTERROG.	You mean Mary? Easily—
VANĚK	You are supposed to be one floor down.
1st INTERROG.	What do you take me for, Mister Vaněk, me, who knows your poems better than you do—
VANĚK	They are not my poems!
1st INTERROG.	Please! I accept the second point, but the first one is unjust. That's a fact!
VANĚK	How did she find us here then?
1st INTERROG.	Since it interests you so much, I'll go and ask her. *(Grabs the screen and quickly departs. The steps are receding.)*
VANĚK	*(To George.)* Can you tell me where the washroom is?
GEORGE	What—?
VANĚK	The toilet.
GEORGE	I don't know. *(Noticing Vaněk's surprise.)* It's my first time here.
VANĚK	That makes two of us. Maybe we could find it together.
GEORGE	Impossible.
VANĚK	How come?
GEORGE	Have to wait for the comrade.
VANĚK	*(Resigned.)*
	(Sound of approaching steps. The door bursts open and in rolls, like a tank, a man Vaněk's age, tall, strong, in rumpled, colourless clothes; he inspires fear; in his hand he holds a writing pad. George jumps to attention. Vaněk slowly gets up. The man falls noisily into the armchair behind the desk, opens the drawer, takes out a clean notepad and a bunch of pencils and throws it all in front of Vaněk. Then, out of his pocket, he takes a sports magazine, opens it and disappears behind it. Bewildered, Vaněk searches for an explanation from George; however, George averts his eyes.)
VANĚK	*(After a while.)* Excuse me—
2nd INTERROG.	*(Behind the paper, laconically.)* Yes!
VANĚK	The gentleman who was here before you, promised to drive me home—
2nd INTERROG.	When you finish writing it!
VANĚK	What?
2nd INTERROG.	Everything!

VANĚK	*(Perplexed.)* I—
2nd INTERROG.	*(Still behind the paper.)* Don't you know how to write?
VANĚK	*(Perplexed.)*
2nd INTERROG.	*(All of a sudden, he throws the newspaper away, gathers the papers and the pencils, grabs one of them, and without looking at Vaněk, starts shooting questions.)* You just dictate it to me! Quick—who was the one who thought up the Charter, who was helping him, where was it written, and how did it get out!?
VANĚK	*(Perplexed.)*
2nd INTERROG.	*(Shouts.)* I am waiting!
VANĚK	*(Comes to, but keeps silent.)*
2nd INTERROG.	I don't hear anything, Mister Vaněk!
VANĚK	Perhaps it is because I am silent.
2nd INTERROG.	*(Roars.)* No more jokes! This is not the theatre; this is the State Security Office!
VANĚK	*(Quietly, but firmly.)* And how am I to know that?
2nd INTERROG.	What?
VANĚK	In the last hour, I got to meet several unknown gentlemen, some who broke down our door, some others who took me down here without uttering a word, one lover of poetry, and this fellow who doesn't know where the—Now, you come barging in and without an introduction start shouting at me. And all this is supposed to make me realize that I am at the State Security Office?
2nd INTERROG.	You guys are all very squeamish when we step on your toes. You weren't that squeamish about us!
VANĚK	What do you mean by "we" and what by "you"?
2nd INTERROG.	Simmer down, I don't go for your speechmaking, I am originally a miner by profession! Quick! Author of the Charter!
VANĚK	Ferdinand Vaněk.
2nd INTERROG.	Hey, hey, we hit the nail on the head!
VANĚK	I am introducing myself. Can I have your name?
2nd INTERROG.	You can't. So, did you write it or not?
VANĚK	*(Sits down and keeps silent.)*
2nd INTERROG.	*(Bangs his fist on the table.)* I didn't allow you to sit down!
VANĚK	Unless you introduce yourself, I consider you an unknown person. I don't need to stand to attention before you; nor do I need to answer you.
2nd INTERROG.	I see, some sort of a wise guy? Who poured all this wisdom into your head? Your employers at the CIA?
VANĚK	*(Keeps silent.)*
2nd INTERROG.	*(Roars.)* I am not going to waste my time with you!!
VANĚK	*(Keeps silent.)*
2nd INTERROG.	So, you know what, Mister Vaněk? Don't think that I am

scared of you because you are not going to hang me from a lamp post—you won't live to see that, Mister Vaněk! My name is Labský and I am asking you to answer my questions. Author of the Charter?

VANĚK   Could I see your identification?

2nd INTERROG.   *(Wants to shout again, but changes his mind, takes out of his pocket a little red book, opens it, closes it, and puts it back.)* Here. Satisfied? Let's get going. Whose idea was it first?

VANĚK   Mr. Labský, there comes a time when one has to educate oneself, and so I have bought myself a copy of the Law on National Security. It says there I have to be summoned for an interrogation if I am not under arrest. Am I under arrest?

2nd INTERROG.   You would like that, wouldn't you? In the evening it would be on the news, and tomorrow, business would boom, eh? Do you need to sell some new anti-socialist play? It's not going too well even in the West now, is it?

VANĚK   Well, if I am not under arrest, I have to be summoned.

2nd INTERROG.   I am issuing the summons now.

VANĚK   Instead of the summons, you are now breaking down the door?

2nd INTERROG.   You shouldn't have barricaded yourself.

VANĚK   I beg your pardon, I didn't bar—

2nd INTERROG.   Our Police confirmed your barricading yourself in; they used force because there was a danger of you taking your life.

VANĚK   Why should I be taking—That's a lie!

2nd INTERROG.   Those golden days are gone, Mister Vaněk, when in the '60's you drove our comrades to suicide! But we are not taking revenge, as you can see yourself; on the contrary, we are risking you accusing us of violence rather than harming you; even though, in my opinion, it wouldn't do culture any harm. Now, quick, let's get a move on—Author of the Charter?

VANĚK   You are trying to provoke me, aren't you?

2nd INTERROG.   You are overestimating yourself, Mister Vaněk! As far as I am concerned, you are just an ordinary citizen like everybody else!

VANĚK   Could you then show me an ordinary summons?

2nd INTERROG.   I could not.

VANĚK   May I ask why not?

2nd INTERROG.   You may not.

VANĚK   I will wait, then.

2nd INTERROG.   All right, Mister Vaněk. Wait. We have plenty of time.

VANĚK   I don't, but for you, I'll make an exception.

2nd INTERROG.   *(Bangs his fist on the table.)* Enough is enough! Man, where do you get the gall? We can see through you. You are a typical product of your class! Daddy owned half of Prague and you would dearly love to get it back! And because of that, you would bring the nation to the brink of disaster, and when, at the last moment, the Party puts things right, you'd play the martyr. Nothing doing, Mister Vaněk. Your days are over. To be or not to be, that's your big concern! *(He walks to the locker, tears off the seals, takes out the key, opens the door and removes a big stack of papers which he puts on the table.)* All this is you, Mister Vaněk! All your misdemeanors, blunders, lies. Everything checked, documented, and prepared for the printer. When your fans in the West read this, you'll be nothing but a big zero there! Even your collaboration with us is in your file!

VANĚK   I would be more surprised if it were not there.

2nd INTERROG.   You will stop laughing when you see this.

VANĚK   If you don't mind, I am not going to look at it till I get that summons.

2nd INTERROG.   What good will it do, since you are here already?

VANĚK   It must have started the same way in the '50's; first, people got reconciled to being arrested without proper papers, and in the end, they asked to be hanged.

2nd INTERROG.   Well, the time is coming again when that will turn out to have been right. Only they had the tough luck to land in jail while such smart cookies as your family had enough money to sail through. You'd like to own half of Prague again, eh?

VANĚK   No.

2nd INTERROG.   Well, in those days you liked it!

VANĚK   No.

2nd INTERROG.   So, you were actually glad when we took it away from you, right?

VANĚK   We never had it.

2nd INTERROG.   How come? What was your father's profession?

VANĚK   A gamekeeper.

2nd INTERROG.   But your uncle—

VANĚK   The same.

2nd INTERROG.   So, who was it among your colleagues? Whose father was a big architect and whose uncle was a big producer?

VANĚK   *(Opens and closes his mouth.)*

2nd INTERROG.   Well?

VANĚK   *(Shrugs his shoulders.)*

2nd INTERROG.   I can easily find out!

VANĚK   *(Shrugs his shoulders.)* I have already told your colleague that I am not going to name any names.

2nd INTERROG.   And what if I won't let you go home?

VANĚK   *(Shrugs his shoulders.)* Well, in that case, I will have to stay here.

2nd INTERROG.	I have plenty of time, Mister Vaněk. Plenty of time!
VANĚK	I don't, but for you I will have to make time.
2nd INTERROG.	Wasn't it Havel, by any chance? It was Havel, wasn't it?
VANĚK	*(Shrugs his shoulders.)*
2nd INTERROG.	Everybody knows that—Havel is a millionaire's son!
VANĚK	Marx was also a millionaire's son. All I know is that Mr. Havel's father built one of the most beautiful parts of the city and his uncle was the founder of the Czech cinema.
2nd INTERROG.	And while they were at it, they were lining their pockets! So, you see, you remembered the author of the Charter!
VANĚK	I never said he was the author—
2nd INTERROG.	Why would you stand up for him when compared to him you're only a proletarian! Even today, he has enough to get himself out of any trouble!
VANĚK	So, why is he banned?
2nd INTERROG.	Why? Because he kept asking for the capitalists to come back!
VANĚK	Where? When?
2nd INTERROG.	He wanted to hang us all from lamp posts!
VANĚK	Show me!
2nd INTERROG.	Would you also like to see us hanging from lamp posts? That won't happen, Mister Vaněk!
VANĚK	Just show me, when and who wanted that??
2nd INTERROG.	The comedy is over, Mister Havel!
VANĚK	Stop calling me Havel!!
2nd INTERROG.	What?
VANĚK	My name is Vaněk!!
2nd INTERROG.	And so?
VANĚK	You are calling me Havel!
2nd INTERROG.	You are all the same bunch.
VANĚK	I'll file a complaint about you!
2nd INTERROG.	*(Laughs loudly and points Vaněk out to George as if Vaněk were a village idiot.)* He will file———ha ha!
VANĚK	*(To George.)* And you will be a witness!
2nd INTERROG.	*(In the same vein.)* And you will be his—ha ha!
VANĚK	*(Excited.)* You are misusing your function and insulting me! You claim I wrote something I didn't write, and you deliberately call me Havel! *(Sound of steps in the hall, enter an elegant, pleasant-looking man of about sixty. The Second Interrogator and George spring to attention.)*
3rd INTERROG.	Couldn't you be a little bit more quiet, comrades? And what is this here?
2nd INTERROG.	*(The change in him is striking, he speaks quietly as if he were embarrassed for Vaněk.)* Well, Mister Vaněk here is sort of

	discussing with me—
VANĚK	*(Still excited.)* I am not discussing anything with you!
2nd INTERROG.	*(Hurt.)* Yes, you have different plans for us—
VANĚK	I don't want to hang anybody!!
2nd INTERROG.	Who is talking about hanging?? See Mister Vaněk—slip of the tongue—
VANĚK	*(Catching his breath, he turns to the newcomer.)* I am filing a complaint against this gentleman! He insists I didn't write something I did, that is to say, that I wrote something I did not—yes, that I did not. And deliberately he is calling me by a name that is not my own!
2nd INTERROG.	*(Shrugs his shoulders as if to show there is no point in quarrelling with Vaněk.)*
3rd INTERROG.	*(Nicely.)* Could you leave us here alone, comrades? *(The Second Interrogator and George nod, bid them good-bye, and leave the room; one set of steps is receding.)*
3rd INTERROG.	What happened to your hand?
VANĚK	*(Slowly calming down.)* Nothing, just an inflammation of the tendons—
3rd INTERROG.	How does a writer get an in—
VANĚK	*(Sharply.)* When he writes a lot. May I ask—
3rd INTERROG.	Of course. Take a seat, Mister Vaněk.
VANĚK	No, thanks.
3rd INTERROG.	You don't want to stand, surely.
VANĚK	Nobody has explained to me yet why I should sit here.
3rd INTERROG.	*(Laughs.)* Good thinking!! Before I forget. *(He shows him his red identification card.)* Just for order's sake.
VANĚK	*(Calms down some more.)* Thank you. The other gentleman forgot what should have been obvious and, furthermore, he was rude.
3rd INTERROG.	The comrades are overworked and nervous these days, you see. They haven't got much time for their families.
VANĚK	I am not with my family either.
3rd INTERROG.	But they—let's leave that for now. *(He picks up a little box from the table.)* A cigarette?
VANĚK	Not now—
3rd INTERROG.	*(Lights up and pushes the box towards Vaněk.)* When you feel like it. They gave you coffee, I see.
VANĚK	I explained before that I am not going to—!
3rd INTERROG.	Are you a health nut or are you suspicious? *(Gets serious.)* So, what is your pleasure, Mister Vaněk?
VANĚK	*(Shocked.)* I—
3rd INTERROG.	I was told you wanted to tell me—
VANĚK	What kind of nonsense is this? The door to my apartment was broken down; I was brought in here without a summons

	and have been waiting for an hour now!
3rd INTERROG.	For whom?
VANĚK	*(With sarcasm.)* For Godot.
3rd INTERROG.	Who is that?
VANĚK	*(Sheepishly.)* I beg your pardon—it's the title of a play.
3rd INTERROG.	Yours?
VANĚK	No, Beckett's.
3rd INTERROG.	I'm ashamed, but I don't know him. Is he one of your group? I mean, the group that signed the Charter?
VANĚK	No, a Frenchman.
3rd INTERROG.	Aha! And we were wondering why it first appeared in *Le Monde*—But that's beside the point. Why are you upset, Mister Vaněk?
VANĚK	Did they break down my door just so they could insult my colleagues to my face??
3rd INTERROG.	Your colleagues—do you know that I was almost one of your colleagues?
VANĚK	*(Doesn't understand.)*
3rd INTERROG.	But as long as the Havels were in power, the best I could manage was to dig ditches. Yes, my first poem was returned because it had ten misspellings. That was capitalism, Mister Vaněk. I experienced it! I bet you will tell me now that Kohout was a Communist. *(Takes off his wedding ring and hands it to Vaněk.)*
VANĚK	*(Doesn't understand.)*
3rd INTERROG.	Just look inside!
VANĚK	*(Looks inside.)*
3rd INTERROG.	Is it still legible? It's been twenty-seven years this year!
VANĚK	*(Reads.)* To Francis from Frances.
3rd INTERROG.	*(Points to.)* December 21, 1950! That date doesn't mean anything to you?
VANĚK	*(Shrugs his shoulders.)*
3rd INTERROG.	Stalin's birthday. We got married on Stalin's birthday, just like those two characters in Kohout's play, what was it called, it went in those rhymes—
VANĚK	*(Shrugs his shoulders.)*
3rd INTERROG.	"Good Love"—no, "Such a song,"[4] or something like that— Well, and today, he's got a young wife, his third one, while I still have the old one! *(Gets gloomy, but quickly recovers.)* Look, Mister Vaněk, maybe politically we are on opposite sides of the barricade, but as an artist and a human being I value you much more than those—ah, let them be—no matter what anybody says!
VANĚK	You better not say this in front of anybody else.
3rd INTERROG.	You don't know me; I'm not any less stubborn than you are

127

and I didn't need to wait for Dubček[5] to come. You think I don't see who those people are who claim to be writers today? All you have to do is to switch on the TV. For example, right now the series from that fellow Franěk, do you watch that?

VANĚK   Yes—

3rd INTERROG.   I am surprised at you, it's such junk! Just the other day I told Frances—Vaněk should get hold of this!

VANĚK   Thank you—

3rd INTERROG.   Actually, what prevents it?

VANĚK   Right now, me sitting here rather than in the Writer's Club.

3rd INTERROG.   You wouldn't need to sit in the Club, but on the Executive.

VANĚK   Well, I must confess, I'd rather sit here.

3rd INTERROG.   Look, that's something I don't understand. Imagine, it wouldn't be Franěk who would set the tone—keep this to yourself! —not even the Bulgarians want to publish his feeble out- pourings— but people internationally renowned like yourself.

VANĚK   You are exaggerating—

3rd INTERROG.   Not really! Let's make a bet that I know what *Le Monde* will publish tomorrow? That the nasty policemen broke down your door. Isn't that a waste of your talent?

VANĚK   But they really did break down our door.

3rd INTERROG.   Try to take a different view of it—you barricaded yourself.

VANĚK   *(Gets up.)* If you are going to repeat that stupid lie—

3rd INTERROG.   *(Also gets up.)* Is it a lie that you barricaded yourself from reality? Pardon me, that's my view—

VANĚK   *(Sheepishly.)* Excuse me, I thought you wanted—

3rd INTERROG.   It's not easy to discuss things with you—

VANĚK   That's a misunderstanding— What reality?

3rd INTERROG.   *(Motions to him to sit down and sits down himself.)* That's the way it is. You barricaded yourself when you are needed most— well, and life itself has come to claim you—! Life needs you, Mister Vaněk.

VANĚK   What does that mean in plain Czech?

3rd INTERROG.   This time, if you would stay outside the Charter, we could finally get rid of Franěk. The union would be taken over by men like Staněk,[6] decent authors, who didn't do anything underhanded; they just couldn't say no. And where Staněk is, as the saying goes, there Vaněk is, and where Vaněk is, there are also the others, of course, everything nice and sensible; we don't want the Franěks to agitate Moscow.

VANĚK   Moscow will be upset as soon as Franěk falls.

3rd INTERROG.   Nonsense! I can tell you— but this is absolutely confidential— *they* are behind this.

VANĚK   Not really!

3rd INTERROG.	It's a fact, and you can be pleased that even they consider you an international figure. You probably have a lot of old friends there?
VANĚK	*(Agrees.)*
3rd INTERROG.	Do they still associate with you?
VANĚK	*(Agrees.)*
3rd INTERROG.	Where?
VANĚK	Excuse me, what kind of a role am I playing here exactly?
3rd INTERROG.	That of a famous Czech writer, Mister Vaněk, whom we would like, in this hour so critical for our literature, to give the opportunity to fulfil his moral duty. Satisfied? Aha! I let them break down your door because I considered it unwise that anybody else should know about this discussion. Today, we have here Patočka, Vaculík, Pavlíček, and even Havel;[7] Mr. Kohout just landed here with his wife, so it won't be noticeable. It's a regular writers' congress here. *(He laughs.)*
VANĚK	*(Just looks at him and shakes his head.)*
	(The phone rings.)
3rd INTERROG.	*(Picks it up and answers sharply.)* Call later! *(Puts down the receiver.)*
VANĚK	This moral duty, what's it all about?
3rd INTERROG.	You will be surprised; it's nothing you would expect. No public confession, no secret collaboration with us—simply to help us change the direction of our culture by your active participation in it.
VANĚK	Like how?
3rd INTERROG.	Mister Vaněk, you have been politically devalued for nearly ten years, and you will lose practically all value by signing that Charter. I am making you an offer—become a hard currency again.
VANĚK	How so?
3rd INTERROG.	*(Takes out his wallet and out of it a little piece of paper.)* Do you know this?
VANĚK	*(After a while.)* I'm sorry, but I have decided not to answer any of your questions. Since you consider me an internationally known author, you shouldn't treat me here as a common thief.
3rd INTERROG.	You really ask patience of people, Mister Vaněk; because of you I have to be patient with Frances, so, why shouldn't I be patient with you, too. This is your signature on Charter 77; it came from luggage found in the car driven by Landovský and Havel.
VANĚK	That's good—
3rd INTERROG.	What's good?
VANĚK	As far as I know, they were trying to deliver the signatures to

	the National Assembly.
3rd INTERROG.	And as you can see, on the way they changed their mind and brought them to us— *(Laughs.)* That's just a joke. Seriously. Look, what if this little piece of paper— *(Pretends to destroy it.)*
VANĚK	But it's known that I have signed it.
3rd INTERROG.	It's not known. If it doesn't come from us it's not officially known. Tonight, what we have decided on will become known.
VANĚK	But it has been already published abroad— *(Quickly adds.)* —you yourself have said that—!
3rd INTERROG.	*(Winks at him.)* I have said; you have said. And you have just given me an idea. We will put in the official report—strictly for us—that your name has been added by your—I am not an expert when it comes to those people, for me the domestic men of letters are enough—Beckett?[8]
VANĚK	That's utter nonsense!
3rd INTERROG.	He's completely unknown to me; you were the one who mentioned his name!
VANĚK	But in a completely different context!
3rd INTERROG.	Mister Vaněk, let's not quarrel. *(Laughs.)* I'm not trying to drag any names out of you. There is something more important I am concerned about. Look, let's say, that your name was added by someone who sent the whole thing abroad; we don't know this person, so we cannot deny it.
VANĚK	And then?
3rd INTERROG.	Then nothing. For the first time, your name won't be mentioned in our report. That's all.
VANĚK	And what am I going to tell my friends?
3rd INTERROG.	Nothing, as far as they know you have signed it. Do you realize how ingenious this is? The whole world will think of you as one of the signatories of the Charter, only, with your consent, we will inform the higher authorities, that it's all a hoax, and that will be sufficient for those who are concerned about you. *(A pause.)* Well, what do you say? What is more important, Mister Vaněk, the fate of literature or a few friends, who are actually going to profit by this act?
VANĚK	Are you not suggesting I betray them?
3rd INTERROG.	Now, now, why the big words? You wouldn't want to get them in trouble—all for a good cause!
VANĚK	A good cause gained by bad behaviour is worthless.
3rd INTERROG.	Did you ever try to examine how worthy of you your friends are?
VANĚK	It's because of them I live in Czechoslovakia. My friends are my country.
3rd INTERROG.	*(Opens the cabinet and sets out a pile of papers next to the*

	first pile.) Here she is.
VANĚK	Who is—
3rd INTERROG.	Your country. It could be published as a collection—Ferdinand Vaněk through the eyes of his friends. Snatches from letters, transcripts of telephone conversations, lists of statements, reports of colleagues, but also whole essays, when your dear friends started talking and writing, whenever your name was mentioned. Here, help yourself! Get to know your country. You'll lose another one of your naïve ideas.
VANĚK	I am not going to look at it.
3rd INTERROG.	Rather than acknowledge publicly that this is your country, you prefer to stand cynically behind it. Or, would it make you sick, maybe—? I wouldn't be surprised. *(Turns over the pages.)* For instance, here your pal, your neighbour, writes—
VANĚK	*(Gets up, resolutely.)* I don't want to hear it!!
3rd INTERROG.	Disillusioned Love? That would be a very nice title for a play.
VANĚK	I don't want you to show me my friends in a moment as intimate as fear. Fear of you! The last one allowed to call a raped woman a whore is the rapist himself!
3rd INTERROG.	Do I look like a rapist?
VANĚK	You don't, but the one who was here before you!
3rd INTERROG.	But it's me who is here now, Mister Vaněk, and I really mean well, why don't you believe me?
VANĚK	You are always addressing me by my name—
3rd INTERROG.	Shouldn't I? Just say so—
VANĚK	That's all right. And I should call you—by your number?
3rd INTERROG.	I don't remember it myself! Of course, I also have a name.
VANĚK	May I guess? Are you by any chance Mister Dunajsky?
3rd INTERROG.	You put me at ease; I was afraid you were clairvoyant. No, I come from Moravia; my name is Odrak.
VANĚK	Aha! Jan would go with that.
3rd INTERROG.	Oh no!
VANĚK	Joseph?
3rd INTERROG.	Wrong! Can you imagine, Thomas, vintage 1918. They named me after Masaryk.[9] You can see, even the policeman has his Achilles' heel.
VANĚK	Thomas is a nice name. Certainly much nicer than Francis.
3rd INTERROG.	Francis? *(Finally, he gets it, looks at his wedding ring at a loss for words.)*
VANĚK	*(Watches him with a mixture of pity and curiosity.)* *(Phone rings.)*
3rd INTERROG.	*(Lifts it up.)* No more calls! *(Hangs up, sighs.)* Look, Mister Vaněk, you are forcing us to do this with that *Le Monde* of yours—but I wouldn't like to think that all the rest was just a game. Sit down, and let's—

VANĚK	I would really like to be clear on one thing—am I under arrest?
3rd INTERROG.	Clearly, Mister Vaněk—no, you are not under arrest; I wanted to have a talk with you, and my offer still stands.
VANĚK	In that case, I would like to go home—
3rd INTERROG.	As you wish. Do you have that paper issued at the gate?
VANĚK	No—that young fellow has it—
3rd INTERROG.	*(Opens the door leading to the hall.)* You, come here!
GEORGE	*(Enters, stands at attention.)*
3rd INTERROG.	Give me his release paper.
GEORGE	Comrade Labský took that.
3rd INTERROG.	Dammit—just a moment, Mister Vaněk. *(Leaves, steps quickly receding.)*
VANĚK	*(Resigned, looks at his watch.)* Did you ask?
GEORGE	Ask what—?
VANĚK	Where the washroom is?
GEORGE	No— *(After a pause.)* I don't have to go yet—
VANĚK	*(In desperation, looks at the washbasin.)* I guess, I will have to—
GEORGE	This one is plugged.
VANĚK	*(Resigns himself.)*
	(Sounds of woman's heels quickly approaching, enter angry Mary.)
MARY	Where's the Chief?
GEORGE	I don't know.
MARY	Did he go home?
GEORGE	I don't know.
MARY	Did someone call him? Twice?
VANĚK	*(Because she now looks at him.)* Yes—
MARY	*(To George.)* It was you who took it, am I right? Next time, you be good enough to ask what I want? I am not going to fly from one floor to the next like a witch on a broom.
GEORGE	It wasn't me—
MARY	*(To Vaněk.)* Was it you?
VANĚK	No. Your boss.
MARY	Naturally—we shall see—*(Goes to the phone, dials, notices the cigarettes, and takes one.)* Sherry? Mary. Hey, any idea where Charlie is? But his Beetle is still sitting here. Look out the window! *(Motions to George to light her cigarette; he doesn't have a match. Vaněk obliges, using his lighter; she offers him a cigarette.)* Yeah, right. If he turns up, holler at him to give me a buzz. And make sure he does. Ta! *(Puts down the receiver, dials again, looks at her watch, notices that Vaněk didn't take a cigarette.)* Don't you want one? *(Sits down on the table.)*

VANĚK	Thank you.
MARY	You don't smoke?
VANĚK	I do, but not here.
MARY	Just go ahead, I am giving you permission.
VANĚK	Unfortunately, I forgot mine.
MARY	*(Telephones.)* Lieutenant Havránek—I don't know which button, I am not in my office—look, this is Mary Havránek, it's urgent! *(To Vaněk—indicating cigarettes.)* These ones aren't bad.
VANĚK	That's very nice of you, but I have decided to accept nothing from you.
MARY	But these are not mine; they belong to the establishment.
VANĚK	Which establishment?
MARY	Well—to the office— *(Into the phone.)* Christ, ask at the garage, he must be somewhere!
VANĚK	That's just it—I have read and also heard from my friends that one—and that includes all of you here—becomes dependent on you and has a tendency then to reciprocate, but, if you could tell your colleague here— *(Embarrassed, points to George.)* You wanted to ask something—
GEORGE	I—? What—?
VANĚK	Remember, I asked you before—!
GEORGE	And I told you— *(Points to the washbasin.)* —it's plugged—
VANĚK	*(Quickly interrupts.)* Where is the washroom here?
GEORGE	We will wait for the comrade.
MARY	Are you looking for the john? It's right across. Go right in.
GEORGE	My orders are to guard him.
MARY	So, you go together!
VANĚK	Thank you, thank you very much— *(Very embarrassed.)*
MARY	Don't mention it. *(Laughs, but then rolls her eyes.)* Christ, they're a bunch of idiots down there.
GEORGE	*(To Vaněk.)* Leave the bag here!
VANĚK	*(About to put it over his shoulder using his healthy hand.)* What's that?
GEORGE	The bag, you leave it here!
VANĚK	If you don't mind, I have my personal things in there and I wouldn't like—
GEORGE	You can't go in with the bag.
MARY	Is Mister Daněk under arrest?
VANĚK	*(Corrects her politely.)* Vaněk—no, I was, as your boss put it, called in for a discussion.
MARY	Explanation, right? According to paragraph 19? You just keep it. *(To George.)* I'll take the blame. *(To Vaněk.)* You don't need to return it. *(Into the phone.)* Rudy? *(Waves to them to leave.)*

(Vaněk leaves the room followed by George; steps receding.)

MARY Look, Rudy, it's a madhouse here today—yeah, you have heard—yeah. But you'll be through at your normal time, right? Good. Look, if I don't call you by four, could you pick up little Rudy? Yeah. And look, buy him two little cartons of yogurt and a croissant. *(Steps in the hall; the First Interrogator enters; surprised, he looks around.)*

1st INTERROG. Where is—where are they—

MARY *(Puts her hand over the phone and hisses.)* In the john! Psst, my old man! *(Into the phone.)* And, Rudy, see to it that little Rudy eats everything; guess where I found some yogurt yesterday? Inside your rubber boots; you would have had a good laugh when you stepped into them. *(The First Interrogator approaches from the back and gives her a peck on the neck; she quickly finishes.)* Rudy, I have to hang up, the boss is coming, he is in a mood to kill us all today! Look, don't you worry, I'll be home by midnight! *(Hangs up.)*

1st INTERROG. *(Straightens up and says with horror.)* Why midnight? You will be home by seven!

MARY With this kind of opportunity? *(She hugs him, but he frees himself, jumps to the wall, lifts the picture of the president, and unplugs something.)*

1st INTERROG. You have gone mad!

MARY Oh? A while ago, I had the feeling that you—

1st INTERROG. Of course, Mary, but today—today—

MARY That's annoying, you can't just give me this garbage about being on duty, comrade!

1st INTERROG. To you, I would never—you, I always, you know that, but today, we have guests—

MARY Like hell you do. Gerry is keeping din-din for you and after that you'll go beddie-bye with her.

1st INTERROG. What on earth are you—

MARY Just like you do every Monday and Saturday!

1st INTERROG. That's—

MARY You've cancelled Thursdays, I understand.

1st INTERROG. Where did that come—

MARY Gerry told Sherry. So, today you are cancelling Mondays!

1st INTERROG. Well, that's—

MARY Look here, Charlie, just so we understand each other. If you can't manage, Deputy Kučera promised to get me out of here. Then you can enjoy your old bag every day! Maybe she will even laugh at your stupid jokes.

1st INTERROG. How come—?

MARY I've had it up to here with all those couches in here!! Are you going to marry me or not?

1st INTERROG.	*(Trying to catch his breath.)* But you are—you are also—
MARY	I will get a divorce one, two, three! *(Steps; in comes Vaněk, followed by George.)*
MARY	*(Sweetly.)* If you need me, I'll be in my office. Until four! *(Bangs the door, triumphantly clanging her heels as she departs.)*
1st INTERROG.	*(Speaks sharply to George.)* How come he took his bag with him??
GEORGE	The comrade permitted him—
1st INTERROG.	*(Closes his mouth; turns to Vaněk; the genial tone is gone.)* Sit down!
VANĚK	If you will allow me—?
1st INTERROG.	No. Sit down!
VANĚK	In that case, I have to repeat that I didn't get the—
1st INTERROG.	*(Out of his breast pocket he quickly takes a folded piece of paper.)* Summons? Here. Sit down!
VANĚK	I would also like to ask you—
1st INTERROG.	The party's over, Mister Vaněk, now we will start an interrogation!
VANĚK	That's why I demand some proof of your identity.
1st INTERROG.	*(Controls himself and quickly shows him his identification.)* Sit down!
VANĚK	*(Sits down.)*
1st INTERROG.	In accordance with paragraph 19 of the Law on State Security, I am asking you to give an explanation of a punishable act against an unknown culprit.
VANĚK	I have to repeat, I am not going to answer any of your questions.
1st INTERROG.	*(Shouts.)* So, the gentleman plans to stay quiet? Where do you think you are??
VANĚK	In a place that's supposed to guard my safety.
1st INTERROG.	You are extremely squeamish when it concerns you! You wouldn't be that squeamish about us!!
VANĚK	What do you mean by "you" and what by "us"?
1st INTERROG.	Why don't you calm down; nobody is going to listen to your speeches here! Are you willing to answer my questions?
VANĚK	As long as you keep shouting, I am not going to answer anything.
1st INTERROG.	*(Stops shouting.)* You know what? To make it easier for you—we will keep you here as long as you decide not to answer our questions.
VANĚK	In that case, I ask to be taken to my cell—
1st INTERROG.	You would like that, wouldn't you? In the evening, it would be on the news, and tomorrow business would boom, eh? Do you need to peddle a new masterpiece? Nobody buys that

	junk of yours, not even the C.I.A., am I right? So, are you going to answer?
VANĚK	*(Keeps quiet.)* *(Steps. Enter the Third Interrogator. The First Interrogator and George don't even get up.)*
1st INTERROG.	*(Visibly surprised.)* What's up—?
VANĚK	Comrade Chief, you promised me—
3rd INTERROG.	Just a moment, Mister Vaněk, get up—
VANĚK	*(Surprised.)* Why?
3rd INTERROG.	Just because I'm asking you.
VANĚK	Very well— *(Gets up.)*
3rd INTERROG.	*(Politely.)* Now, if you would kindly turn around for a moment—
VANĚK	As you wish— *(Turns around.)* *(Behind his back, the Third Interrogator points to the picture of the President while looking at the First Interrogator; the first Interrogator slaps his forehead and plugs in something located under the picture; he grins apologetically.)*
VANĚK	May I ask—
3rd INTERROG.	*(Sharply, just like the Second Interrogator and now the First Interrogator.)* No, you may not, Mister Vaněk. Now it's we who want to know. Are you going to answer or not??
VANĚK	This reminds me very much of the '50's—
3rd INTERROG.	That's really enough! Man, where d'you get that insolence? We sure can see through you! First, you force the whole nation to get married while reading *Sweet Love*,[10] and when the Party restores order at the last minute, you begin to play the martyr. Nothing doing, Mister Vaněk, the game is over! Prague won't belong to you any more! *(Lifts up the pile of papers that the Second Interrogator took out of the cabinet.)* Here are all your misdemeanors, blunders, sins. When your dearly beloved friends read this, you will be just a big zero for them.
VANĚK	My pals will get a good laugh hearing that I am co-operating with you. May I go to my cell?
3rd INTERROG.	You would like that, wouldn't you, to have it broadcast this evening, and tomorrow business would boom. Do you need to find a publisher for your new play? Have you written *Sweeter Love* or, maybe, *Sweetest Love*?
VANĚK	Well, gentlemen, I have now realized that the purpose of all of your so-called mistakes is to rob me of my identity. And, so there won't be any misunderstanding, since I didn't make a statement about my signature: my signature on the Charter is valid. The Charter is a legally based initiative to uphold the Helsinki agreement, and Czechoslovak law number 120, concerning the citizens'—

3rd INTERROG.	What Charter—?
1st INTERROG.	We will get to your women in a moment, Mister Vaněk!!
VANĚK	I beg your pardon—
3rd INTERROG.	You are clearly under the impression, Mister Vaněk, that you are here for political reasons, but you are here because of a common criminal act, one that is not going to bring you any glory!
VANĚK	What is this again—?
1st INTERROG.	You got angry, because somebody here called you Mister Havel.
VANĚK	And what's that—
3rd INTERROG.	You don't like Mister Havel?
VANĚK	On the contrary.
1st INTERROG.	Does he like you?
VANĚK	Why don't you ask him since he is here?
3rd INTERROG.	And what is your relationship to Mrs. Havel?
VANĚK	Gentlemen, what is the reason for this—
3rd INTERROG.	The reason for this interrogation is a punishable offence that we will acquaint you with in due time, but the reason for our astonishment is your moral profile. This is what your famous friendship looks like: with Mister Havel you write the so-called Charters—
1st INTERROG.	—and with Mrs. Havel, you jump in the sack!
VANĚK	*(Leaps up.)* I beg your pardon??
1st INTERROG.	Does that seem normal to you—to jump into the sack with the wife of your friend?
3rd INTERROG.	For us normal people, who followed your advice and still have their first wives, for us, to put it in a nutshell, Mister Vaněk, this is morass!
1st INTERROG.	How will your pals view all this when it comes out?
VANĚK	*(Comes to.)* They will just laugh at you and even ordinary people won't swallow that—
3rd INTERROG.	I think the last laugh will be on you when this comes out! *(Out of the pile he pulls a big photograph and hands it to Vaněk.)* Well?
VANĚK	*(Just stares at it without making a sound.)*
1st INTERROG.	One wouldn't suspect a poet of this, Mister Vaněk!
3rd INTERROG.	This could be titled Barebacked Love, Mister Vaněk!
1st INTERROG.	Is that how you got your sore tendons, Mister Vaněk!
3rd INTERROG.	Do you know that joke, Mister Vaněk, about the guy who is asked why he has his hand in a cast, and he replies, "Well, I put my hand in a snatch and Mister Snatcher caught me?"
VANĚK	You should be ashamed—!
1st INTERROG. and 3rd INTERROG.	*(To George.)* We are supposed to be ashamed—ha ha ha!

137

VANĚK	You are teaching the young some nice things!
1st INTERROG. and 3rd INTERROG.	*(To each other.)* We are teaching them—ha ha ha!
VANĚK	*(Upset.)* And all this under the portrait of a man who was once given a life sentence in exactly the same way and today is President of the Republic!
1st INTERROG. and 3rd INTERROG.	*(Have tears in their eyes laughing.)* President—ha ha ha!

(Sound of steps, door opens; enter the Second Interrogator, followed by Mary lugging a typewriter; the First Interrogator, the Third Interrogator, and George jump to attention.)

2nd INTERROG.	*(With an indulgent detachment, the same as the Third Interrogator used previously.)* Would it be possible to conduct this in a somewhat quieter manner, comrades?—What is this here?
3rd INTERROG.	*(As if ashamed for Vaněk.)* It's just that Mister Vaněk here is having a discussion with us—
VANĚK	*(Still upset.)* I, with you— *(All of a sudden, he calms down.)* You are really provoking me—only you are forgetting, gentlemen, that history does not end today.
3rd INTERROG.	Yours does, Mister Vaněk!
1st INTERROG.	You are not going to hang us from lamp posts anymore, Mister Vaněk!
2nd INTERROG.	*(Trying to calm all of them down.)* There, there, comrades—! *(To Vaněk.)* You know, Mister Vaněk, it's you who is forcing us to behave like this. These days, the comrades hardly see their families. So, what decision have you made, Mister Vaněk? Are we going to part amicably, or do we start writing?
VANĚK	You can do what you like. I have already asked to be taken to my cell.
2nd INTERROG.	There, there, Mister Vaněk. Grey is all theory, eternally green is the golden tree of life![11] Look, politically, we stand on the opposite sides of the barricade, but as far as I am concerned, as an artist, you are in a class by yourself. I don't care what anybody says. You are internationally known, and all of us here hold the fate of Czech literature in our hands. You yourself publish in all those different *Le Mondes*, claiming there is only one literature, and Franěk, Staněk, and Vaněk are part of it. Now, you have the opportunity to change from words to action. *(He takes out of his wallet the paper with Vaněk's signature and pretends to destroy it.)* You are familiar with the offer, it's fair and valid. Well? I've done my part, now it's your turn—!

VANĚK	You know my answer. My signature is valid too.
2nd INTERROG.	*(After a pause.)* Very well, then— The masquerade is over; it's better to show your real face—Mary! Take this down.
MARY	*(Inserts the form, at the same time looking ostentatiously at her watch and at the First Interrogator.)*
ALL OF THEM	*(They light cigarettes; nobody offers a smoke to Vaněk.)*
2nd INTERROG.	Ready? Let's start. Ferdinand Vaněk—you can copy the particulars from the summons—excuse me, Mister Vaněk, *(Takes his paper from Vaněk and later on puts it in his pocket.)* begun on January 11, 1977 at 3:50 P.M., got it?
MARY	*(Types, using all her fingers without looking at the paper, but looking frequently at the First Interrogator who tries to avoid her, embarrassed.)*
2nd INTERROG.	Namely: *(Recites.)* I am informing you that according to paragraph 100, you can refuse to answer, should it incriminate you or any person close to you; should your statement not correspond with the truth, you may be prosecuted for perjury, do you understand, Mister Vaněk? First question— *(Phone rings; Mary reaches it first.)*
MARY	Yeah, Mary. Is it Sherry? Yeah— *(Looks at the First Interrogator.)* He is!
2nd INTERROG.	*(Desperately.)* We don't have time, let them phone—
MARY	Sure. Just put her through. *(Innocently.)* It's your wife—
1st INTERROG.	*(Goes to the phone as if to the guillotine.)* I can't now, Gerry, I'll buzz you—what? I'll probably be stuck here this evening—
2nd INTERROG.	*(Frightened.)* Of course not! You will be home by six—
1st INTERROG.	*(Deflated.)* Yeah, I know—Gerry, honey, I just want to—! *(He wanted to add something but she has hung up; he sits down, looks at Mary who ignores him and pays attention only to her typing.)*
2nd INTERROG.	So—question one. Disclose everything you know about the distribution of pornographic pictures showing you and Havel, Olga, birthdate, address, fill that in later.
VANĚK	Nothing.
2nd INTERROG.	I want to make it clear to you that making those pictures is strictly your and Mrs. Havel's private affair. We might not like it—and, I would guess, our citizens won't either—it's disgusting, but not punishable by law. It becomes a criminal act only when it is distributed to two or more parties—and that's really the question!
VANĚK	Gentlemen, I was of the opinion— *(Then he sees the Second Interrogator motioning to Mary to type.)* Don't type that! That at least you can afford the luxury—to consult a professional, for instance, a psychologist. What you are doing here with me is rank amateurism. Showing me a falsification!

1st INTERROG.	So, you are accusing us—Now, watch it! Mary—
VANĚK	I am not accusing you; I am saying that it's a fake. Photomontage! Any psychologist will tell you that a person confronted with such a bald lie will only harden, not collapse.
2nd INTERROG.	You are claiming, then, that it's a fake, and I am even willing to believe you. Those pals of yours are capable of much worse—
VANĚK	Would you be so kind as to leave my—
2nd INTERROG.	But, how are you going to prove it? Today, not even our people in the lab can recognize a photomontage.
VANĚK	Who needs any proof?
2nd INTERROG.	Ah! The comrades haven't told you? This pornographic picture was offered for sale to several citizens, even to Western diplomats. One of them recognized you and was so shaken, he offered it to our press.
VANĚK	How touching.
2nd INTERROG.	Perhaps. But not as amusing as you think. The satirical weekly *Scrimmage* plans to use it in their next issue with the caption the Charter's Naked Truth—as long as the censor doesn't interfere, yes, the same one you complain so much about. What do you say, Mister Vaněk, should he interfere?
VANĚK	*(Keeps silent.)*
1st INTERROG.	You are not going to talk to us this time, Mister Vaněk? You were so talkative before!
VANĚK	I—I was very angry, when you arrested me with such fanfare. One is not used to that—but the more I watched you playing these games with me, the more I had the feeling I was on stage. Even a bad actor believes in his character. You believe only in your anonymity, but that is full of holes, something always shows through. You *(To the Third Interrogator.)* are really Francis, who got married Dec. 12, 1950 and your number is 536666; you *(To the First Interrogator.)* have a wife by the name of Gerry, drive an old sportscar and are a member of the Legion, and you— *(To the Second Interrogator.)* Chief, Number 548366—I have an unhealthy memory for numbers—judging from your recitation, you, I would say, more likely you did bit parts in local theatre—
2nd INTERROG.	*(Nervously.)* Don't you worry about us, Mister Vaněk; you should be more concerned what Mister Havel and your wife will do.
1st INTERROG.	Or should we have a really serious discussion about our offer? *(This time, for a change, it's he who takes out of his wallet the paper with Vaněk's signature and pretends to destroy it.)*
3rd INTERROG.	Fortunately, a bad deed can be made good by good behaviour.

VANĚK	*(Achieving inner peace.)* Gentlemen, I am very concerned about my good reputation, but I would rather be—excuse me—rolling in the shit, than extending you a hand—that should be the greatest service I could offer Czech literature.
2nd INTERROG.	Have you finished?
VANĚK	And one more thing. This fake has one blemish on its beauty that will make a mockery of the whole thing in the eyes of our friends and families. That's enough for a start. As far as I am concerned, that's it, I'm finished with you three gentlemen, for good, you have forced me into saying this.
2nd INTERROG.	Look here, don't threaten us! Those golden days when you owned half of Pra—
1st INTERROG.	Just a moment! What kind of blemish?
VANĚK	*(Keeps silent.)*
1st INTERROG.	What blemish on its beauty?
VANĚK	*(Keeps silent.)*
1st INTERROG.	It's in your own interest! If you can prove it, we would, naturally—
VANĚK	*(Keeps silent.)*
1st INTERROG.	As you wish. Mary, read the question again.
MARY	*(Gets up, combs her hair in front of the mirror.)* Time is up.
1st INTERROG.	Now, wait a minute, we haven't finished—!
MARY	I have to pick up my little boy from kindergarten. *(She begins to pack her things, evading the eyes of the First Interrogator.)*
2nd INTERROG.	*(Looking at the First Interrogator.)* How about your husband taking a turn?
MARY	That's not possible. *(She dials a number.)* Comrade Kučera? Mary here. So could I get a ride with you then? And one more thing, I'd like to drop him at my aunt's in Davle— *(Joyfully.)* You would?
2nd INTERROG.	*(Suddenly.)* Mary, it can't be helped! You just have to stay!
MARY	*(Into the phone.)* Just a moment, they are here— *(To the First Interrogator.)* What?
1st INTERROG.	Your husband really couldn't? I too can drop you at Davle!
MARY	*(Looks innocently into his eyes.)* But your wife—
1st INTERROG.	*(Looks at the other two.)* We'll somehow—
BOTH	*(Nod.)*
MARY	*(Into the phone.)* Jeez, comrade, I am terribly sorry, it's such a madhouse here today, maybe next time, all right? Thanks. You're sweet. *(Hangs up triumphantly and reads.)* Tell us all you know about the distribution of pornographic pictures, showing you and Havel, Olga, birthdate, residing, I'll fill that in.
VANĚK	*(Keeps silent.)*
1st INTERROG.	Mister Vaněk, we have the full authority to keep you here!

VANĚK	*(Keeps silent.)*
2nd INTERROG.	Keep you here for a very long time!
VANĚK	*(Keeps silent.)*
2nd INTERROG.	Really a very long time!
VANĚK	*(Keeps silent.)*
2nd INTERROG.	As you wish. We are not going to fool around with you! Mary, write: witness keeps silent, does not answer questions. Concluded and signed at 4:00 P.M. Got it? Give it to me. *(Puts it in front of Vaněk and hands him a ballpoint pen.)* Sign here!
VANĚK	*(Doesn't react.)*
1st INTERROG.	Well, surely you can sign this!
VANĚK	*(Doesn't react.)*
2nd INTERROG.	You have to sign it!
VANĚK	*(Doesn't react.)*
3rd INTERROG.	Mister Vaněk, this could have terrible consequences for you!
VANĚK	*(Doesn't react.)*
1st INTERROG.	Well, then—let's go, comrades, this we have to take to the boss! *(All three leave. Their steps receding.)*
MARY	*(Gets up and helps herself from the official cigarettes.)* I'll just be a minute. *(Vaněk gives her a light.)* You really don't want one?
VANĚK	No, thanks.
MARY	*(Picks up the photograph lying on the table.)* My, that's hot stuff. That Mrs. Havel, what's her bust measurement?
VANĚK	I beg your pardon??
MARY	I mean, is she more or less— *(Expands her chest.)*
VANĚK	Less, definitely—
MARY	This one has at least two sizes on me. *(Smirks.)* That's where the blemish is, am I right? *(Leaving, but returns.)* Mister Daněk—
VANĚK	*(Tired, but patient.)* Vaněk.
MARY	Yeah. Really, aren't you scared?
VANĚK	*(Surprised, hesitates, then answers.)* Yes, I am.
MARY	You sure don't show it.
VANĚK	My bigger fear is—of fear.
MARY	*(Tries to understand, shrugs her shoulders, and leaves.)*
VANĚK	*(To George.)* Could we at least sit down?
GEORGE	*(Shrugs his shoulders.)*
VANĚK	*(Sits down, looks at his watch, takes it off, shakes it, and gives up.)*
GEORGE	Couldn't you sign it for me?
VANĚK	What?
GEORGE	*(Points to the table.)* This document—

VANĚK	Why?
GEORGE	That would be a shot in the arm—
VANĚK	Young man! I am not here to speed your climb up the corporate ladder!
GEORGE	Pardon me—
VANĚK	But I am going to give you good advice: look around and use your brain!

(As they wait, they again hear familiar sounds. In the yard, somebody is keeping time, One-two, three-four, scores of shoes make thumping sounds. Solitary steps are coming closer, whistling echoes in the hall. Enter a friendly looking man, around thirty, dressed in the uniform of an ensign of a transport corps; under his arm, he carries a rolled-up object; he is eating a pear.)

4th INTERROG.	*(To Vaněk.)* Have a seat! No stage fright, you can do it! Everything nice and easy. *(Unrolls the poster with a picture of a car engine and hangs it on the switch under the portrait of the President.)*
VANĚK	I have a driver's licence!
4th INTERROG.	You have—Can I see it?
VANĚK	*(Puts his bag on the table and with one hand, tries in vain to find it, then remembers.)* You took it from me!!
4th INTERROG.	You are here for the refresher exam, Mister driver. *(Takes a piece of paper out of his pocket.)* On June 20th of last year, at 7:28 P.M., you failed to give the right of way, in front of the National Theatre—and that's the reason you are here now. Let's get going: car engines are as a rule, well?
VANĚK	*(Doesn't know.)*
GEORGE	*(Sits down, looks around and, maybe, is even thinking.)*

THE END

Hamburg
Haus von Nikolai
Oct. 5, 1981

NOTES

1. See note 1 to Introduction.
2. Rudolf Slánský, top man in the Czechoslovak Communist Party, fell into disgrace during the Stalinist period and was executed in 1951 after a show trial. In 1962 he was declared innocent of all major crimes and officially "rehabilitated."
3. Gustav Husák, President of the Czechoslovak Socialist Republic since 1975.
4. Kohout is ironically playing with references to two of his early plays *The Good Song* (1952) and *Such a Love* (1957). The latter was an international theatrical success.
5. See also note 3 to *Permit*.
6. We recognize the successful, "normalized" writer from *Protest*. See also Note 2 to *Permit*.
7. Jan Patočka (1907-77), Czech philosopher and historian of culture and philosophy as well as translator of numerous philosophical works into Czech; in his seventieth year he assumed the arduous role of Spokesman for Charter 77. He died of a brain hemorrhage a few days after a lengthy police interrogation. Ludvík Vaculík (born 1926), Czech novelist and prose writer (prohibited from publication in Czechoslovakia); his novels *The Hatchet* and *The Guinea Pigs* have been translated into English; in 1976 he was awarded the George Orwell Prize. František Pavlíček (born 1923), Czech dramatist and author of television and radio plays (prohibited from publication in Czechoslovakia.)
8. Samuel Beckett's short play *Catastrophe* is dedicated to Václav Havel.
9. Tomáš Garrigue Masaryk (1850-1937), founder and first president of Czechoslovakia.
10. See note 4.
11. The Second Interrogator is trying to show off his culture by quoting Goethe's *Faust*.

PAVEL LANDOVSKÝ

Arrest

Translated by Peter Petro
in collaboration with Anna Mozga

CHARACTERS

Ferdinand Vaněk, 40 (?), writer
Rudolf Pejchl, 50, compositor
Harry Soumar, 66, former officer   PRISONERS
Laco Horňak, 22, Gypsy robber
Elemer Matte, 28, Gypsy robber, deaf and dumb

George Fragrance, dark-haired prison guard   PLAYED BY
Mike Blondie, fair-haired prison guard   THE SAME
                                                ACTOR

PLACE

A Cell in Pankrác Prison, Prague

(A regulation-size cell (12' x 7') in Prague's Pankrác Prison— remand section. Right, four bunks with mattresses of dark blue foam rubber, stacked on top of each other. Above the bunks, a window, barred and covered with perforated sheet-metal. Left, a beige metal door, a 1' x 1' section of which can be opened from the outside. Above this little window, a peephole. Beyond the door, part of the corridor with other cell doors. Against the back wall, a sink and, for personal belongings, two khaki-coloured army-lockers. Further, a cast-iron toilet, a table made of light metal tubing, four stools, and a heating-radiator. Various shades of green predominate. The prisoners wear brown training suits with patches of a faded reddish hue. Underneath the suits, grey shirts and white underpants; below, green socks and black slippers. In the evening the prisoners change into picturesque yellow pyjamas with brown collars. The light in the cell is always on. At night the more courageous prisoners cover their eyes with handkerchiefs.

When the lights come up, Fragrance is alone in the cell, searching through the prisoners' belongings, lifting up the mattresses, etc. After a while, the sound of feet pounding from the corridor. Fragrance bolts from the cell, assumes position beside the door, and closely watches the group of four prisoners entering from downstage and trotting into the cell. They have just returned from a forty-five minute walk in the courtyard.

When Soumar, Horňak, Matte and Pejchl have entered the cell, Fragrance bangs the door shut and locks it. Then he moves to the next cell to which, judging from the sound, another group of prisoners is returning. He locks up. The process is repeated at regular intervals. In all, the sounds of prisoners running along the corridor and of doors being slammed last several minutes.

HORŇAK *(Continues jogging on the spot for a while. He is young and full of Gypsy desire for movement and freedom. A walk is obviously not enough for him.)* I tell you, God, always when I see snout of asshole Fragrance I want to wipe it away. I whack him like this—wham! *(He demonstrates.)*

SOUMAR We've got five minutes for the hole.
(Soumar lifts up the sink and Horňak rips the pipe on which the basin sits out of the wall. The fact that the pipe is loose has been cleverly concealed by bread stuck around the opening.

With the agility and speed of a monkey Horňak climbs up onto the top bunk and with the aid of the pipe begins making a hole in the sheet-metal behind the bars.)

HORŇAK O my shit, I not know swines use tin so hard!

SOUMAR Shut up and work. If you can join two of the holes, it'll do. *(To Pejchl, ironically.)* Mr. Pejchl, would you be so kind as to take position at the spyhole?

PEJCHL *(An indecisive man with greedy eyes.)* I wouldn't bother with any holes in any windows. It could mean trouble.

SOUMAR But your big trap's always ready for a fag. Just remember, when we haul up tobacco from the guys below, you'll get bugger all.

PEJCHL *(Reluctantly puts his eye to the peephole, trying to look into the corridor.)* But it's covered from outside.

(Entering the corridor from downstage, Fragrance, pushing Vaněk ahead of him. Vaněk carries some blankets and his personal belongings, consisting of a carton of cigarettes, a box with mainly food in it, and writing materials. He walks slowly, dragging his feet.)

FRAGRANCE Move it, Vaněk, get your ass in gear. You're not on vacation — You're doing it on purpose, crawling along like — like in slow motion.

VANĚK Commandant, sir, I beg your pardon, I am not doing it on purpose — These slippers I was issued are at least four sizes too large.

FRAGRANCE No clowning around, Vaněk, you should've reported that. Just get the lead out, and no talking back! *(They disappear down the corridor.)*

PEJCHL I say — it's covered from outside.

HORŇAK *(Puffing with exertion.)* Take good look; is a crack on the right. When I take back bowls in the morning, I stick in piece of bread.

MATTE *(Deaf and dumb, he pushes Pejchl away from the door and watches the corridor with his sharp eyes, issuing some sounds to indicate that the air is clear.)*

PEJCHL *(Happy to be relieved from his task, sits down on a stool.)*

SOUMAR *(Still holding the sink, turns to Pejchl.)* Pejchl, move your butt and get me the supports from behind the radiator; my hands are getting numb. They're just stuck on with bread.

PEJCHL *(Reluctantly does as he is told.)*

HORŇAK Is the shits; I need hacker! *(He starts furiously hitting the metal.)*

PEJCHL *(Scared.)* Cut it out, you idiot, or we'll all end up in solitary!

SOUMAR *(Gleefully.)* Only solitary? We could get five more years!

	They'll throw the attempt-to-escape article at us, with the section on impermissible arming in the cell, and no judge'll give a damn that we were only fishing for smokes. A hole is a hole, and that pipe is actually a heavy weapon. *(He sets the sink on the two pieces of wood Pejchl has stuck into the wall in place of the pipe. At first glance nothing out of the ordinary is visible. To Pejchl.)* Don't lean on it, you jerk, it's just hanging there. *(To Horňak.)* How's it going?
HORŇAK	I bust it in one spot, but I have to bend tin so we can push through magazine. They want picture with chicken in bathing suit for tobacco. *(He continues working, huffing and puffing.)*
PEJCHL	May I roll a cigarette?
HORŇAK	No cigarette until hole is finish! Else I break you head with this pipe you fuck-your-mother! *(Continuing to work, he sings plaintively.)* Hey-hoo, my lords what you do, gypsies in prisons like tiger in zoo, lords what you do, tiger in zoo, hey-hoo—
SOUMAR	What they've done? Locked you up for two armed robberies plus aggravated violent assault causing grave bodily harm.
HORŇAK	*(While working.)* I tell you, shit, when I get out, I find slut that get me in, and I cut her up into little bits.
PEJCHL	*(Contemptuously.)* When you get out, maybe she'll be in. Ha ha.
HORŇAK	You playing with death, Pejchl!
MATTE	*(Suddenly turns from the door, signalling danger.)*
	(Horňak quickly slides down the bunks, hides the pipe under a mattress, sits on a stool, grabs a book and pretends to read. Soumar stands with his back to the sink and his hands behind him, so he could hold the basin, if necessary. Pejchl is shaking with fright and Matte stands at attention. The key is heard turning in the lock and the door opens. Fragrance looks into the cell without fully stepping in, since, like every guard, he is afraid to enter a cell in which there are Gypsies.)
SOUMAR	*(Regulation shouting.)* Commandant, sir, cell number two hundred and ninety-two reporting four persons!
FRAGRANCE	*(Through his teeth.)* Good. *(To Horňak.)* Horňak, pack your things, you're moving.
HORŇAK	Commandant, sir, but I —, is after my first trial, and Matte here, you know, he need me, he—
FRAGRANCE	No discussions, Horňak. You've got five minutes to stand by the door with your things ready.
	(Horňak hangs his head, saddened by the news. Fragrance bangs the door shut, secures it with the bolts and with quick

151

	strides disappears down the corridor.)
SOUMAR	*(Alert.)* He didn't turn the key, which means he'll be back in a moment.
PEJCHL	I'm curious to see who they'll dump in here.
SOUMAR	*(Maliciously.)* Well, it's not gonna be one of your buddies from the Party rag's editorial board, that's for sure. You were the only sucker there.
HORŇAK	Geez, was very lucky this.
	(Matte points his behind at the door, slapping it and smiling contemptuously. Horňak gathers up his blankets, puts them on the table, and starts carrying his modest belongings from the locker.)
HORŇAK	I leave you tobacco. Maybe I lucky and move to good cell.
SOUMAR	I thought I'd piss myself laughing when you grabbed that book like you were reading. Can you even read?
HORŇAK	You not believe this, but now I can. When they put me in jail I know nothing, but in interrogation time I meet dissident and he teach me. He even teach me count. I think Vaněk is name. God, I say, do he have cigarettes! Whole floor is smoking. Nice guy. Every night he give me lesson, even draw map of the world for me. So now I know everything, even French. Come on alley voodoo? You see?
SOUMAR	I know him. A month ago we waited together for an hour in the line-up for X-rays—yapping about everything under the sun.
HORŇAK	We put it together, quick. *(He points to the sink and takes the pipe from under the mattress.)*
SOUMAR	Yes, we better—in case they send us some ninny who's into good behaviour and squeals before we know what's happening.
HORŇAK	And this Vaněk, he tell me about crimination against Gypsies, he know all about it, what they do to us, how we always have to go where they want. I have brother-in-law in Budějovice and I cannot work there and have to work in Ustí nad Labem under name of my brother Geza. And he know it all, why they don't leave us alone, he explain it all so beautiful I forget, so complicated is.
	(During the following, Horňak and Soumar put the pipe back into place while Pejchl sticks the wooden supports back under the radiator. Matte watches at the peephole.)
PEJCHL	Nice swine, your Vaněk. Don't have to tell me about him. I know. We were setting articles about him in the printing shop. He had dough coming out of his ears from his plays, and his daddy was an exploiter. Don't have to tell me about him.
HORŇAK	*(Sentimentally.)* Nice guy. He teach me read, write and count.

	I want to teach him neck jab, but he don't want to.
PEJCHL	What's a neck jab?
HORŇAK	Is a punch in the neck, after which even two-hundred-pound guy will nicely make his bed on floor. But he say he never fight and that is against violence.
PEJCHL	Oh, I just love his kind—money coming out of his ears and all the while protesting to be a meek little lamb! *(Soumar and Horňak start kneading pieces of bread in their hands and Pejchl burns pieces of newspaper, adding the ashes to the bread to colour it black. The resulting paste is stuck on the wall around the pipe. These actions are carried out mechanically while the prisoners are talking.)*
HORŇAK	*(Climbs up to the window.)* I fix hole now, you can finish tomorrow. Just bend this pieces here. *(He disguises the opening. Then sadly.)* If I keep on this floor, I try to leave smokes for you under cap-box during exercises. *(Meanwhile Blondie is making his way through the auditorium. He wears jeans and carries a fashionable jacket. One can see that he is not too enthusiastic about going to work. He disappears down the corridor.)*
SOUMAR	*(To Pejchl.)* How can you envy Vaněk his dough, Pejchl—he earned it with his brains, but you had to steal, because you're stupid.
PEJCHL	*(Sits down heavily and motions Matte, who is rolling a cigarette from a box of communal tobacco, to roll him one as well. Matte gladly gives him his.)* Why stupid? Everybody's getting rich. Every Sunday the editor-in-chief takes his family in the government car all the way to a cottage in Moravia, and the chauffeur sleeps in the hotel and waits till Monday, how d'you like that? The things I know about him—they'll be happy if I keep my mouth shut during the proceedings.
SOUMAR	Better keep it shut, or they'll give you fifteen years instead of three.
PEJCHL	Bloody bastards, all of them—feeding us this line about how we as Party commissars have all these privileges, but the minute I got into trouble they made themselves scarce.
SOUMAR	Surprise, surprise! And such a wonderful idea it was—printing counterfeit bus passes on a government press!
PEJCHL	Everybody's getting rich.
SOUMAR	But why?
PEJCHL	Because there's not a damn thing to buy in the stores.
SOUMAR	*(Slyly.)* How come? I find that hard to believe.
PEJCHL	Because those son-of-a-bitch thieves who can bribe butchers and that buy it all up.
SOUMAR	*(Pretending not to understand.)* And what do they do with

	the grub?
PEJCHL	Well, what do you think they do? Stuff their faces!
SOUMAR	They eat it all?
PEJCHL	Yes of course, every bit of it.
SOUMAR	*(Obviously entertained.)* So there's not enough to go around?
PEJCHL	No!! *(He doesn't understand the line of questioning.)*
SOUMAR	That means, if there isn't enough for everybody, there couldn't have been too much of it to start with. *(He can't control himself any longer and bursts out laughing.)*
MATTE	*(Also laughs, because he can see that the nice Soumar is amused and the not-so-nice Pejchl is frowning. He starts jokingly hitting Pejchl's shoulders, motioning that he would like to shadow-box, and making the guttural sounds of a deaf-mute. Pointing at himself.)* Matte! *(Pointing at Pejchl.)* Policeman! Bang, bang, bang Matte! *(Pointing at himself again.)* Bang, bang!
PEJCHL	Fuck off, dirty Gypsy!
	(Entering the corridor from upstage, Fragrance and the shuffling Vanĕk, who is still carrying his bundle.)
FRAGRANCE	Stop, Vanĕk! *(He carefully studies a piece of paper. To himself.)* I must be crazy! Where am I going to put you?
VANĔK	Beg your pardon?
FRAGRANCE	*(Looking up.)* What—? *(Realizing he had been thinking aloud.)* Look, Vanĕk, it's none of your business. Turn to the wall and wait for my orders. *(He opens a little box in the wall, containing a telephone, and pushes a button. Shouting into the receiver.)* Mike?—George here— Have you changed?—I can't put him there—We have to leave three cells empty on the second floor—But then there'll be five of them!—Look, my bus is leaving in ten minutes, you finish it off; you were late anyhow. *(He angrily bangs down the receiver, locks the box, opens the cell and enters. Horňak is standing by the door, his things ready.)*
FRAGRANCE	*(To Horňak.)* What's this? Where do you think you're going?
HORŇAK	You say I have to move.
FRAGRANCE	You say, you say—! Well, do you hear me saying it now? *(To Pejchl.)* Where's the dice? Before exercise you were playing dice, so better hand them over, or else!
PEJCHL	There are no dice here.
FRAGRANCE	Then I'll make a thorough search, and if I find them I'll put you in the cooler for talking back to me.
SOUMAR	*(Standing in front of the sink.)* Pejchl, immediately hand over the dice to the commandant!
PEJCHL	*(Finally understands, reaches into one of his socks and gives Fragrance five playing dice made, of course, of bread.)*

FRAGRANCE	*(Chuckling victoriously.)* Next time it'll be worse! And if you complain about insufficient bread rations, I'll remind you of these, Pejchl. *(He steps out of the cell and shuts the door.)* *(In the cell, a general sigh of relief. In the corridor, Vaněk still stands facing the wall.)*
FRAGRANCE	*(While locking the door.)* Vaněk—attention and wait!—I have my eyes everywhere! *(He quickly disappears down the corridor.)*
VANĚK	*(To himself.)* Idiot! *(He puts down his blankets and sits on them.)*
MATTE	*(Pointing to himself.)* Hungarian. Matte Hungarian—Box, box, box—bang, bang, bang. *(He is making side steps and miming a boxing-match. One can see his boundless pleasure in and need for movement.)*
PEJCHL	*(Sits down.)* I'm not going to listen to that. This one's a deaf and dumb retardo and the other one's going to incite rebellion by spreading false rumours about the economic situation.
SOUMAR	Better cut out the incitement, Pejchl, or you might just accidently fall down the stairs during the morning walk. And—judging by the looks of you—it wouldn't exactly improve your health. Not to mention the fact that I've no idea what's happening on the outside, since I haven't been on the outside for fourteen years. *(He laughs, but it is a dangerous sort of laugh that sends shivers down Pejchl's spine.)**
MATTE	*(Has finished boxing and, laughing, motions Soumar and Pejchl to move to the window, because he has to use the toilet.)***
PEJCHL	Ah, shit! *(He turns on his chair so as to face away from the toilet. Soumar sits down next to him with a discreet matter-of-factness.)*
HORŇAK	*(Almost sadly.)* Fucking son of a Fragrance bitch, I meet you outside and you come home like steak tartare, asshole.
MATTE	*(Sits on the toilet, picking his nose.)*
	(Pause.)
SOUMAR	They won't move anyone in before lunch.
PEJCHL	What day is it today, Thursday? Could be spinach.
HORŇAK	Or beans.
PEJCHL	I don't give a shit for their beans. They're undercooked.
MATTE	*(Pulls up his pants and flushes the toilet. Then he touches*

* *Only a person who has been in prison will know the fear of someone sharing the cell with a man who has spent fourteen years behind bars.*
** *In jail, the customary thing to do in such a situation is not to take any notice.*

155

*Horňak on the shoulder and by tapping his wrist and pretend-
ing to eat asks whether it's lunchtime yet.)*

*(Sound of footsteps in the corridor. Vaněk quickly stands up.
In the cell, Horňak touches his nose twice, signals "meal,"
and points to the bottom of the door. Matte understands,
blows his nose, and kneels by the door, sniffing the air,
apparently without success. In the corridor, Blondie and
Vaněk approaching. Vaněk is again carrying his bundle. He
stops in a disciplined fashion, and Blondie quickly opens the
cell door without first checking the peephole as regulation
demands. Matte is completely surprised and terrified.)*

BLONDIE   What's this horsing around, man? You want to get whacked
          with the stick? *(Realizing what's going on and that Matte
          can't understand him, he good-naturedly adds.)* It's the beans.

SOUMAR   *(Clowning.)* Thanks, commandant, sir.

HORŇAK   *(Aping him.)* Thanks so much, commandant, sir.

BLONDIE   *(To Vaněk.)* Well, Vaněk, do you want to keep standing in
          the door forever? Or maybe you don't fancy your new residence?

VANĚK   Pardon me. *(He enters.)*

BLONDIE   Man, this looks like a Gypsy camp. And smells like a monkey-
          cage. Get some air in here, will you.

SOUMAR   *(Clowning.)* Is it allowed?

BLONDIE   Well, if I say so, it is.

VANĚK   Excuse me, commandant, sir, but I didn't get the paper today.

BLONDIE   Not my fault, I just started my shift. It's all a mess, maybe we
          didn't get any.
          *(Meanwhile Horňak, acting on a signal from Soumar, has
          climbed onto the bunks and opens the vent. Blondie exits,
          slides in the bolts, then opens them again, and re-enters the
          cell. He takes something out of his pocket.)*

BLONDIE   *(Putting the dice on the table.)* Next time, play on a towel, so
          no one can hear it. *(To Vaněk.)* I can lend you the paper from
          the office, if you remind me at lunchtime. But you'll be
          disappointed, not a tiny little thing about you today. *(He
          winks at Vaněk, exits, secures the door, and vanishes down
          the corridor.)*

SOUMAR   At least we've got that bimbo on today. Ought to be a quiet
          afternoon. *(To Vaněk.)* My name's Soumar.

VANĚK   Vaněk, Ferdinand. We met at X-ray, didn't we?

SOUMAR   I thought you'd have forgotten.

HORŇAK   *(From the window.)* Make ready, Vaněk, we have chess-
          tourney in afternoon.

PEJCHL   *(Stands alone, staring at Vaněk. Some cumbersome thought
          process is going on in his head.)* This means, if Horňak

156

washed the floor this morning, then tomorrow we'll have to start again in the order of beds, don't we, so that it'll come out right.

SOUMAR   Right. And for a change we'll start from the door. That means, it's your turn tomorrow.

PEJCHL   No way! I did it this week when Matte went to court. And anyway, I should get Hornak's bed. Let the new guy sleep by the crapper.

HORŇAK   You want to eat fist? What is bed you mean? Is still my bed!

VANĚK   I'm not particular about where I sleep. *(To Soumar.)* If you want a cigarette, just help yourself. I've got enough; and I asked for more to be picked up next shopping.

HORŇAK   *(Breathing in deeply.)* Such good air, you guys, like in mountains. *(He sings.)* Three days they run after me, three days no catching me; let them run another three, still there be no catching me—

PEJCHL   *(Reaches for the carton of cigarettes.)*

SOUMAR   *(Slapping Pejchl's wrist.)* Only if you sleep by the can.

PEJCHL   *(Afraid of authority, hesitates.)*

VANĚK   Let him take one if he doesn't have any.

SOUMAR   Stay cool, Vaněk, and screw him. Let his Party buddies send him some, if he's doing time for them.

MATTE   *(Approaches the carton, smiling, indicating that he would like a cigarette.)*

VANĚK   Go ahead, take some.

SOUMAR   He doesn't understand a word you're saying.

PEJCHL   Two sticks—I do your cleaning and sleep by the crapper.

VANĚK   I don't understand.

PEJCHL   For two cigarettes I'll do your cleaning and sleep by the crapper.

VANĚK   Look, I wouldn't want you to get into any trouble on my account. Just take some; they're to be shared.

SOUMAR   *(Chuckling.)* I like it! Jail is a bridge that spans all the contradictions in the world. Ha ha! May I have the pleasure of introducing you, gentlemen—*(To Vaněk.)* This is Comrade Thief. *(To Pejchl.)* And this here is Mr. Author.

PEJCHL   *(Unsure of himself.)* Thanks for the smokes.

VANĚK   Don't mention it. What sort of book do you have here? May I have a look?

PEJCHL   Some Russian bullshit. I don't read that.

HORŇAK   *(Bragging.)* Is quite good. I read one.

SOUMAR   *(Hands Vaněk four books.)* In case you've read them, we can exchange them with the other cells at dinner time, if Blondie's on duty and we do it on the quiet.

VANĚK   *(Obviously delighted with the reading material but trying to*

	adjust his language to that of his cell-mates.) Piss on it! Dostoyevsky's *From the House of the Dead.* Read it when I was fifteen—couldn't understand much then.
SOUMAR	And now you don't need to understand.
VANĚK	Your knowledge of—I mean, you've read them?
SOUMAR	During my term I've read everything any prison library has to offer.
VANĚK	*(Looking at the other titles.) Proud Destiny.*[1] *The Leopard.*[2] Gee, you're lucky to get books like these. I don't know why I always ended up with such rubbish. I'd get anthologies of military songs from the '50's and the collected works of Lenin and Stalin.
SOUMAR	Looks like something Fragrance would do to bug you and make you blow your lid.
HORŇAK	*(Closes the vent and jumps down from the bunks. Spreading his arms theatrically.)* Vaněk! Long time no see! Right now, tell me what you do last three months we not see each other. You know, I still have map, only no Australia; Dr. Benda[3] tear it off when he need paper to write something. *(Meanwhile Fragrance is making his way through the auditorium on his way to work. He disappears down the corridor. A while later, Blondie, in civilian clothes, whistling contentedly and playing with his car keys, takes the same route, but in the opposite direction.)*
VANĚK	I'll draw another one for you, if we stay together. What was your sentence?
HORŇAK	Just four year. I think it be more. Other robbery they cannot prove, because Pole I hit won't come to interrogation. The money he say I take from him, you see, he don't want to say where he get it from. He probably steal it.
SOUMAR	I'd love to find out who finally gets to spend all that money you guys keep pinching from each other. *(He finds a pair of glasses, puts them on, and carefully reads the book titles.)*
PEJCHL	*(His ear to the door, listening attentively.)* Lunchtime, gentlemen! *(Indeed, the noise of lunch bowls rattling is heard from the corridor.)*
PEJCHL	We mainly have to get some fresh bread, so we can plug those holes under the sink.
VANĚK	What holes?
SOUMAR	Never mind, I'll explain later. *(Sounds of a key turning in the lock and of both bolts being opened. Matte and Pejchl quickly place the table near the door. From an invisible trolley in the corridor five portions of soup, beans with salami, and five thick slices of bread are handed in. Food being a serious thing in prison, the proce-*

dure is quite a ceremony. A special atmosphere begins to reign. The behaviour of prisoners at mealtime is not unlike that of animals in captivity. Matte is nervous, Pejchl fidgets—he is sizing up the portions, trying to get the biggest ones. All eat in silence, concentrating.)

SOUMAR   *(To Horňak.)* When they come back for the dishes, we'll have a good fifteen minutes to fix that hole.

HORŇAK   *(With his mouth full.)* After such beans I punch hole with my ass.

PEJCHL   Why tempt fate, when we've got plenty of smokes anyway?

SOUMAR   *We*, Pejchl??

PEJCHL   But he said we could take some.

SOUMAR   *(In a fit of rage hits Pejchl quite hard on the forehead with his spoon.)* And suddenly you don't mind that they're his!

VANĚK   Why should he mind?

SOUMAR   *(Burps and significantly closes the topic.)* He knows why.

VANĚK   Do you have anything against my cigarettes, Mr. Pejchl?

PEJCHL   *(Giggling.)* —Mr. Pejchl! It sounds so silly, doesn't it?—Mr. Pejchl—Last time someone addressed me like that was at City Hall when I got married.

SOUMAR   *(Laughs maliciously.)* —Well, and for thirty years after that they called you Comrade Pejchl or Rudi. But now it's coming, now you'll never be without titles again. At court it'll be: Defendant Pejchl, get up, and before that, they'll lead you in in chains, like a bear. *(He laughs maliciously.)* And your old lady'll be sitting in the front row. And then it'll be: Pejchl-sentenced-to-five-years, be quiet, you didn't fulfil the norm, package and visit refused.

(Matte stacks the dishes at the door and tries to engage Vaněk in a little boxing. Vaněk wants to be accommodating, but, being an intellectual, he is clumsy. He stumbles over a stool and falls on the floor. To Matte this is very funny. Only the fact that the bolts are now sliding back and the dishes are being collected saves Vaněk from receiving a good thrashing at the hands of the exuberant Matte.)

SOUMAR   *(As soon as the door is bolted.)* Vaněk, glue your eye to the peeper!

VANĚK   Pardon?

SOUMAR   Well, watch if somebody's coming.

VANĚK   *(Repeats to himself, amused.)* Glue your eye to the peeper. *(He does so.)*

(The procedure with the sink is repeated.)

SOUMAR   See anything?

VANĚK   Not a thing. It's covered up on the other side.

PEJCHL   *(Taking the supports from under the radiator.)* Ah, shit,

159

	there's a thin crack on the right. Horňak covered it up with bread.
VANĚK	*(With disarming politeness.)* Pardon me, dear colleague, but I didn't notice right away — *(Happily.)* I see it now — a sort of thin crack!
PEJCHL	*(Mutters.)* I'm no colleague of yours —
SOUMAR	You can say that again, brown-noser.
HORŇAK	*(From up on the bunks.)* Not argue, fuck on it, and Matte give me stool.

(Soumar conveys the message to Matte by pointing first to a stool and then to Horňak. Matte grabs a stool and climbs onto the bunks with it. He then holds the pipe while Horňak uses the stool as a hammer.)

PEJCHL	Who's arguing? I only want to note that I'm in for something different than *Mister* Vaněk here, to make that perfectly clear. I'm no anti-state element —
SOUMAR	*(Maliciously.)* But a pro-state thief. *(He laughs.)* History is repeating itself, only in light blue. In 1931 I was in jail with a manager who'd swindled away a trainload of wheat. He wasn't talking to me either, because I was a Communist then.
VANĚK	*(Still at the peephole.)* Are you a thief?
PEJCHL	He's just shooting his mouth off. They did me in.
VANĚK	Who, they?
PEJCHL	Who, they?! The others, of course. Everybody's getting rich, and I'm up shit creek.
VANĚK	I think it is only the poor who are enriching themselves — but I should add that poverty is not a simple thing. It can be either a state or a feeling; and that's quite a difference. As a state, it's the best thing that can happen to anyone, but as a feeling it's an evil which will destroy all of us.
PEJCHL	State! Feeling! What bullshit!

(Suddenly the metal between the two perforations Horňak and Matte have been trying to connect breaks, and Matte falls off the bunks. Though hurt, he happily dances around in the cell, issuing sounds of joy.)

SOUMAR	So that one could say, my distinguished philosophers, that the poorest of the poor, one who has lost everything, even his voice, has enriched himself with a hole. This is —
VANĚK	Pardon me — Mr. Soumar — or —
SOUMAR	Just call me Harry.
VANĚK	Yes — Pardon me, Harry, but why did they lock you up?
SOUMAR	Why? — As a matter of fact — well, I never thought about it, why — I'm in jail — I guess it's not important. To be more precise, as an amateur lawyer, I should be — it's probably not relevant.

VANĚK	It might be indiscreet of me to ask you like that.
PEJCHL	Shit, speak Czech, will you?! All this "irrelevant," "indiscreet"—one feels like an asshole here.
SOUMAR	Shut up, you—you—mental basement!
PEJCHL	Let's put the sink back, at least, or there'll be trouble.
SOUMAR	Suit yourself, comrade, you have an opportunity for independent action, if you know what that is.
PEJCHL	*(Waves his hand and begins exchanging the two pieces of wood for the original pipe Horňak hands down from the bunks.)*
SOUMAR	What I'm in for? Maybe I called a policeman a schmuck. And then one thing followed another, just like that.
VANĚK	Mr. Soumar—I mean, Harry—I know it's not important, we're simply in jail, we chat, time flies—but, I mean, don't you care about anything in life?
SOUMAR	Me?
VANĚK	You!
SOUMAR	*(Laughs like an idiot and playfully gives Pejchl a boot in the pants, eliciting great mirth from Matte.)* All I cared for in my life was life— *(Starting to clown.)* True, sometimes it was somebody else's, but always life.
PEJCHL	Are you stupid or something? You kicked me in the ass!
SOUMAR	Really?
VANĚK	Did you kill anyone?
HORŇAK	*(Sings.)* They kill, o kill two babes in the wood, Ursiny they hang, Kapusta they shoot.
SOUMAR	What?—What, what? Kill? Mmn. Perhaps— *(Silence.)*
PEJCHL	Con tales.
VANĚK	And how come you're in the remand section when you're meant to be serving time?
SOUMAR	*(Chuckles.)* Because it's nice here. Quite a turnover, always something new, one finds out what sort of tricks people are up to, gets to know dissidents and even *(He slaps Pejchl on the back.)* the working class. It's much like a first-class hotel, you know.
VANĚK	How old are you, Mr.—I mean, Harry?
SOUMAR	Oh, you wouldn't believe me anyway, so why ask? How about you?
VANĚK	Look, I'm on the other side of forty as well.
SOUMAR	*(Chuckling.)* Forty! When I was forty, I was standing on Place Pigalle in Paris, barracks bag in hand, pockets bursting with cash, and my life in front of me—and look how awful I ended up. That stint in the foreign legion did me in. Yes, my boy, I've still got two years to do from my last sentence, and if

	they add on another two I'll be seventy on the dot when I get out of prison.
PEJCHL	*(Swerves around, his mouth hanging open. Holding that posture.)* What?
VANĚK	That's impossible!
SOUMAR	O yes, it's possible. I was born in 1914.
VANĚK	But that's absolutely fabulous!
SOUMAR	*(Pleased, executes a hand-stand and a few perfect push-ups. Though a little out of breath, he is undeniably in good physical shape.)* Jail's the healthiest place on earth!
MATTE	*(Taking Soumar's performance as a signal for general merriment, also tries doing a handstand.)*
VANĚK	If so, Harry, then you could say, turning the entire country into a prison would be the healthiest thing for everybody.
SOUMAR	Exactly. After all, they've done just about that. The only problem's the supplies.
PEJCHL	People stuff their faces too much.
VANĚK	And think too little.
SOUMAR	*(Starting to laugh.)* Vaněk, tell me the truth, did you ever write anything on a full stomach?
VANĚK	*(After a while.)* I always fell asleep.
SOUMAR	You see.
PEJCHL	*(Has finished camouflaging the loose pipe.)* What does he see?
MATTE	*(Playfully hitting Pejchl.)* Pejchl — box, box, box — bang, bang, bang — Matte —
PEJCHL	*(Punches Matte, shouting.)* Stupid Gypsy, get back to your hole!
MATTE	*(Far from taking offence, continues with his antics.)*
PEJCHL	*(While Soumar and Vaněk continue in their conversation.)* Guess I'll ask to be moved from this cell.
SOUMAR	After fourteen years in jail, my brain has decided that this is the very kernel of the whole Communist system.
VANĚK	What do you mean — Harry?
SOUMAR	Like I said, Ferdie — When the Party and the government cram people's throats, the people burp with contentment, sit on their asses, do a little screwing, but you won't get them to work — not even with a whip.
VANĚK	That's true. I read somewhere that certain African tribes used to kill hippopotami and eat the whole thing up in one go — And half the people died from it. But then, we can't look at the world in such simplistic terms.
SOUMAR	And why not? Isn't that the way it is?
VANĚK	But the efforts humanity has made over millenia, you can't just take that and throw it —

SOUMAR	Wait a minute, I'm not through yet! Well, and when people get hungry, they start thinking and very quickly find out what sort of dirty business this whole socialism really is.
PEJCHL	People are a bunch of swine.
SOUMAR	Yes, my dear author, and the Communists don't have it easy. *(Chuckling.)* Just take a look at this specimen. *(He points at Pejchl.)* His brain's as smooth as the kidneys of a little bunny rabbit—not a dimple.
PEJCHL	Why a—a rabbit?
SOUMAR	Because it guzzles nothing but water, you oaf, so its kidneys stay real smooth.
VANĚK	But in '68 I had the time of my life, and that was also socialism.
SOUMAR	I wouldn't know about that, I was shut up—I only read the papers—and the law code.
VANĚK	Sorry, Harry, I'm really at a loss arguing with you. I've taken a lot of seminars, but this, talking to ordinary people—that's different.
SOUMAR	Ordinary people, eh? All my life I've been in uniform, either outside or in the clink! What's ordinary about that?
PEJCHL	*(Crosses to his locker and takes out writing utensils. He sits down at the table and writes, shielding the letter with his free hand to prevent the others from seeing what he is writing.)*
MATTE	*(Stares for a while, then begins walking for exercise.)**
VANĚK	Good point. *(Lowering his voice.)* And what did they lock you up for? You can tell me the truth.
HORŇAK	*(Is quietly listening to the conversation.)*
SOUMAR	*(Growing serious.)* One could say, for being a trifle oversensitive.
VANĚK	What do you mean?
SOUMAR	Well—crossing of state borders with a weapon. And they threw in espionage for good measure, as usual. I had it planned really well, only I slipped on account of my conscience—for the first time in my life, Vaněk—But I'm not sorry I did.
VANĚK	What do you mean, on account of your conscience?
SOUMAR	You see—I was co-driver on a lumber truck transporting wood from the border area, and I found out that the cook in the military outpost had keys to a gate through the barbwire fence, because he kept a vegetable garden on the other side. So I got myself this cook's uniform, and the next guard tower was about two hundred yards away—all they'd be able to see

---

* Unlikely as it may sound to an outsider, a prisoner under stress can walk up to twenty miles a day in his twelve foot cell.

was the white outfit. Behind the vegetable patch was a trench and the forest. A real Mickey Mouse job. In the morning, I figured, the cook was alone, so I crawled into the kitchen after him and hit him over the head with a stick—not too hard. But he's like a bull, just shakes it off and throws a meat cleaver at me—split my left shoulder wide open. So I pull out my gun and he gets scared—Still could've brought it off nicely, though, if I'd only let him have it. I could've walked all the way to Germany like on a promenade, but man, all of a sudden—he kinda looked at me like an animal—wasn't none of his fault—besides, I'd known him for six months. And there he was, holding a butcher knife in his hand, sort of whining quietly and I—I just couldn't—for the first time in my life—*(Abruptly shouting.)* Shit, Matte, quit that running back and forth!

MATTE   *(Does not hear and, smiling happily, continues his pacing.)*

VANĚK   *(Quietly.)* And why couldn't you, do you think?

SOUMAR   Don't know—I guess because it's home.

VANĚK   See, and that's exactly where other people do the most swinish things.

SOUMAR   That's just it.

VANĚK   Just what?

SOUMAR   Like I said, right—even a bad egg like myself can suddenly go soft when it comes to snuffing somebody out in your own country—That's it, pal, that's why they can control it so easily.

VANĚK   But they're still afraid, tremendously afraid—of everything, including themselves.

SOUMAR   And does that surprise you?

VANĚK   Yes, a little.

SOUMAR   All right, let's take it theoretically, from a purely legal point of view. I know the criminal code by heart—all these years, you see, and what else is there to read?

VANĚK   Completely by heart?

SOUMAR   Want to test me?

VANĚK   Well, no, but I'm surprised.

SOUMAR   Look, for me 1968 and the whole fucking mess since then is absolutely clear and simple, even though it didn't really touch me in any way. I was cooped up then and I'm cooped up now. Listen carefully. *(He recites, as if he were reading.)* Part two, special section, chapter one. Criminal acts against the Republic. Sub-chapter one, criminal acts undermining the foundations of the Republic. Section ninety-one, treason. A Czechoslovak citizen who in contact with a foreign power or agent commits the criminal act of sedition of the Republic, terrorism, or sabotage, will be punished by loss of liberty for twelve to fifteen years or by death. Section ninety-two, disruption and sedition of the Republic. Paragraph one. An individual who intends to disrupt the socialist sytem and the administration of government, territorial integrity or defence capability of the Republic or to destroy its *independence*, a) takes part in acts of violence, etc., and now! b) is engaged in other dangerous activities undermining the foundations of the Republic or its important international interests, will be punished by loss of liberty for eight to twelve years. And now, watch it! Sub-chapter two. Punished by loss of liberty for twelve to fifteen years or by death, anyone who a) as a member of an organized group commits the offence outlined in paragraph one, b) by so doing causes grave bodily harm to others or death, c) in the execution of such an act causes damage of considerable magnitude or effects other serious consequences, or d) commits such an act during military mobilization. *(He straightens up. Victoriously.)* Now, what do you say?

HORŇAK   *(Sadly.)* This no fun. I don't understand. I better catch shut-eye under bunks. If trouble, kick me. *(He indicates to Matte what he wants him to do and dives under the bunks, where he falls asleep.)*

VANĚK   *(Puzzled.)* What do you expect me to say, Harry?

SOUMAR   Hell, Vaněk, it's plain as day! Don't you see? After all, *(Quoting.)* anyone who as a member of an organized group and in alliance with a foreign power conducts activities undermining the foundations of the Republic and causes damage of considerable magnitude or effects other serious consequences—will be what? Sentenced to death, you dumbo!! And what else was that bunch of nuts that are running things today doing a week before the invasion, if not that?

VANĚK   *(Startled.)* Well, yes, if you look at it that way.

SOUMAR   Well, how do you want me to look at it, when I'm locked up for fourteen years on the basis of that same criminal code?

VANĚK   But politics is something entirely different; there are all kinds of special angles, all sorts of dispensations and diplomatic concessions.

SOUMAR   There's only one law and it's for everybody. So don't be surprised there's state terror; the lawmakers have to protect themselves against their own laws somehow.

VANĚK   It sounds nice, but—

PEJCHL   *(Has been listening for a while.)* Nothing but prison gab, but a little risky perhaps.

SOUMAR   For who?

PEJCHL   Well, I wouldn't want to point a finger.

SOUMAR	No, my boy, you'd have to point it at yourself. *(He laughs.)* Cause if you stool, you won't live till tomorrow. Besides, I'm finished. *(He signals Matte to roll him a cigarette.)*
MATTE	*(Does so, because in his eternal silence anything is better than inactivity.)*
VANĚK	Finished. Yes, that's true, isn't it, when a person is finished he can do just about anything.
SOUMAR	Except what he can't do on his own.
VANĚK	The stiff attack!
PEJCHL	That some kind of thriller?
VANĚK	No. But once, when I was doing my military service, during anti-nuclear training, I was stuck in a warehouse, writing poems or whatever, and there was this instructional poster for units subjected to nuclear radiation, something I won't forget to the day I die.
SOUMAR	Tell us about it. *(To Pejchl.)* What's that you're scribbling, mushhead?
PEJCHL	That's my business!
SOUMAR	Just don't let me check it out, or I'll rearrange your face a bit. *(To Vaněk.)* How was that with the attack?
VANĚK	It was instructions for the commanding officers and it said, literally, that should a unit be hit by about eighty degrees of Geiger, it's already dead. That is, it's not dead yet, but it will be, six hours later. In such a case, according to the instructions, the commanding officer and his unit are to launch what's called "the stiff attack."
SOUMAR	So what?
VANĚK	Nothing. Only, while you were quoting those laws, it reminded me of something.
SOUMAR	Well, I guess that's it—but no solving it here. Fucking mess, in little things and in big ones, too. Look at Matte. *(Matte notices that they are talking about him.)* Last week he went to court, three years they slapped on him. Only that that guy, the court expert who interprets for all the deaf-mutes, knows only Czech. Matte was constantly trying to let him know that he doesn't understand Czech, but that ass interpreted it as a confession, the judge sentenced him, and that was the end of that.
VANĚK	But they can't do that! If it were a political case, I wouldn't say anything, it's all rigged, but with criminal acts there has to be justice.
SOUMAR	Not really.
PEJCHL	*(While writing.)* You hear that stomping?
VANĚK	No.
PEJCHL	Then I must be hearing things.

VANĚK	And what did it say in the judgment?
SOUMAR	Not a single mistake in it, and none in the deposition by the court interpreter either. O yes, one tiny giveaway slipped through—that Matte is Hungarian. Ha ha ha!
VANĚK	Could I have a look at that judgment?
SOUMAR	No, you can't.
VANĚK	Then I'm sorry, Harry.
SOUMAR	The reason you can't is because it's all gone up in smoke. It was typed on such fantastically thin copy paper.
PEJCHL	*(While writing.)* Damn, there is something going on in the hallway! You hear it?
	(Everyone listens. Sound of something being dragged along the corridor.)
SOUMAR	Sounds like they're moving something. What are you writing? A letter to the comrades? Just watch you don't get too chatty and accidently let something slip about that hole.
PEJCHL	That hole doesn't bother me.
SOUMAR	Just reminding you. You know, with people who fake bus passes on the Party rag press one can't be too sure.
PEJCHL	Stuff it, grampa.
VANĚK	*(Has been thinking.)* How come you burned the judgment, Harry?
SOUMAR	Well, we used it for rolling cigarettes.
VANĚK	But how could you do that?! The poor guy has to appeal! If there's no politics involved he has a chance.
SOUMAR	Matte! *(Accompanying his words with sign language.)* Here—Vaněk—you Matte—wants to help—in front of court— against the police—*
MATTE	*(Laughs and waves his hand. Pointing at himself.)* Matte—bang, bang, bang—box, box, box—police—Matte—nothing do—
SOUMAR	See, Vaněk, he doesn't want to.*(He giggles.)*
MATTE	*(Pulls Vaněk along and takes a set of chessmen made, of course, of bread from under the radiator. He puts them on a stool that has a chess board painted on it.)* Matte—chess, chess—
VANĚK	*(Unable to refuse, sits down by the chess board.)*
SOUMAR	Those three years won't do him any harm, you know, 'cause if you listen to Horňak, he's pulled off so many heists in his life he'd be good for a hundred and fifty.
VANĚK	But in this case he's innocent, after all, and one can't simply—*(He decides against continuing the argument, waves his hand, and moves with a pawn.)*

* *In sign-language, court is "big head," police "hand in hand-cuffs."*

MATTE	*(Makes a Bobby Fischer-face, deliberates for a long time, and also makes a move.)*
SOUMAR	*(Behind Pejchl.)* And what are we concocting here, my dear representative of the ruling class?
PEJCHL	That's my private business.
SOUMAR	Listen, Mr. Comrade Pejchl, here only your shit is your private business, if you'd like to know.
PEJCHL	*(Is startled by the sharp tone.)*
VANĚK	Leave him alone, Harry. We've got to respect each other, we're all in the same boat.
SOUMAR	Leave that up to me, all right, respecting others has got me into trouble more than once — In 1940, when I was in a Soviet camp in Siberia, I also — *(Vaněk and Pejchl look up.)*
VANĚK	You were locked up in Russia too?
SOUMAR	Yeah — twice. Once as a member of the Comintern, that was before Spain, and the second time before they formed us into the first Czechoslovak army unit — And, for good measure, in between I did almost a year's stint as a member of the International Brigade in a French camp, with a shot wound in my leg. For a change. So don't bug me about why I want to know what's going on around me. *(To Pejchl.)* Now, what's this all about? But lickety-split!
PEJCHL	*(Fearfully.)* It's a letter to my wife.
SOUMAR	Let's see it.
PEJCHL	*(Jumps up and with three leaps tries to reach the emergency bell.)*
SOUMAR	*(Gets there before him, covers the button with his hand, and giggles. Then calmly.)* I can be that smart too. *(He kicks Pejchl aside.)*
PEJCHL	*(Groans with pain.)*
SOUMAR	A letter to your wife, you say? And that's why you wanted to ring the guard. Come on! What's in it?
PEJCHL	*(Quietly.)* I want to be transferred to another cell instead of Horňak.
SOUMAR	*Why?*
PEJCHL	*(Reluctantly.)* Because of Vaněk, for political reasons.
SOUMAR	*(Stares at Pejchl for a moment.)* Well, fuck my grandmother. For crying out loud!
VANĚK	*(Gets up.)* And why shouldn't he? It's his affair.
SOUMAR	*(Steps away from the bell.)* Be my guest. There's the bell.
PEJCHL	*(Hesitates.)*
	(Silence. Matte lifts his head and pulls Vaněk by the sleeve to make him move. Vaněk does, and Matte again ponders his response at great length. Soumar watches, chuckling.)

PEJCHL	I've been a Party man since 1945, I believe in it, and if I did anything wrong, the comrades'll understand. But undermining the foundations of socialism, that I won't stand for—I just won't stand for it.
SOUMAR	*(Realizing the futility of arguing.)* Oh, and I suppose by counterfeiting bus passes you were supporting that socialism. Idiot!
VANĚK	*(Calmly.)* You have anything against me, Mr. Pejchl?
PEJCHL	Yes! *(Startled by his own fierce tone.)* Not against you personally, but I've read reports about how you were preparing the restoration of capitalism, and that I won't stand for. Unlike you, I know the meaning of Party discipline.
SOUMAR	*(Amused.)* O yes, but here you're not in the Party but in jail, you jerk—Haven't you got that yet? *(To Vaněk.)* Vaněk, take me away from this guy, or I'll knock his head against the wall until he wakes up.
VANĚK	Mr. Pejchl, I interceded only for those people who were unjustly prosecuted.
PEJCHL	Nobody can be unjustly prosecuted in this country. All that's just copying the Western propaganda.
SOUMAR	Amen. Believe, and your faith shall heal you—Only thing is, I don't know if it applies to mental disorders as well. *(As before, Matte pulls Vaněk by the sleeve, Vaněk moves, and Matte again contemplates the situation.)*
PEJCHL	You may be a decent person, but you stand on the other side of the barricade.
VANĚK	Don't be angry with me, Mr. Pejchl, I guess it's really my fault—You see, I didn't notice that there was a revolution in our country or even that there were any barricades.
PEJCHL	*(Shouts emphatically.)* Revolution goes on all the time!
VANĚK	Mr. Pejchl, I respect every opinion, and I would really appreciate it, if you would *truthfully* answer me just one question.
PEJCHL	I refuse to talk to you.
VANĚK	Very well, but I'll ask all the same. Do you want to be transferred because you are afraid that sitting in the same cell with me might hurt the world revolution or because it might get you into trouble? That's all. *(The question remains hanging in the air. Pejchl stands biting his lip, trapped.)*
SOUMAR	I'll do a few miles before supper. *(Silence—except for the ticking of a clock which gets gradually louder. Blondie leisurely walks along the corridor, locking the cell doors, which, during lunch and until the dishes have all been collected, are secured only by the two bolts.)*
VANĚK	Why was he unlocking?

PEJCHL *(Glad about the change of topic.)* Maybe he was locking up. *(The ticking gets louder. Suddenly, the sound of heavy pounding on a cell door in the distance. The inmates start and grow attentive. A desperate voice from the same direction.)*

VOICE I'm here—here I am. *(Again, the sound of heavy pounding with a metal object on a cell door.)*

SOUMAR *(Stops walking.)* My God, what is that?

VOICE I'm here, comrades—Give it to them!

HORŇAK *(Jumps out from under the bunks.)* Who? Who they beat? O my, o my, my ass!

PEJCHL *(Fearfully.)* What could it be—what could it be?

SOUMAR *(More calmly.)* Probably some con in the next section going crazy. They'll soon fix that.
(Silence.)

PEJCHL *(Lights a cigarette, shaken. Plaintively.)* They'll drag me in like a bear, in chains—and my wife will be sitting in the first row—You shouldn't have told me that, you shouldn't have told me that—it's really horrible—
(From the back of the corridor, sounds of a horrendous stomping of hobnailed boots and a jumble of voices.)

VANĚK *(Jumps up. Uncertain.)* What will they do to him?

MATTE *(Unaware of the commotion, continues sitting like a grand master, pondering his next move.)*

SOUMAR Give him a good thrashing!

VANĚK What do you mean? They're not allowed to do that! Beating people simply won't do.

SOUMAR *(Stoically.)* Well, normally it's not done. The guards prefer to deal with the prisoners nicely, but if somebody flips out, then it's actually the best service they can do him.

VANĚK What do you mean? That's nonsense. It's against all ethical principles.

SOUMAR Look, Ferdinand: If you're hysterical and someone smacks you one, you'll come around in no time and be normal again. Because only social human beings are capable of defiance—not lonely lunatics.

VANĚK Thanks—thanks, but I dont want to—I refuse to—

SOUMAR A lot of good that's going to do you.
(Sounds of doors being slammed and of a terrific stomping. Pejchl circles the cell in fear.)

SOUMAR *(With his ear to the door.)* Now they're lugging him into the cellar. They'll give him a good going-over, and we'll have peace and quiet.
(Silence.)

VANĚK *(Hollers.)* They have no right!!

SOUMAR *(Clowning.)* Article forty, April 24, 1974. Concerning the

Committee on National Security. Section three. Means used by the agents of the Committee on National Security in performing their duties. Paragraph thirty-two, use of benign means. Section one. For the keeping of public order, particularly when averting an attack by rioters or other dangerous individuals on his/her own person or other persons, or while overcoming opposition aimed at frustrating the efficacious performance of duties, tasks, or appeals; further, when preventing the escape of an arrested or summoned person, an agent of the Committee on National Security is justified in using the holds and restraints of self-defence, tear-inducing agents, truncheons, handcuffs, police-dogs, water jets, vehicles for repelling the crowd, blows with a weapon, verbal warnings, and warning shots in the air. Section two. By generally binding legal regulation the Ministry of the Interior is permitted to—

HORŇAK   When they run after me, pig always hit me with handle of shovel.
(Sound of heavy pounding with a metal object on a cell door.)

VOICE   *(As before.)* I'm here—here I am. *(More banging.)*

PEJCHL   *(Collapses.)* I can't handle it, not this—this, this, I can't—What's going on?

MATTE   *(Looks up from the chess board, laughs, and nudges Vaněk to continue playing.)*

VOICE   I'm here, comrades—beat them!

HORŇAK   *(Happily.)* They do it—Well, fuck my grandmother off, I want to go there too.

SOUMAR   *(Watches the shaken Pejchl, amused. Then, with a malicious expression but seemingly unconcerned.)* Well, this looks like a riot.

VANĚK   A what?

SOUMAR   A prison riot.

PEJCHL   *(Very fearfully, whispering as if praying.)* They'll drag me in like a bear, in chains, and my wife will be sitting in the front row—

SOUMAR   No, they won't. For a rebellion you get shot.
(Sounds of a machine-gun round being fired and of a terrific stomping and a jumble of voices.)

PEJCHL   What have I got to do with this—what have I got to do with this?

VANĚK   Listen, the cell doors are being opened!

SOUMAR   *(Less confident.)* O-oh! This looks like a real jam.

VANĚK   Why? What could it mean?
(As before, a round of machine-gun fire, stomping, jumble of voices.)

VOICE	Beat them—comrades—
HORŇAK	*(Sings.)* He-ey, the maple a-blooming, the time is to rob—
VANĔK	Wait a minute! *(His ear to the door.)* Did he say, "Beat them, comrades" or "Beat the comrades"? Listen, somebody there's shouting in Russian!
HORŇAK	—the maple leaf fallen, the time is to stop.
SOUMAR	*(Listening at the door.)*—And German—
PEJCHL	What have I got to do with that? Why couldn't I just forget about those blasted bus passes?!
SOUMAR	*(To Pejchl.)* That's what they'll want to find out from you. *(Seriously.)* If those fucking rebels have machine-guns and keys, they'll be opening all the cells, and if someone refuses to get in on the act *(Trying to scare Pejchl.)*, they'll pump him full of lead.
PEJCHL	Holy Mother of Jesus!
MATTE	*(Finally gets up from the chess board. Seeing Pejchl close to tears, he assumes they are playing some kind of game. He laughs and starts shadow-boxing.)* Box, box, box—bang, bang, bang—
VANĔK	*(Stops Matte and through clumsy signs tries to explain that something is going on in the corridor.)* Matte—you—I— Soumar—Pejchl—bad—shooting—all—rebellion—
HORŇAK	*(Takes over and, using sign language, quickly explains the situation to Matte.)* Bang, bang!
MATTE	*(Grows serious, sensing the tension of the others.)* *(Prolonged silence. Then, more machine-gun rounds, stomping, voices.)*
VOICE	Here, comrades—our boys are here— *(Sound of a hand-grenade exploding.)*
SOUMAR	*(Yelling.)* Quick—push the bunks against the door and block them with the table and the stools, so we can hold off the first attack! Vanĕk, stuff the blankets between the window bars to make it darker.
VANĔK	*(Climbs onto the bunks and carries out Soumar's instructions. It gets darker.)* Enough? *(The others have meanwhile turned the table sideways, placed it against the door, and wedged it with the stools.)*
SOUMAR	Okay. Now the bunks. Mattresses against the door, and then the bunks. *(The mattresses are stacked vertically between the door and the table. The bunks are shoved against the table. In the corridor, the stomping and shouting is repeated. The sounds of gunfire and of cells being unlocked is getting closer.)*

VOICE	My asvabadili vas!!!*
SOUMAR	Holy shit! *(He takes down the sink and arms himself with the pipe.)*
HORŇAK	*(Grabs a stool.)* Let's go—I want first one!
MATTE	*(Sniffs at the door. He coughs to indicate that he can smell smoke.)*
	(Silence. Coming down the corridor, Blondie, mechanically unlocking one cell after the other without opening them or even looking through the peephole. The prisoners prepare for an attack. Blondie unlocks their cell, turns to the one opposite and unlocks it too. Meanwhile, the weight of the barricade has pushed the door open and the mattresses tumble into the corridor. Blondie swerves around. Everyone stares at him as though he were an apparition.)
BLONDIE	*(Recovering his wits.)* Good heavens, what are you doing, you idiots? Do you realize the amount of trouble you're in for? *(In a truly commanding manner, yelling angrily.)* Put those bunks back under the window immediately! Down with those blankets, or I'll call the commando and show you a merry-go-round like you've never seen before. No more Mr. Nice Guy!
VANĚK	Commandant, sir, we thought this was an uprising and wanted to protect ourselves.
	(Vaněk's last words are drowned out by the sounds of machine gun-fire, stomping and shouting of "My vas asvabadili!" All at once Blondie understands. He laughs.)
SOUMAR	*(The pipe still in hand.)* Well, what am I supposed to think, locked up in this hole, when there's some kind of war going on in the corridors?! When one doesn't know a damn thing!
BLONDIE	*(Calmly.)* Hardly a war. Vávra, the movie director, is shooting *The Liberation of Prague* trilogy in the next section, and you can hardly expect a state artist to get permission from each and every con and ask if perhaps the gentlemen have any objections. And now get cracking! Everything in its place! I'll be back to check in five minutes. You're lucky. If anybody else had been on duty today, you'd be shipped off to solitary, all of you. *(He pushes the mattresses back into the cell and slams the door.)*
	(Silently, the prisoners begin restoring order.)
SOUMAR	Bloody Vávra.
VANĚK	I know him personally.
SOUMAR	Shooting *The Liberation of Prague* trilogy!!

---

*   Translator's note: "We have liberated you!!!" in Russian.

VANĚK	And he won't stop shooting until everything's shot. *(Another round of gun-fire, stomping, voices.)*
VOICE	I'm here—here—beat them, comrades!
VANĚK	*(Sarcastically.)* Doesn't seem to be going too well, this liberation—if they have to keep repeating it. *(The cell is almost in its original shape. Soumar and Vaněk reattach the pipe gone unnoticed by Blondie and put the sink back on. Matte picks up the chessmen strewn all over the room, and Pejchl, turning away from the others, puts the finished letter under his shirt. Blondie opens the door.)*
BLONDIE	How's it going? Come get your supper. *(Matte and Vaněk move the table to the door, and five bowls of tea, plates of cheese, and five thick slices of bread are handed in.)*
PEJCHL	*(To Blondie, in a loud voice.)* Commandant, sir, I ask that you accept a letter!
BLONDIE	*(Severely.)* In the morning. You know very well that the mail's taken during the morning report.
PEJCHL	*(Venomously.)* It's a letter to the Deputy Supervisor on day duty, and you have to accept it, commandant, sir.
BLONDIE	Give it to me! *(Pejchl removes the letter from under his shirt and hands it over. Soumar crosses to Pejchl and with all his weight stomps on the latter's foot. Pejchl screams out loud. Blondie pretends not to have noticed the incident.)*
VANĚK	Commandant, sir, may I ask a question?
BLONDIE	What is it?
VANĚK	Commandant, sir, is the actor Vrabec also appearing in this movie?
BLONDIE	*(Winking at Vaněk.)* Of course he is, Vaněk. *(He shuts and bolts the door.)* *(Silence—except for the sound of stomping, shooting, and shouting.)*
SOUMAR	*(To Pejchl.)* So what? Out of fear for your grub or for the sake of ideological purity?
PEJCHL	Oh, leave me alone, I'm no fighter and my heart will suffer as a consequence. I've got two small girls, my son's doing his military service, my wife has bad lungs. I worked hard all my life, never stole a thing—this is the first time—that I—did— *(Nervous, he takes a cigarette butt and tries to light it.)* I received two honourable mentions in the printing shop—I know how to work—nobody can take that away from me—not you and not them—I worked like a horse all my life—and was as poor as a church mouse—I just couldn't any more—The food those three kids put away—And now they'll drag me in

	like a bear, in chains. *(He starts to cry.)*
VANĚK	*(Gives him a lighted cigarette.)* Here, take it, Mr. Pejchl. *(To Soumar.)* What a shame—
SOUMAR	Well, I suppose— *(To Pejchl.)* But they'll still drag you around in chains like a bear on display in the market square, and your wife'll be sitting in the front row! *(This for Pejchl's letter.)*
	(The usual mealtime procedure—The meal taken silently, then the door, dishes, and the locking up. All sit quietly. The ticking of a clock grows louder. Then, the sound of a siren as permission to use the bunks. The prisoners change into their pyjamas and take down the bunks. Matte cleans his teeth, Vaněk smokes, Pejchl has pulled the blanket over his head.)
SOUMAR	*(Sings.)* Over high mountains the sun has passed, praise be to God, this day bites the dust.
	(The ticking of a clock grows louder. The light in the cell is dimmed. After a while, coming down the corridor, Blondie.)
BLONDIE	*(Opens the door and hollers.)* Pejchl, pack your things; you're moving. On the double!
PEJCHL	But I'm in my pyjamas!
BLONDIE	No talking back, just throw your things in the blanket, and off you go. You wanted it, so they processed your request straightaway. *(To Horňak.)* Horňak, stop gawking and make your bed; you're staying.
HORŇAK	*(Happily embraces Matte.)*
BLONDIE	*(To Pejchl.)* Move your tail, Pejchl, for heaven's sake. *(To Vaněk.)* I heard something about you on the radio again; didn't catch it all. Anyway, it'll be in tomorrow's paper.
PEJCHL	*(His things ready.)* Commandant, sir, should I change?
BLONDIE	Just come along as you are. I'll lock you up only a few doors down. And hurry up, 'cause I'd like to make it home too.
	(As Pejchl passes Vaněk, the latter holds out his hand. Pejchl shifts his pack to the left hand and somewhat clumsily and bashfully accepts the offered hand. He hesitates for a moment.)
PEJCHL	*(Mumbles.)* I know—somehow things are always a bit different.
	(Pejchl steps into the corridor, and Blondie locks up. Both disappear into the back. Silence.)
SOUMAR	*(After a while.)* He sure softened up, eh?
VANĚK	He's a poor devil after all, when you think about it.
SOUMAR	But a disciplined one.
HORŇAK	Screw Pejchl, and look at Matte do show. *(To Matte.)* What was in train—choo-choo-choo—bang, Matte, go!
MATTE	*(In wild pantomime narrates how he set fire to a haystack and, when the entire village population had run to extinguish it, robbed the abandoned houses, with a pitchfork killed a big*

175

*dog that attacked him, stowed away on a train, picked the
pockets of some card-playing passengers, got away by jump-
ing off the moving train, and was never found out.)
(While Matte performs, Fragrance is walking along the corridor,
peeking into the cells. When he gets to their cell, he looks in
for a moment and then vigorously pounds on the door.)*

FRAGRANCE   Hey, what the fuck's going on in there?! Want me to come in
and teach you a lesson?
(Silence. Fragrance moves on.)

SOUMAR   How come that shit's here again?

HORŇAK   Is Blondie's short shift. Long one is day next to tomorrow.
Tomorrow is turn of Horseface.

SOUMAR   Well, I'm delighted.
*(Siren, announcing bedtime. The prisoners climb into the
bunks. The light grows fainter still—night intensity. The
ticking of the clock gets progressively louder, until it is
almost unbearable for the audience. Sounds of contented
snoring. Suddenly Vaněk starts from his sleep and jumps out
of bed.)*

VANĚK   *(In panic.)* Help, help!
*(The others wake up, asking, "What's going on?", "What is
it?", etc.)*

SOUMAR   What's wrong, Ferdinand, what happened?

VANĚK   *(Slowly grasping the situation.)* I had a terrible dream. It was
something dreadful.

HORŇAK   You all wet, Vaněk, what is dreadful thing?

VANĚK   You're going to laugh, but I dreamt I was in jail!
(Pause.)

SOUMAR   And why not? Weren't jails made for everybody?
*(Fragrance rushes into the corridor. He can't decide which
cell to enter because everything is quiet. It is dawn.)*

THE END

NOTES

1. *Proud Destiny* (1947) is a novel by Lion Feuchtwanger (1884-1957) which compares the complex patterns of power play of the French and the American Revolutions.
2. *The Leopard* (1958) by Giuseppe Tomasi di Lampedusa (1896-1957) is an historical novel about Sicilian society in the nineteenth century.
3. Dr. Václav Benda (born 1946) is a Czech writer and philosopher. In 1977 he lost his position with Charles University, and in 1979, as one of the speakers for Charter 77, he was sentenced to four years in prison.

JIŘÍ DIENSTBIER

Reception

Translated by Dr. Josef Skála
Adapted by Anna Mozga

This play, inspired by *Audience* and by my stay, together
with its author, in a place where life takes off the social
mask, is dedicated to Václav Havel on the occasion of his
first New Year's Day out of jail—1984.

1 January 1984

The author would like to thank all those who at various
stages during the creation of this work contributed to it
by offering their thoughts and criticisms; in particular,
Luboš Dobrovský, Václav Havel, Sergej Machonin and
Zdeněk Urbánek.

CHARACTERS

Brewmaster
Ferdinand Vaněk, a writer
Bavarian
Swing
Gopher
Biftek
Chief Officer

PLACE

Prison Office

ANNOUNCER

(Announcer's voice begins to be heard over the house speakers shortly before the house lights go down.)
The play you are about to see is fictional. It describes none of the thousands of prisons glowing like pearls on the diadem of our civilization. The imaginary characters of our chamber-drama find themselves in the entrance hall to an exclusive institution. This place is unfortunately not yet available to everybody, simply because of its limited capacity. Do not despair, however; it will suffice to look out of your window onto the street on which you live, to peep through a keyhole into the adjacent office, or to put your ear against the wall separating you from your neighbour. The play you are about to see is fictional. It describes none of the thousands of prisons—
(The voice tapers off. The house lights go down.)

(Brewmaster's office in prison. The office walls are chalk-white, obviously freshly painted. Stage left, a door and a filing-cabinet; stage right, a window. The back wall is almost completely covered by a cork board displaying countless name plates, numbers, and notices in a variety of colours. A small part of the board is taken up by clippings of newspaper articles and photographs. Above the board, a slogan in big red letters occupies the entire width of the wall. It reads: MAXIM GORKIJ: MAN—IT HAS A PROUD RING. Two office desks and three chairs centre stage. On top of each desk, a typewriter and piles of papers. In the corner, a sink and, adjacent to it, a small table. On the table, a hot-plate with a tea-kettle on it, a number of old marmelade jars, and a few pots and pans.
When the stage lights come up, Brewmaster is sitting at his desk. His hair is clipped short and he wears an old army uniform. The uniform is neatly ironed and fits well. On his chest is a large brass badge with the inscription EW (Exemplary Worker). He is sipping tea from a marmelade jar and looking at a large magazine centrefold. After a while there is a knock at the door. Brewmaster quickly folds the picture and hides it among the papers on his desk. He punches a few keys on his typewriter.)

BREWMASTER

Come in! *(He continues typing.)*
(Entering hesitantly, Vaněk. His hair is cut very short and he wears an army surplus uniform similar to Brewmaster's only his is grotesquely ill-fitting: the jacket is too large, the pant legs are too short, and the shirt has many buttons missing. He

	closes the door behind him and assumes the "at attention" position.)
VANĚK	Sir! *(He hesitates.)*—Mr. Commandant, prisoner Vaněk. I came as ordered, sir.
BREWMASTER	Put on your glasses, Vaněk. Don't you know that you report only to guards?
VANĚK	Sorry, but the pedagogue in admissions said—
BREWMASTER	Ah, don't give a shit about what he says. He thinks just because he used to be a deputy minister he can play the big cheese around here.
VANĚK	Yes, sir.
BREWMASTER	*(Gets up and pats Vaněk on the shoulder.)* Now ain't that somethin'—he doesn't even recognize me!
VANĚK	*(Stares at him.)*
BREWMASTER	Well, why the hell should you remember? After ten years! Guys like me don't make it into the papers.
VANĚK	*(Startled.)* Mr. Brewmaster!
BREWMASTER	And anyhow, in your life the brewery was only a short detour.
VANĚK	So you've also—
BREWMASTER	And no need to mister anyone here. A con's a con.
VANĚK	Yes.
BREWMASTER	Gee whiz, now ain't that somethin'? Tell me, would you ever—would you've ever expected this?
VANĚK	*(Seems to be comparing their uniforms.)*
BREWMASTER	Yeah, people sure look different in civvies than in these duds. *(He examines Vaněk's uniform.)* Christ, look what they done to you! Well, what the hell! Lock you up they can, but let you out they must! *(He sits down and looks through his papers.)*
VANĚK	I don't think I would have expected you—
BREWMASTER	Anyone can get busted. Justice is justice.
VANĚK	I'd rather have met you somewhere nicer.
BREWMASTER	Like in the brewery, maybe?
VANĚK	*(Swallows.)* Maybe.
BREWMASTER	Who knows, if you'd given me a hand with that stupid report— maybe I'd still be Head Brewmaster and you could still be rolling them barrels—
VANĚK	But how could I possibly report on myself?
BREWMASTER	And you didn't bring Bohdalová,[1] either. You know, the actress.
VANĚK	I did ask her to come.
BREWMASTER	Busy, was she?
VANĚK	I really—
BREWMASTER	Come on, you wanted to quit!
VANĚK	No, I had to have an operation. For a hernia.
BREWMASTER	Those were the good times, eh? Sherkezy[2] is here too.

VANĚK	The guy who was on full barrels?
BREWMASTER	Yeah. That Gypsy son of a bitch. Why don't you sit down?
VANĚK	*(Cautiously sits down.)* What happened to him?
BREWMASTER	Some chick. You know how it goes. He slugged a guy for screwing one of his personal cunts. Hit 'im with a heavy chain, you know. And that bastard almost kicked the bucket.
VANĚK	Pardon?
BREWMASTER	But they managed to pull him through. Lucky for Sherkezy.
VANĚK	I see.
BREWMASTER	*(Gets up, unbuttons his shirt, and reveals a colour tattoo of Hradčany castle emblazoned on his chest.)* See this? That's what I call poetry. Eh? Hradčany castle. And in livin' colour! *(He quickly buttons up his shirt.)* Sherkezy is good. Can't drink here, so he discovered other talents. *(Pause.)* I always wanted to be a brewmaster in Prague. In the Urquell brewery. Oh, heck! Couldn't even make it to Pardubice. *(He sits down.)* But who gives a shit! The Prague brewery ain't what it used to be either. Did you know they now use sugar instead of malt?
VANĚK	Really?
BREWMASTER	That's what they say. The malt's only for export. Geez, what a brew! Well, you never liked beer anyhow. *(He looks through his papers.)* You oughta ask Sherkezy. He'll make you one too. Sure, he's a coloured bastard all right, but in the brewery we all used to be one gang. And there's no match for him when it comes to tattooing, no matter what!
VANĚK	Isn't this a bit suspicious? I mean, us sitting here together like this.
BREWMASTER	What's wrong with it? Gotta do your admission papers, don't I?
VANĚK	I see.
BREWMASTER	Want some coffee?
VANĚK	You can—you have—
BREWMASTER	Yeah, sure. If you play your cards right, you get what you want—even in the slammer.
VANĚK	That's what I've been missing most.
BREWMASTER	Even more than broads?
VANĚK	I thought it was forbidden.
BREWMASTER	It is. *(He hands Vaněk a jar with coffee.)*
VANĚK	*(Smelling the coffee.)* Won't we get into trouble?
BREWMASTER	Bet you never had coffee in a marmelade jar before, did you?
VANĚK	*(Slowly takes a sip.)* Ah, is that ever good!
BREWMASTER	*(Takes a sip of tea.)* Anything can get you into trouble. If you let it. Swing and Biftek are on duty today. If you don't rub them the wrong way, everything's okay. Besides, they don't

usually bother people in the office. Who'd do their work for them?

VANĚK　Maybe I could help a bit too. With the typing. *(The door flies open and Bavarian enters. His uniform is well-ironed like Brewmaster's, and he has an identical badge on his chest. He is about thirty. He carries some papers which he proceeds to put on Brewmaster's desk.)*

BAVARIAN　*(To Brewmaster.)* Here's the laundry papers. *(He looks at Vaněk.)* That him?

VANĚK　*(Gets up, and they shake hands.)*

BAVARIAN　I'm Bavarian. *(He pushes Vaněk back into his chair.)* I knew the pen would be good for something. Tell me, where else would a small-time district bureaucrat meet a celebrity like yourself?

VANĚK　Oh, I'm just another rookie.

BAVARIAN　Every connection's good for something.

VANĚK　Just ask Brewmaster here.

BREWMASTER　*(To Bavarian.)* Get with it!

BAVARIAN　You'd better keep all your connections under wraps—all of them and especially a connection like this. If you don't, everybody'll be pissed off. Got to keep a low profile, so people swallow all the bull about you trusting them, and then business improves right away. *(He grabs a folder with papers.)*

BREWMASTER　*(Laughing.)* Look who's talking. You're about as unnoticeable as a fart during the pope's sermon. *(To Vaněk.)* Know why they call him Bavarian?

BAVARIAN　So I was a sucker! Young and green. With two BMWs parked in front of my house, the neighbours kept blowing the whistle on me, till even bribes didn't work any more. There's always something you can pin on a department store manager. Obvious, isn't it? *(He exits.)*

BREWMASTER　Don't trust anyone here. You understand? Better drink up. Some rat might sneak in. You seem to get special treatment everywhere.

VANĚK　*(Quickly sips the hot liquid.)*

BREWMASTER　You don't have to scald your tongue.

VANĚK　You'd think that at least here everyone would hate informers.

BREWMASTER　Everyone does. The ones that fink on him, that is. *(Pause.)* See, everybody wants parole. And there's always the question of who gets to be kingpin and who cleans the shithouse. It's the same in here as out there. You never know who's the prick that finked on you. *(He takes a sip of tea.)* What kinda help are you talking about?

VANĚK　If it is in my power, I try to be of service to anyone who requires my help.

BREWMASTER	*(Laughing.)* Even the head screw?
VANĚK	I think I can play the game.
BREWMASTER	Don't make me laugh. What are you gonna say when the warden calls you to his office and asks: "What's new, Vaněk"? What'll you tell him? See what I mean? You'll say you don't know nothin'. Or you'll start spouting off some rubbish you've seen on TV. But what he wants to hear is who was cooking in the cell at night or what Sherkezy collects for his tattoos. And if you're not singing that tune, he'll know you're trying to pull one over on him. Even a fucking idiot can see that kinda thing around here, so don't ever try to say you didn't see nothin'.
VANĚK	He couldn't expect me to inform on anyone.
BREWMASTER	What d'you mean, inform? Remember how you got A's in school? Do you? By telling the Miss what she wanted to hear.
VANĚK	Mmn.
BREWMASTER	You only get marks for information you can sell. That's life. If you didn't get your education at home or in school, you'll get it here. You get to be real educated when you share everything you know with your supervisor. Otherwise a super'd be useless, see?
VANĚK	Like saying that you gave me coffee?
BREWMASTER	Something that can be forbidden can also be allowed. Depends who's doin' it. *(He looks at Vaněk.)* And I never gave you no coffee, anyhow.
	(The door opens and an elegant young officer enters — Swing. A riot-stick and a walkie-talkie which screeches almost continuously hang from his belt. He walks and stands with a peculiar swinging motion. Brewmaster jumps up and stands at attention. Vaněk clumsily follows his example.)
BREWMASTER	*(Shouting.)* Lieutenant, sir. Prisoner Brewmaster plus one —
SWING	Okay, Brewmaster. *(He looks around, notices Vaněk's uniform, and gives him a slight shove.)* Look what they've done to you, man. You have till tomorrow to swap with somebody. *(He notices the coffee. To Brewmaster, pointing at Vaněk.)* Buddy of yours?
BREWMASTER	Worked together in the brewery long time ago.
SWING	Turned some trick together you mean, Brewmaster?
BREWMASTER	Well, a few beers with the broads from the packing plant once in a while.
SWING	A few beers, you say?
BREWMASTER	You know how it goes, Lieutenant. That's life.
SWING	Never mind. What's for dinner?
BREWMASTER	Gruel, sir. Won't get more than half the inmates for that one.
	(An angry voice over the walkie-talkie. Swing fiddles with the

	knobs for a while and then shouts into the device.)
SWING	On my way! *(He switches the walkie-talkie off.)* Look, Brewmaster: There's soccer on TV. I want everything quiet, you hear. *(He walks toward the door and stops.)* Oh yeah, Brewmaster. They called from the pig-farm. Haven't got enough feed. Make sure that someone takes round the leftovers from dinner, will you. *(He is now in a good mood. Pointing to the jars of coffee and tea.)* And get rid of these. *(He exits.)*
	(Brewmaster sits down. Vaněk, still standing, finishes his coffee and proceeds to wash the jar in the sink.)
BREWMASTER	Don't bother with that.
VANĚK	I wouldn't want to create any problems for you.
BREWMASTER	*(With a gesture of dismissal.)* We're lucky. He can watch his TV no sweat. But if it was pastry with custard for dinner, every man and his dog would show up. And Swing'd be fidgeting like he had itching powder up his ass 'cause he'd have to be in the kitchen to kick out the defects.
VANĚK	Which ones?
BREWMASTER	You know, the ones that didn't shave, guys with long hair, buttons missing, or dirty boots, or anyone who gets on his nerves.
VANĚK	I see.
BREWMASTER	To make sure there's enough leftovers to feed them stupid pigs.
VANĚK	*(Puts the clean jar on the desk and sits down.)*
BREWMASTER	They don't like guys that know each other from the outside.
VANĚK	You didn't have to tell him.
BREWMASTER	Wake up, Vaněk! If I keep quiet about it, he smells a rat right away. No sir! Even the best cop doesn't like anybody pissing over his head. *(He thoughtfully plays with the badge on his chest.)*
VANĚK	A decoration?
BREWMASTER	Ain't that somethin', eh? The badge of an exemplary worker.
VANĚK	Gee.
BREWMASTER	Wouldn't have guessed, eh?
VANĚK	*(Smiling.)* You've always been a good worker.
BREWMASTER	I know. Otherwise you wouldn't bother.
VANĚK	*(Tries to protest.)*
BREWMASTER	Too bad there ain't no barrels to roll here. Nothin' to brew either. *(He pulls out the magazine picture and unfolds it.)* See, here she is.
VANĚK	*(Squinting at the picture.)* Who?
BREWMASTER	Don't tell me you don't even recognize her!
VANĚK	*(Still looking at the picture.)* My glasses—

188

BREWMASTER	You don't need glasses to recognize this one!
VANĚK	*(Finally.)* It's Georgina Bohdalová!
BREWMASTER	*(Delighted.)* So she's with me all the time. Been for a year already.
VANĚK	I did ask her, really.
BREWMASTER	She just laughed, right?
VANĚK	She had many invitations.
BREWMASTER	Well, why the hell would she— *(He folds up the picture and puts it into a drawer.)* Let me tell you, Vaněk, here any woman's picture goes to your brain and to other less appropriate places. But you don't care, do you?
	(Bavarian enters and puts some papers on Brewmaster's desk.)
BAVARIAN	Just need the machine shop papers and it's finito. *(He crosses to the cork board with a piece of paper in his hand and starts rearranging the coloured cards.)*
BREWMASTER	*(To Vaněk.)* I'll tell you something. In some ways it's better in here than on the outside. There you keep coming up with stupid ideas, you always want things, and you bullshit yourself into thinking you can actually get them. When all you really are is a piece of shit. You know bugger all. Not even whether you'll get busted or not. And here? Here you either make it or you don't. If you make it to the office, you're in the office. If you get thrown in the hole, you're in the hole. You always know what's what. If it wasn't for parole, it'd be easy.
BAVARIAN	*(Has finished rearranging the cards. To Vaněk.)* Will they give the amnesty?
VANĚK	I beg your pardon?
BAVARIAN	They've got to. They signed the Hague Declaration—International justice, see? Universal laws.
VANĚK	That doesn't make sense.
BAVARIAN	You've been in solitary for too long. Couldn't have heard about it in there. *(To Brewmaster.)* The machine shop wants some poem on their wall. Got anything that's already okayed? *(Brewmaster fishes in a folder and hands over a newspaper clipping. Bavarian takes it and exits.)*
VANĚK	You select poems?
BREWMASTER	Wouldn't have guessed, eh? Florian's always kosher. He's in the papers all the time. Besides—he's a State Artist.
VANĚK	I see.
BREWMASTER	*(Puts the clippings in order and returns the folder to his desk.)* Let me tell you something. Everybody oughta do time— at least a year—and everything would be totally different.
VANĚK	Jail seems to be an existential necessity for twentieth-century man.

BREWMASTER	That's it. Anyone can have bad luck. *(He drinks.)* We got tipped off that the pigs were on the way, so everybody hid their records, but I was on holiday in the Tatra mountains. Someone had to be sacrificed.
VANĚK	And they let you—
BREWMASTER	I've always been fair and square.
VANĚK	I know.
BREWMASTER	You can think what you like.
VANĚK	Of course, one can't inform on one's accomplices. That would mean being one of them.
BREWMASTER	Like I always say, honesty's profitable. I'll collect my due from them when I get out. All they managed to nab was some copies. Had all the original documents stashed away, I had.
VANĚK	Good for you.
BREWMASTER	Yeah, sure. If the pigs had got their hands on them or if I'd squealed, they would've called us an organized racket. But as a small crook all I could get was a fiver. *(He glances at his papers.)* You want the laundry job?
VANĚK	I've never worked in a laundry before.
BREWMASTER	The ironing's even dry—warm and dry. That's the most important thing in the clink.
VANĚK	Do you think it might be possible?
BREWMASTER	Anything's possible. We're just regular guys, you know.
VANĚK	I would really be grateful.
BREWMASTER	Even more regular here than outside. But sometimes it's the other way round. D'you know Eva?
VANĚK	*(Searching his memory.)* The director's secretary? The platinum blonde with the big— *(Indicates breasts.)*
BREWMASTER	You mean the one with the fantastic tits? No, that's not her. I mean the one from the packing plant. We had a thing going, you know. Used to be a barmaid.
VANĚK	I don't think I remember.
BREWMASTER	She's got a fantastic pair too, by the way. Even better. Got herself into trouble and had to drop out of sight for a while. So I helped a bit and got her the job in the packing plant. That holiday in the mountains—she was there with me. You been to the Tatra?
VANĚK	A long time ago.
BREWMASTER	It's poetry, right? Hills, forests, valleys, brooks, fresh air. We decided to sign up for life.
VANĚK	Congratulations.
BREWMASTER	Got nailed as soon as we hit town again. *(He sighs.)* Only they can't make dumplings. No Slovak knows how to cook dumplings. But Pilsener or Budweiser you can get everywhere.

	(He takes a sip of tea.) Will you write me a poem to send to her?
VANĚK	*(Fidgeting.)* I wrote some poetry a long time ago. But not like this. I doubt that I could do it.
BREWMASTER	Rubbish! It doesn't have to be anything like Florian's. We'd neither of us have a clue, anyway. Just make it beautiful.
VANĚK	Perhaps you shouldn't talk so much. It's risky.
BREWMASTER	Nobody's going to shit bricks on account of some poem.
VANĚK	No, I meant—what you said about the documents.
BREWMASTER	You think I'm stupid? I wouldn't tell nobody.
VANĚK	And what about a few minutes ago?
BREWMASTER	That's different. You're an old buddy, right? Well, okay, sometimes even a pal can sink you. But you're different, you're a political. You don't know how swell it is to have you here.
VANĚK	Thanks. But I would rather—
BREWMASTER	There wasn't anybody to talk to, to tell one's deep thoughts to, one's worries, personal problems and stuff.
VANĚK	They say we should be getting an advance on our pocket money.
BREWMASTER	Tomorrow morning at the cashier's. Just wait. Vaněk, it'll happen to you too! *(The door opens and Gopher enters. His uniform is crumpled. He wears a blank expression on his face.)*
BREWMASTER	What's up?
GOPHER	Can I take those shirts?
BREWMASTER	Pick them up this evening. *(He points to the door. Gopher hesitates.)* Shove off, will you! Don't you see I have a new acquisition here?
GOPHER	*(To Vaněk.)* So you're new here, sucker? There's going to be a three-year-general, in case you didn't know.
VANĚK	Beg your pardon?
GOPHER	Amnesty, faggot!
VANĚK	I haven't heard anything specific.
GOPHER	It's a fact. One of the cons told me, and he don't bullshit around. His aunt's niece on her husband's side sits in the President's office, you sucker. *(To Brewmaster.)* Do I get a smoke? *(Brewmaster takes a package of cigarettes from a drawer and throws it to Gopher. The package falls on the floor. Gopher picks it up and exits quickly.)*
BREWMASTER	*(Disgusted.)* No privacy here. If no one else turns up, then this garbage bum has to crawl in.
VANĚK	He takes out the garbage?

191

BREWMASTER	No, he eats it. Right out of the kitchen bin where everybody else dumps the grub they can't swallow.
VANĚK	Does he work in the laundry?
BREWMASTER	No, why?—He washes my stuff 'cause he's a gopher. You'll have one too. Cons are either kings, mice, gophers, or suckers. Most of them mice. Faceless numbers; place is swarming with them. The gophers are like small businessmen, capitalists. Work for the kings and get paid in smokes or tobacco and dough. The suckers clean the shithouse and give blowjobs, if a king wants. You'll obviously be a king.
VANĚK	I don't think so. A mouse, more likely—like most of the others.
BREWMASTER	*(Laughing.)* Like what others? You never gave a damn about what the others did, not even on the outside. A regular guy tries to make things a bit easier for himself and makes sure he don't lose his spot. Listen, your principles ain't gonna get you nowhere. Even you'll come around to that.
VANĚK	I'm not saying that some improvement wouldn't come in handy.
BREWMASTER	Congratulations! You see, you can't afford to become a bum. You never hit nobody and you never stole nothin'. You were run in on account of the truth, and you've got to behave like it. *(Pause.)* And don't forget me, if you wind up with an empty tin from that imported tea.
VANĚK	You'll get a full one.
BREWMASTER	No, I couldn't take it. Not for the time being. Maybe when you've established yourself a bit. An empty tin'll do. I'll put it on my desk where everyone can see it. Shows my class, you know.
VANĚK	*(Hesitantly.)* How did you know—
BREWMASTER	Everybody knows that being in the mill on account of saying what's true is totally stupid. On the other hand, people who do time for the truth are reliable. Like murderers.
VANĚK	What?
BREWMASTER	Obviously. Killers get stretches so long, it's pointless turning into a rat. And for politicals, there's no parole. So why would you bother? Cons don't do nothin' that ain't useful. Too bad there's not much hook-up with the killers. You'll meet the doctor. Told his wife three times not to fuck around or he'd do her in. The fourth time he blew her away and the guy along with her. And then goes and gives himself up. Bet he's sore he didn't just kick her ass in instead. *(He takes a sip of tea.)* Politicals are different. Usually talk all the time. Your pal Neubauer[3] was here too, you know. Everybody kept

192

asking him the height of Kilimanjaro, what's the chemical formula for pot, what city in Zimbabwe has six letters, what's the proper way to screw, and how to learn English in a month, 'cause every kindergarten graduate wants to join the Green Berets or the South African commandos and shoot everybody that's yellow, black, or red. He even spent hours yapping with the garbage bum on account of that jerk wanted to take the Gilette way out.

VANĚK   I'm not a missionary.

BREWMASTER   That's what you think. You smoke them American cigarettes, have imported soap and tea and a foreign electric razor. You went to school and the papers write about you.

(Bavarian enters, carrying some papers. He stops at the desk and listens while arranging the papers.)

BREWMASTER   Some guards'll come after you like a chicken after a spit to catch you smoking in the locker room or somethin'. So they get ahead. But they wouldn't dare punch you. Anyhow, you'll be on your best behaviour, won't you? Work hard? Sure. It's no big deal, you'll see. Same as on the outside. Sometimes there's no gas, sometimes the oxygen runs out, then the crane breaks down, the electricity goes off, or the sheet metal's missing. D'you fight?

VANĚK   Never.

BREWMASTER   Fix?

VANĚK   I'm most certainly not a drug addict.

BAVARIAN   *(To Brewmaster.)* Swing's been asking for you.

BREWMASTER   Why the hell didn't you tell me earlier? *(He grabs his cap and exits running.)*

BAVARIAN   *(Laughing.)* And we from the house committee will assign you duties like choosing TV programmes and movies—nothing but candy jobs, and we'll only ask you to do some cleaning if there's nobody else to do it—but all smut-free work, of course.

VANĚK   I don't think it would make a great deal of sense to refuse a favour.

BAVARIAN   There's no telling when the shoe'll be on the other foot, and an experienced con never makes an enemy of another who may get his nose in the feed trough some day.

VANĚK   I never intended anything of the sort and I never will. I only say and write what I think.

BAVARIAN   What you think! What's important is what people believe. And not even the guards will believe what you say. At any rate, you probably have influential friends.

VANĚK   A lot of good that does me here.

BAVARIAN	*(Laughing.)* I realize you won't tell me your plans. In here you naturally have to lead a decent existence. And watch out for everybody.
	(Brewmaster enters out of breath.)
BAVARIAN	What did he want?
BREWMASTER	*(Sits down.)* It's one: zilch.
VANĚK	I beg your pardon?
BREWMASTER	Slavia's down one goal. He thinks that I'm a Slavia´ fan. Probably 'cause I wanted the brewmaster's job in Urquell. I wasn't gonna argue about it.
BAVARIAN	You're losing your marbles over that parole.
BREWMASTER	*(To Vaněk, angrily.)* Look who's talking. This bastard arranged his parole even before he got here, and now he's the clever one. Plenty of dough, mother somewhere up in the system—
BAVARIAN	In a ministry. *(He takes some papers and exits.)*
BREWMASTER	The deficit they charged him with was just a small piece of what he swiped. And do you think he lost any of it? All he had on him was a few grand and one of the BMWs. The old one. The new car, the house with the swimming pool, and a cottage in the Beskyd mountains are all registered in his ex-wife's name. She's as clean as a water-lily, so they can't confiscate anything of hers.
VANĚK	But he seems interested in the amnesty.
BREWMASTER	Sure. Amnesty would be now; parole's in two years. He can't sleep thinking of that. *(He drinks.)* You know how to make your bed?
VANĚK	I've always had a sense of order. *(Interested.)* How many get parole?
BREWMASTER	Look who's talking. You and parole! Not unless you come up with a TV speech like that actor or director or whoever he was. But I know you, you couldn't. Not you! You never change. Never listen. Even then, with that Holub or whatever his name was—
VANĚK	You probably mean Kohout.[4]
BREWMASTER	Yeah, Kohout, sure. You didn't even stop seeing Kohout. I kept telling you. And who was right? Me, an ordinary brewery stud with none of your schooling and your movie star connections. I was right. Where's your Kohout now? Well, where is he?
VANĚK	He went to Austria on an official business trip.
BREWMASTER	See? Spreads his wings over the beautiful blue Danube. And in the right direction too.
VANĚK	Actually, they pushed his car over the border. He was returning home.
BREWMASTER	Bullshit! He ain't stupid, that's all.

VANĚK	You also got arrested.
BREWMASTER	*(Sighs.)* It's all right, this. *(Pause.)* With one exception: the broads. You know, women are always trouble. On the outside 'cause you've got them, and here 'cause you don't. You have a wife?
VANĚK	Yes.
BREWMASTER	Kids?
VANĚK	No.
BREWMASTER	You always know how to do things. If your old lady takes off, at least you don't have to pay child support.
VANĚK	Excuse me, but—
BREWMASTER	They all whore around, you know. *(He sighs.)* After all, what broad wants to have moss growing you-know-where. *(He gets up and paces around nervously.)* Bavarian's the only one who doesn't mind. She's got the real estate and he the hidden millions. Like love birds. But is that love? It's strictly business. And what about me? Don't you see, Vaněk, I had to get nailed to find out how jealous I am. At my age! If she'd only stick around, faithful or not. You know, some of them keep pretending for years, come for visits, write letters, and the guy thinks he's got a home. Just before he gets sprung, there's a letter. She met another man. She's in fact been living with the guy for years, but now it finally comes out. Well, what would she do with an ex-con anyway. Somebody who's got to stay clean as a whistle, work his butt off, and be scared to take even a bit of cement home. *(Pause.)* Nine out of ten get divorced. And I'm not even married to Eva yet. Jesus, I might end up giving my savings to some hooker in the park behind the railway station. *(Dreamlike.)* And you know, Vaněk, we're real smuthounds.
VANĚK	Beg your pardon?
BREWMASTER	I mean Eva and me. Like I would lie on the carpet and pretend to be asleep. And she'd come out of the bathroom starkers and jump on my face—
VANĚK	*(Trying to stop Brewmaster.)* Look, these are intimate things—
BREWMASTER	*(Still dreamlike.)* And I'd keep lickin' and lickin'—
VANĚK	*(Angrily.)* That's your private affair!
BREWMASTER	*(Stops, feeling offended, and sits down.)* Sure, sure, doesn't interest you. Just wait! You'll go crazy sooner than you think!
VANĚK	Dreaming doesn't get you anywhere.
BREWMASTER	Who can dream? You'll be awake at night. Not a wink. Whole nights! Won't be able to shut your eyes. Come morning, you'll be imagining how to take apart a motorcycle and put it back together again just to get sex off your mind.
VANĚK	I only know how to pedal.

BREWMASTER   Even better. Maybe you'll be able to drop off if you concentrate on that. *(Short pause.)* Vaněk, d'you think I'd be able to do it?

VANĚK   Well, it probably—

BREWMASTER   If I don't manage parole, I'll be fifty when I get out. At that age, without practice, and after a five-year break? Just the other day I read in a magazine, *Young World*, that organs which don't get used shrivel up. Like legs of people who don't walk but only move their asses in and out of cars all the time.

VANĚK   *(Trying to console Brewmaster and cheer him up.)* It definitely wouldn't apply to this.

BREWMASTER   You're afraid too, right?

VANĚK   Of course it depends on your physical and psychological shape.

BREWMASTER   And you expect to get out of here in any great shape?

VANĚK   At least in some respects. Regular sleep, less time and opportunity to smoke, and without alcohol, your liver gets a break.

BREWMASTER   *(Cheerfully.)* That's right. Like I say, it's swell to have you here. *(He takes a piece of paper from a folder in front of him.)* Have a look what they wrote about you in here: "To be placed in the work division inside the institution. Do not allow to join the house committee. Should be put on duty during political, educational, and instructional activities." Quite somethin', eh? You have to have special treatment everywhere.

VANĚK   *(Emphatically.)* Is the laundry indoors?

BREWMASTER   Get with it! Would I give it to you if it wasn't?

VANĚK   I see.

BREWMASTER   What did you write?

VANĚK   Plays.

BREWMASTER   I was in the National Theatre once. With the brewery. Saw the *Strakonice Piper*.[5] Not bad. Just that the fairies were a bit dumpy. I've got an idea! They wouldn't show none of your plays anyhow, but you could do a skit for me. You'll get to bone up on your writing and I'll get points for parole. Maybe something to celebrate the first of May or the Day of Liberation.

VANĚK   They celebrate that even here?

BREWMASTER   And how we celebrate! Even on the outside they don't do it like this any more. If I wrote a skit—I mean, if you wrote one for me, like so it shows my positive attitude to re-education, we could rehearse it and put it on in the classroom. As long as it's ideologically clean, it could even be funny, so everybody can laugh it up a bit.

VANĚK   I'm afraid I wouldn't know how.

BREWMASTER	Rubbish. You're a writer, ain't you? Do you write plays or don't you?
VANĚK	All I wanted to say is that it might not turn out right. I've never written anything for a specific occasion. What if it did you more harm than good? They could find some irony it it. You never know what they'll pick up on. Or if someone finds out that I did it for you.
BREWMASTER	C'me on, you wouldn't rat on me! You'd have to do it so seriously like you was the one getting parole. *(He sighs.)* When they sent me from reception to a cell and I crawled out of the sack first morning, I got tripped up by a leg. Get the picture? A wooden leg plunked on the floor next to a bunk. I scramble over to the sink, and there's this guy shovin' in a glass eye. And another freak brushing his teeth, and he's got this dinky little hand and it's no bigger than a cat's prick. Like nobody was complete in that cell. And then they started calling each other Peggy, Hawkeye, an' Hook. And some guy that was absolutely huge and farted all the time was called Baloun. I tell you, it was too much poetry even for an ordinary brewery stud like me. That morning I swore to God that once I got out I'd be the best-behaved member of the working class there ever was. In here things are even worse than on the outside.
VANĚK	I'll get used to it.
BREWMASTER	I see. What you're saying is that you won't write it. You never have to ask for no favours. You think: "I'm no common thief." *(He gets up.)* But watch it! I'm not one neither. A thief takes from his fellow man. Everyone hates his guts. He does his time cleaning the crapper. But I'm in here on account of stealing the communal property of the socialist system. Guys like me help people get things they can't get from this fucking system. *(He gestures.)* It may mean more to write a play or sign some petition. But what's bad about getting beer for a dry pub? It would spoil anyhow, if nobody delivers it. All right, one gets dough on the side. But you have to admit that we fight the system too. We do it different, but we're fighting. We're almost like politicals. Except that we can get parole and join the inmates' committee. *(Pause.)* I'll tell you something. It's no big deal to look down on parole if you can't get it for yourself.
VANĚK	*(Quietly.)* I was offered an exit visa to New York during the trial.
BREWMASTER	No kidding. I ask myself all the time how you could be so stupid. *(He looks at Vaněk.)* Or is it 'cause your plays don't

	get put on much abroad?
VANĚK	The invitation to New York was for the première of one of my plays.
BREWMASTER	Even in New York you get special treatment.
VANĚK	How could I go and leave my friends in prison?
BREWMASTER	But now they're out, are they?—Well! Your being a hero sure did them a lot of good! Who knows! Maybe if you'd left, the cops would've been satisfied, and the others would long be home.
VANĚK	But this is my home!
BREWMASTER	The slammer? Jesus, I don't think I can take this any more.
VANĚK	No, I don't mean that. I can go home from here but not from exile. It means that I'm more at home in prison than I would be in New York.
BREWMASTER	Well, it's all the same to you. The longer you stay here, the more they'll write about you in the papers and the more they'll do your plays. Jail is like publicity for you. Even better, it's publicity paid for by them that put you in the clink. Your bank account grows. But what about me? The only thing growing for me is arrears on my alimony payments. You'll become a star like that pop singer, Karel Gott,[6] or a celebrity like Havlíček.[7] You won't have to give a damn about anybody. But I'll be lucky if I get a helper's job in some brewery. Rolling barrels. Me, a brewmaster! *(The door opens and Bavarian enters.)*
BAVARIAN	*(To Vaněk.)* You always have to have some action around you. Right now they're distributing your picture to the screws, so they'll recognize you. They're supposed to report anybody who talks to you or sits with you in the dining room. Did Brewmaster tell you about the other thing?
VANĚK	I don't know what—
BREWMASTER	*(Ignoring Brewmaster's gestures of protest.)* See, we're supposed to make friends with you and report on you to security. *(Both Brewmaster and Vaněk look embarrassed.)*
BAVARIAN	No big deal! He probably didn't have a chance to tell you yet. And, of course, neither Brewmaster nor I are meant to know about the other one being involved in this.
VANĚK	What do they want to know?
BAVARIAN	*(Laughing.)* Every little fart. Don't worry, we'll figure out something. *(To Brewmaster.)* Give me a slogan—fast. They want to have it in the classroom tonight. Got any that made it through the censor's? *(Brewmaster finds a file among the papers on his desk and feverishly looks through it. Bavarian, meanwhile, crosses to the filing-cabinet and takes out a box full of red letters.)*

BREWMASTER	Maybe this: "GORKIJ: MAN—IT HAS A PROUD RING."
BAVARIAN	*(Still rummaging through the box.)* That's up there, stupid!
BREWMASTER	*(Turning to look at the slogan.)* Who cares? *(He looks through his papers again.)* How about this: "ALEXANDER HUMBOLDT: RELATIONSHIPS BETWEEN PEOPLE MAKE LIFE MEANINGFUL"?
BAVARIAN	Too long.
BREWMASTER	Here we are! "GOETHE: MAN GAINS BY HIS LOSSES."
BAVARIAN	That's long too.
BREWMASTER	It's no longer than Gorkij.
BAVARIAN	*(To Vaněk.)* It's terrible. These writers—a gasbag every one of them. *(He grabs the box and the paper with slogans and exits. There is a moment of embarrassed silence.)*
BREWMASTER	You see? Man gains by— *(He cannot remember the rest.)*
VANĚK	*(Resignedly.)* His losses.
BREWMASTER	Good, eh? *(Pause.)* The bastards made me feel so low that Sherkezy had to cook up some dope for me. Want tea?
VANĚK	Is it allowed?
BREWMASTER	*(Puts some tea in the jar and pours hot water over it.)*
VANĚK	One can manage to do without. Especially if doing me such favours could harm your position. You have it quite nice here. You work toward your parole—
BREWMASTER	Nobody bothers to rat about tea. *(He hands Vaněk the jar.)* I got so stoned on that junk I let Sherkezy tattoo the Hradčany castle on my chest. Ain't that somethin', eh? This place can get a guy so freaked out, he turns himself into a walking billboard. *(Vaněk sips his tea. Brewmaster sits down and looks through his papers.)*
VANĚK	How did you know—about the cigarettes?
BREWMASTER	Want to smoke? *(Vaněk takes a package of American cigarettes from his pocket. They both light up.)*
VANĚK	Or about that imported soap?
BREWMASTER	Oh yeah. *(He takes a puff on his cigarette.)* This kinda news gets around real fast. Sometimes damn fast. How about this? You only got here yesterday, but the Voice of America already announced it two days ago. The foreman from the mine listened to it on the graveyard shift with the regular miners.
VANĚK	That's incredible!
BREWMASTER	So they raided your locker, right?
VANĚK	Somebody must have wanted a smoke.
BREWMASTER	Get with it! They were looking for something hidden in your papers.

VANĔK	I see. Stealing cigarettes was just a cover-up. That's how they do it.
BREWMASTER	Bullshit. The sucker stole them on his own. Without orders. Unfortunately, your brand hasn't been seen here for years. The kings caught up with him, smashed his face in, and reported him to Biftek. For stealing from a new number. *(He laughs.)* Biftek happened to be stoned at the time, so he pushed the guy's kisser in a bit more. That got security pissed off, 'cause one of their covers was blown. They hid the poor bastard in solitary for the time being. Their own fault, choosing such assholes. Real poetry, eh? *(A pregnant pause.)*
VANĔK	And the other thing—is it true?
BREWMASTER	*(Indignant.)* Who d'you think you are? Reports are made on everybody from time to time, so why not on you? Especially on you, a guy who lets himself be in the newspapers all the time.
VANĔK	*(Resignedly.)* But I don't let myself—
BREWMASTER	Look, on the outside, you can fool anybody you like. But here the cards are all on the table.
VANĔK	How come he wasn't afraid?
BREWMASTER	Who?
VANĔK	Bavarian.
BREWMASTER	'Cause we're Commies.
VANĔK	What?
BREWMASTER	No private property. Everything's shared—dough, grub, tobacco.
VANĔK	How does he know he can'trust me?
BREWMASTER	They'll all trust you—even if they snitch on you. After all— parole is parole! That goes for the screws too. Even if they let you have it. Every sergeant wants to be a sergeant-major.
VANĔK	You talk as if there weren't any decent people here.
BREWMASTER	Just a few of us. But the majority—! Take Peggy, for example. Try telling him that he's an informer, and he'll clobber you to death with that wooden leg of his. He's no rat, no sir! He just likes to show everybody that he knows everything. Even the police. Like he's telling them: "There ain't nothin' you can do about it anyhow." All they have to do is play real cute, you know, chat him up a bit, give him a pack of smokes, and he tells them anything they want to know.
VANĔK	Why doesn't somebody let him know what's going on?
BREWMASTER	*(Sighs.)* Once they did a documentary on the brewery. I spent the whole day taking people around, pouring free beer down their throats. That was okay. But d'you think they included one word about me? These newspaper people couldn't even

200

	understand how much it would've meant to me. Vaněk, I've realized something. The world's never going to be the way we wise guys would like it. It'll just be good enough for them fucking idiots. Look, in spite of your grand ideals, you see only a small chip of life. Like when the sun's got an eclipse: a fuzzy bit o' light around the edge of a big black hole. You ever seen an eclipse?
VANĚK	*(Impatiently.)* Of course.
BREWMASTER	Poetry, right? *(Pause.)* Well, look at it this way. In the brewery you was full of principles. And how did you end up?
VANĚK	That's my business.
BREWMASTER	Don't you never say that again. Neubauer got two guys parole. Security couldn't believe their eyes when they saw what details they had in their reports on him. He was the one that did them. Even read the letters they wrote home, so he'd have the same bad grammar, spelling and stuff. *(Pause.)* In the brewery maybe I didn't even have to bother. Maybe they would've kept quiet about it, if I'd come up with something else instead. *(Pause.)* But here, if I refuse to co-operate with security, it means I don't care what they want. And when it comes to making out a report on me, they won't give a shit about what I want.
VANĚK	*(Stubbornly sips his tea.)*
BREWMASTER	If I don't write it, someone else will. He'll have to. So he'll just make it up. And you'll be stuck with inspection after inspection and one problem after the next. Even if they don't find nothin' wrong, they'll throw you in the hole just because they're hot under the collar. Or maybe on account of a dirty plate.
VANĚK	I won't leave any dirty dishes.
BREWMASTER	*(Clutching his head.)* Jesus, you drive me bonkers. Have you ever seen a screw that couldn't find anything wrong? A little cobweb in the corner when you're on cleaning duty? *(The door flies open and Sergeant-Major Biftek storms in. His uniform is crumpled and his face purple. Brewmaster jumps up and Vaněk clumsily does the same.)*
BREWMASTER	Sergeant-major, sir, prisoner —
BIFTEK	*(Agitated.)* Stuff it! The chief's coming. Anything messy around here?
BREWMASTER	Everything in order, sergeant-major, sir.
BIFTEK	Tidy up a bit more. Get rid of the jars. You'll certainly win points with the old man when he sees the refreshments you provide for Vaněk. For Vaněk of all people! *(To Vaněk.)* You look like a scarecrow in that outfit! *(Biftek storms out in a panic. Brewmaster quickly hides the*

two jars in his desk. He checks to see if his pockets are buttoned up, organizes papers on his desk, and tidies up everything he can think of. Vanĕk would like to help, but realizes that he would only be in Brewmaster's way. He at least checks his buttons and then hesitantly sits down. Brewmaster continues with his erratic efforts for a while and then sits down at his desk and prepares to start typing.)

BREWMASTER   Education?

VANĔK   I beg your pardon?

BREWMASTER   What schooling do you have? Elementary school? *(He punches a few keys on the typewriter.)*

VANĔK   Yes, elementary school.

BREWMASTER   And then?

VANĔK   High school. Theatre college.

BREWMASTER   *(Types.)* You can actually study theatre? *(He types.)* Some personal information's still missing. Mother's maiden name? *(The door flies open and the Chief Officer enters. He is a confident fifty-five-year-old in civilian clothes. Behind him are Swing and Biftek, trembling. Brewmaster jumps up. Vanĕk does the same, tipping over his chair in the process. He would like to pick it up but decides against it when he sees that Brewmaster is already standing at attention, shouting his report.)*

BREWMASTER   Colonel, sir, Prisoner Brewmaster plus one filling out the reception forms.

Chief OFFICER   *(Looks around. Then, turning to Vanĕk.)* Pick it up!

VANĔK   *(Tries to pick up the chair.)*

Chief OFFICER   So that's you!

VANĔK   *(Still fighting the chair.)* I beg your pardon?

Chief OFFICER   No begging here. Don't you know how to report?

VANĔK   I beg your pardon. Prisoner Vanĕk.

Chief OFFICER   *(To Swing.)* As soon as we've finished, take him back to supplies and exchange his uniform.

SWING   Sir, I've already ordered him to swap with someone. He has till tomorrow to do it.

Chief OFFICER   I said take him back to exchange it.

SWING   Yes, sir!

Chief OFFICER   Otherwise, tomorrow the foreign radio stations will broadcast that we're taking away his human dignity. Isn't that so, Vanĕk?

VANĔK   I can easily trade with someone. It's no trouble.

Chief OFFICER   You heard me. *(To Brewmaster.)* Where did we assign him to?

BREWMASTER   *(Obligingly.)* Sir, I believe we need a convict for the laundry.

Chief OFFICER   Watch it, Brewmaster, or you might end up in the laundry

	yourself. *(Sharply.)* Nothing like that! He'll be put in a production job with quotas to meet. *(To Vaněk.)* What can you do? Besides your perversive activities, I mean.
VANĚK	*(Stubbornly.)* I've never perverted anything. Besides, I was only convicted of subversive activities.
Chief OFFICER	*(Contemptuously.)* We won't argue about it, Vaněk. And we most certainly won't discuss semantics. *(To Brewmaster.)* So what, Brewmaster? Should we give him the choice?
BREWMASTER	*(Obligingly.)* I'll take him to the workshop first thing in the morning.
Chief OFFICER	But it'll be a production-line job, you hear? Working in one spot. No service duties, no running around with a tool-box. *(To Vaněk, with a sneer.)* You'd only be carrying around petitions anyway, right? What do you think, Brewmaster?
BREWMASTER	*(Laughs politely.)*
Chief OFFICER	*(To Vaněk.)* You'll tell no one here about your activities. If I find out anything, you get thirty days in solitary. I won't tolerate any continuation of your criminal activities. The same applies to thieves who teach fellow convicts how to crack dead bolts. Is that clear?
VANĚK	*(With difficulty.)* Yes, but—I beg your—
Chief OFFICER	I said, no begging here. Here you obey the rules. Institution rules apply to you as well as to me. Your job's to listen: mine is to educate.
VANĚK	As you know, prisoners are inquisitive. It would be difficult to—
Chief OFFICER	I'm not even going to try to re-educate you, Vaněk. That would be a waste of time. You'd obey only until your time's up. Provided you survive that long—with your health. What do you want?
VANĚK	It would be difficult not to tell the others the reason for my being here. Even a casual—
Chief OFFICER	All you will do is give them the number of the paragraph and read from your sentencing that you were found guilty of subversive intentions against the Republic because you are an enemy of our social and state system. Is that clear?
VANĚK	How inconceivable—
Chief OFFICER	Who's Kathy?
VANĚK	*(Hesitates.)*
Chief OFFICER	You got postcards from some Kathy even before you arrived here.
VANĚK	A friend.
Chief OFFICER	You will write to her that she's not to send anything else. Because you wouldn't get it anyway. Even better, you'll pass a message to her. Write home and say that nobody is allowed to

	write except your immediate family.
VANĚK	*(Shyly.)* Excuse me, but I couldn't possibly—
Chief OFFICER	What couldn't you possibly?
VANĚK	I couldn't possibly forbid people who weren't convicted of anything to write to whomever they please.
Chief OFFICER	You will forbid nothing. You'll just let them know that I forbid it. I'm sure they'll understand and won't want to cause any problems for you. *(He looks at his watch. To Swing.)* Make sure Vaněk gets his dinner.
SWING	*(Rocking from side to side.)* Yes, sir!
Chief OFFICER	I don't want to catch you making any notes here either. It would make you a millionaire when you get out, wouldn't it, Vaněk? This isn't a writer's colony. *(To Brewmaster.)* What do you say?
BREWMASTER	*(Obligingly.)* I'm not allowed to brew beer here either.
Chief OFFICER	*(Laughs. Then, sarcastically.)* Brewmaster, bread and rice was being fermented in the workshop again. If I find out that you had a hand in it, you'll have every reason to be sorry.
BREWMASTER	*(Alarmed.)* Colonel, sir, really—you have to believe me, I know absolutely nothing about it.
Chief OFFICER	Don't b.s. me, Brewmaster. Unless someone has a grudge against you—
BREWMASTER	Yes, sir, I beg your—
Chief OFFICER	Begging?! Has Vaněk infected you already?
BREWMASTER	Oh no, sir, certainly not. *(He is completely terrified.)*
Chief OFFICER	That would be a fast beginning. *(He looks over his shoulder at Swing and Biftek. Then to Vaněk.)* You are forbidden to discuss your criminal activities not only with other prisoners but also with guards. Is that clear? It would be in your best interest to keep quiet as much as possible.
VANĚK	*(Cheekily.)* Perhaps it would enhance my isolation if I were to spend my free time after work in some secluded spot, reading perhaps, or writing a play.
Chief OFFICER	What?
VANĚK	It wouldn't be anything about prison, nothing political, nothing which could offend anybody.
Chief OFFICER	*(Gradually getting more and more agitated.)* You mean, something about nothing? Vaněk, stop making an ass of me! You, an internationally acclaimed writer, writing about nothing? You wouldn't even know how. All you know how to write is malicious slander. *(Shouting.)* You political sons of bitches!
VANĚK	*(Straightening up.)* I beg your pardon.
Chief OFFICER	*(Trying to compose himself.)* You know what I mean. Slippery as a snake. You don't know how to accept your guilt like a man. Yes, I made a mistake, I accept my punishment, and I

	will reform myself.
VANĚK	I can't admit to a guilt I don't feel.
Chief OFFICER	*(Shouting.)* Anybody who refuses to think our way is a criminal! Under martial law I'd have you shot! *(Trying to calm down.)* Well, we don't have martial law just yet. But you better count on not being able to move a finger without me knowing about it. *(He exits in a hurry.)*
SWING	*(To Vaněk.)* Report to me in the dining room.
VANĚK	I can skip the gruel.
SWING	You heard the chief. *(He exits.)*
BIFTEK	And the game is over by now, and we don't know the score. *(He storms out, slamming the door behind him.)* *(Brewmaster slowly sits down. Vaněk remains standing, leaning on a chair.)*
BREWMASTER	Now you've seen what swine they are. Goddamn cocksuckers!
VANĚK	Better be quiet. It could be bugged.
BREWMASTER	Slimy rats! You teach them how to ferment bread and rice to get a drink one can get stiff on, and the buggers snitch on you.
VANĚK	Maybe it was an accidental discovery. By a guard.
BREWMASTER	I'm sure those wankers let Peggy have a drink.
VANĚK	I beg your pardon?
BREWMASTER	Stop begging.
VANĚK	Sorry.
BREWMASTER	I'm dead sure they let him have a drink. Don't you see? They want to ruin my parole! *(In despair.)* Tell me! There's going to be an amnesty, right? A three-year-general. Or whatever. We have signed the Hague agreement!
VANĚK	That's nonsense!
BREWMASTER	*(Tortured.)* Good news never makes sense.
VANĚK	*(Hesitantly.)* You can only rely on yourself. If you really believe that it might help you, then let's try and trick them somehow.
BREWMASTER	How could it help me? With you all one gets is trouble.
VANĚK	I'll write the Liberation skit for you.
BREWMASTER	Wake up, man! Didn't you hear? Just try and look at a pencil, and they'll be on top of you like a ton of bricks. Even if it's a completely clean letter home, some screw'll pick it to pieces.
VANĚK	I could do it in the can.
BREWMASTER	Sure! And they'll search your stuff and you get thirty.
VANĚK	That would be my problem.
BREWMASTER	*(Plaintively.)* As soon as they see it's a skit for Liberation Day, they'll know you wrote it for someone else. And anyhow, you're not allowed to write.
VANĚK	They'll have to prove it was for you.
BREWMASTER	They don't have to prove nothin'. They'll just figure on other

possibilities, and the result'll be more cons gettin' fucked around. When I come up for parole, no one'll mention that you wrote a skit for me. They'll just turn it down on account of seriousness of crime. Or because I didn't make enough points. They could also hit me with a fast disciplinary action. *(Pause.)* Looks like I'll even have to make up that poem myself. Now tell me. What the hell do I put in the reports about you?!

VANĚK   I'm sure you can get out of that somehow. For example, you could say that I suspect you of being an informer. That I'm being polite but only talk business. Or maybe a bit about our common experiences in the brewery.

BREWMASTER   *(Desperate.)* Only you can afford not to understand!
(Bavarian enters. He looks at the two with interest and puts the box of letters on the desk.)

BAVARIAN   *(Chuckling.)* You two wouldn't be here if you hadn't pulled some job. *(A gesture of dismissal in Brewmaster's direction.)* Nothing you can do about this notorious crook. *(To Vaněk.)* But you guys, you're aces. Public protests! And what good does it do you? You stick out like a sore thumb. No problem either locking you up or exporting you like raw lumber. *(Pause.)* Besides, I don't get it. I'd be out of the country in a minute flat. Over there it's different business. Not like this chickenshit here where you get charged with illegal enterprise. *(He grabs some papers.)* We are the public. There are millions of us. By the time you get around to changing anything, there'll be nothing left to change. Because we'll already have stolen it. *(He walks toward the door and stops.)* Christ, I'll survive the three months until amnesty. I'll survive somehow. They've got to give it. Bet you a carton of smokes they will. *(He exits.)*
(A short pause.)

VANĚK   You really want to do the reports?

BREWMASTER   *(Dejectedly.)* You've got to understand! I do want to contribute to our common struggle. Do I have any other choice? Parole is parole.

VANĚK   Once you start collaborating with them, there's no escape. The cage is locked. That's the worst life sentence you can get. And you passed that sentence yourself. Time after time you'll be reminded of it. Always and everywhere. It is an action which violates all moral values.

BREWMASTER   I couldn't even give you the laundry job. A stupid hot and wet job! Couldn't give you the opportunity to keep in training a bit with your writing. Not even with stupid skits and poems. And you'd still stick up for me—instead of looking out for number one.

VANĚK   After all, it wouldn't hurt me. I don't think it's against the law to make reports about oneself. I wouldn't have to feel obliged to anybody. And I could tailor the information to suit my own intentions. Even in these rather unusual circumstances. But could we really do it?

BREWMASTER   I'll get you a brand-new shirt! I'll get you a gopher! I'll smuggle in some real money for you!

VANĚK   I think you'll give me a heart attack. Does everybody have to come out of here a worse man than he went in?

BREWMASTER   Well, what do you think? People are the worst punishment. Everywhere. It's the same here as on the outside.

VANĚK   I don't think so. A large jail is better than a small one. At least on the outside you have some opportunities.

BREWMASTER   Sure, like in the brewery. You have the opportunity to drink beer.

VANĚK   You can make love.

BREWMASTER   Vaněk, if they ever find out that you dictated the reports, it'll be the end of me.

VANĚK   No need for them to find out. You'll have to anticipate any suspicions they might have. You could tell them that I was too intelligent and almost discovered the truth. So you pretended to collaborate with me in order to gain my trust. That way you can get much more out of me.

BREWMASTER   I could also say that you seem to be losing your reluctance to co-operate with the police.

VANĚK   Crap! Here you've got to take your destiny into your own hands in a manner entirely different from the way you do outside.

BREWMASTER   We really will fool them! And I'll be able to say to myself: "Brewmaster, you've finally joined our common march. You've got rid of at least a bit of your selfishness. Now you can feel proud to look at your muzzle in the mirror because the stupid slogan: 'When man gains something it has a proud ring'— that's you!"

VANĚK   *(Angrily.)* It's bloody well time you got out of this cage!

BREWMASTER   Tell me that she'll wait for me.

VANĚK   Didn't you get her that job in the bottling plant?

BREWMASTER   But anyway, you quit! Sure, you're the one with newspaper articles about you. But there's also the disadvantages. You can't join the inmates' committee. No parole. Always given special treatment. *(He looks toward the window and crosses to it, interested.)* See? A full moon. That's poetry, right? A full moon behind bars.

(Vaněk grabs Brewmaster and pushes him back into the chair

at his desk. He sets the typewriter at an angle but in such a position that it would be possible for Brewmaster to start typing, if necessary. He finds some clean sheets of paper and puts them in front of Brewmaster. Then he shoves a pencil into his hand.)

VANĚK   *(Pointing to the typewriter.)* If someone comes in, you'll continue with my mother's maiden name.
(Brewmaster stares at Vaněk and then begins frantically writing what Vaněk dictates. During the following, the stage lights gradually go down, and the house lights gradually come up. Vaněk dictates fast and in an official manner.)

VANĚK   The subject under surveillance entered the reception office at 16:45. He officially introduced himself to the informant because he did not recognize the latter. After being appropriately instructed, he recognized the informant to be his former superior, dash, Brewmaster, from their common past place of employment, dash, brewery. In the course of further conversation the informant offered to use the less formal first names, the intention on the part of the informant being to induce a more casual atmosphere which would lead the subject to abandon his reticence. The subject accepted the offer. The emphasis on informal interaction was further stressed by the informant's remarks about their past common interests, among them the well-known actress Bohdalová, beer, the barrels the subject used to manoeuvre at his former place of employment, the convict Sherkezy Lajos, bracket, currently serving a sentence in this institution, bracket, who is of gypsy extraction and with whom, it should be pointed out, both the subject and the informant worked in one gang at their former place of employment, dash, the brewery, full stop. The positive shift in the subject's mood was reinforced by the provision of refreshments, dash, a cup of coffee, dash, which, according to his own confession, had been missed by the subject to a much greater extent than the company of females.
(During the following, Vaněk's voice gradually tapers off.)
The reception interview continued with instruction for the subject in his various responsibilities as determined by the institutional rules and regulations as said rules pertain to the appropriate rehabilitation process, for example, the proper style of making one's bed and keeping one's personal effects in the required order, the appropriate work discipline and effort—

THE END

Prague 1983

NOTES

1. The Brewmaster is referring to a request he made when he was Vaněk's superior in *Audience*. See also note 2 to *Audience*.
2. See note 1 to *Audience*.
3. Dr. Zdeněk Neubauer (born 1942) is a Czech natural scientist and philosopher. Apart from about 50 papers in microbiology, he has published philosophical essays in *samizdat* editions; for example, *Being and Subjectivity: Ricoeur's Essays* (1986).
4. See note 4 to *Audience*.
5. *The Strakonice Piper* is a play by Josef Kajetán Tyl (1808-1856).
6. See note 3 to *Audience*.
7. Karel Havlíček Borovský (1821-56), a Czech author and journalist who reacted against the linguistic excessess of Romanticism, gave the Czech language its modern character. He wrote numerous poems, epigrams, and articles against the ruling House of Habsburg and was tried and banished to Brixen (now Italy) from 1851 to 1855.

PAVEL KOHOUT

Safari

the last (?)* one-act play about the life
of the writer Ferdinand Vaněk

Translated from the German[1] by Anna Mozga

* Editor's interrogation mark

CHARACTERS

Moderator
Actress
Journalist
Playwright
Critic
Poet
Ferdinand Vaněk

An Assistant
A Waiter
possibly: Cameramen

PLACE

A Television Studio, Vienna

(*Darkness. Signature tune of a television programme. Over the sound system a very "moderating" female voice.*)

MODERATOR A very pleasant good evening to all our viewers and welcome to today's edition of "Dead Centre," the television journal in which you will again encounter people and issues currently—as the title of our programme suggests—dead in the centre of attention, at least for all those who claim to be culture fans. We are happy to have with us today a very distinguished panel—our regular viewers will be familiar with their faces and for newcomers we will, as usual, superimpose the names of the participants—and for this we owe thanks to our no less distinguished guest, who during these past few days has created a considerable stir worldwide: the famous writer and dissident from Prague—Ferdinand Vanick.

(*Feeble applause as the lights go up. A television studio, furnished as is usual for programmes of this kind. Two armchairs and two sofas, all covered in finest light-brown leather. Spotlights, always focusing on the person speaking. In semidarkness, cameras mounted on dollies—if possible, real ones— and manned by operators. In this case, the images just "transmitted" can even be shown on TV screens in the auditorium. Everything is spoken over the sound system.—On the long glass table, microphones, glasses of soda water and wine, and various snacks. From time to time a Waiter appears noiselessly, takes an order uttered sotto voce and brings coffee or refills the glasses. Also from time to time a fullbosomed Assistant enters with white slips of paper for the Moderator. Then the eyes of all the men present, including Vaněk, follow her breasts there and back—either consciously or involuntarily. Sitting around the table: The Moderator— apparently more concerned with a thousand things going on back stage than with the conversation itself. She is continually looking toward where we assume the director to be, her lips and fingers giving various signals. The Poet she observes with a mixture of love and hate. Whenever Vaněk begins to speak, she nervously checks her watch. The Actress—dressed casually, in rags almost; but they are rags from an expensive boutique. Whenever the others are on camera, she discreetly checks her appearance in a small mirror she takes from an oversized shoulder bag and applies lipstick. The Journalist— skinny, conservatively dressed, chain-smoking, and drinking coffee almost non-stop. The Playwright—corpulent, sporting badly wrinkled overalls and incessantly munching peanuts. When the dish in front of him is empty, he helps himself from*) *the bowls intended for the others. The Critic—in a black silk suit one size too small for his robust frame—perhaps intentionally so. He is correcting galley-proofs. The Poet—wearing jeans and a tight sweater. He yawns often and even dozes off. Two or three times the Assistant whispers in his ear while he stares down her plummeting neckline. Then he writes a brief reply and winks at the camera, as if conveying a message to someone. Ferdinand Vaněk—dressed inconspicuously. His manner indicates shyness. He tries to concentrate but is always distracted somehow. Now he acknowledges the applause by getting up and taking a bow, obviously embarrassed.)*

MODERATOR   Mr. Vanick, for many years, your name has—do please keep your seat, Mr. Vanick.

VANĚK   Yes— *(He sits down.)*

MODERATOR   For many years, Mr. Vanick, your name has been a household word to many of us, a synonym—if I may say so—for courage, morality, identity, integrity, and other character traits few in East and West alike can boast of nowadays. Already having gained worldwide recognition for your early plays, you rose to even greater fame as one of the—if I may say so—spokespersons of the so-called Prague Spring. For over fifteen years you have been among those intellectuals who have refused to come to an arrangement with the new regime, something you have had to pay for repeatedly; publication of your work was banned, and you yourself were degraded to the status of—if I may say so—an un-person. This kind of pressure was intended to drive the troublemakers into emigration. When the plan turned out to be an utter failure, people like you and Vaklaf Havell were imprisoned for several years; others, like Pavel Cohoot and Pavel Landowski were driven into exile by force. Your fate, Mr. Vanick, is perhaps the most spectacular of all. One week ago you went to sleep in your Prague apartment as you would on any normal evening—so you claim—and woke up in a sleeping bag in our Danuvian marshes which are at present occupied by conservationists wanting to put a halt to government plans for a hydro-electric power station in the area.[2] Our viewers will be familiar with the problem.—Almost instantly the Czechoslovak Press Agency issued a statement that you had voluntarily and with the assistance of imperialist agents fled the Republic—probably in a diplomatic courier-case—and that you have therefore been summarily sentenced to another three years' imprisonment for defection. This term will have to be served even in the event of your voluntary return, a price—if I may say so—no normal person would be willing to

	pay. Have I explained this correctly, Mr. Vanick?
VANĚK	*(Embarrassed.)* Well—
MODERATOR	Well, as correctly as it can be explained in a few words, of course. Anyway, it was sufficient to get you invited into this distinguished circle of colleagues from the West—who agree with me that the experiences we are eager to hear about—in human terms as well—are among the most important we have to and wish to confront these days. You are—quite literally—in the centre. It's a great pleasure to have you with us.
	(All applaud briefly. Again Vaněk gets up and takes a bow, obviously embarrassed.)
MODERATOR	In the name of those present as well as in the name—do please keep your seat, Mr. Vanick.
VANĚK	Yes— *(He sits down.)*
MODERATOR	I am sure I also speak in the name of our viewers if I now ask you to summarize these experiences from the East and contrast them with your first impressions of the West. That will give us—if I may say so—a good lead into our controversial topic. Please, Mr. Vanick.
VANĚK	Yes— *(He gets up.)*
MODERATOR	*(Has just received a slip of paper from the Assistant and nods at someone.)* Oh, excuse the interruption, the phone numbers we have just projected on your screens are to give you, dear viewers, the opportunity to direct questions at our guest for yourselves. Don't miss this unique chance to conduct your own interview with one of the most important witnesses of our time. Please, Mr. Vanick.
VANĚK	I—
MODERATOR	Do please keep your seat, Mr. Vanick.
VANĚK	Yes— *(He sits down and absent-mindedly bows again but then collects himself and begins in earnest.)* I—
ACTRESS	Pardon me if I'm interrupting, but I mean— *(To the others.)* I may not be a— I'm just an— but still, I mean we shouldn't—in such an impersonal—It isn't just a matter of—We're not faced with a—I see my— *(To Vaněk.)* I just want to cry! *(All laugh.)*
ACTRESS	Why are you laughing? Did I say anything—? After all, I'm not a— *(To Vaněk.)* I'm an actress, you know.
VANĚK	I know—
ACTRESS	*(Pleased.)* Ah—you know. Then you know that it's not my job—the actor needn't necessarily—you can't expect me—in a word: I'm not a writer, you know.
VANĚK	I know—
ACTRESS	Yes, you know. Then you probably also know that I unfor-

217

	tunately—I never had the opportunity—the good luck, that is, to play—but you know, there are so many plays!
VANĚK	I know.
ACTRESS	I mean, unfortunately. Unfortunately, there are so many. I mean—the bad ones. There are so few plays which directly— even as an actor one is, above all, a citizen—You see what I mean?
VANĚK	*(Nods.)*
ACTRESS	All I'm trying to say is that even though I've never had the good luck—the opportunity, that is, to play—but when this thing happened in '67—this—misunderstanding with the Russians—
JOURNALIST	If you mean the Russian occupation of Czechoslovakia, as I presume you do, that was in '68.
PLAYWRIGHT	More of these catchwords from your anti-communist head- line bin!—as if Western Europe wasn't occupied by the Yankees.
ACTRESS	My opinion exactly, but I want to tell—we were playing *Hamlet* that evening. I was Ophelia, that's the—you know—
VANĚK	I know—
ACTRESS	I know. Mex, my ex-husband, was Hamlet—you probably know him too?
VANĚK	*(Shakes his head, embarrassed.)* No—
CRITIC	You haven't missed much.
ACTRESS	Pardon?! Well, the production may have had its flaws, Mr. Grumpo, but it survived—I'm trying to say—people remem- ber it to this day, which is more than can be said of your malicious review.
CRITIC	It is alive and well in you, as we've just seen.
MODERATOR	Mr. Grumpo—I think—Lydia—I think—perhaps we shouldn't bother Mr. Vanick with problems not directly related to today's—
ACTRESS	But I want to relate to today, Lola, if I might only finish! Well, where was I?
PLAYWRIGHT	You were playing Ophelia.
ACTRESS	Yes. *(To Vaněk.)* Believe me, we'd rather not have played at all that evening, or else a play which—our feelings—but, as I said before, we had to play—and then Mex had the great— well, just imagine—you know *Hamlet*?
VANĚK	Yes—
ACTRESS	Yes. Well, he kills my father, drives me mad, accuses his uncle, insults his mother, fights, drinks poison, zap, over. Then the scene with Fortinbras, and four captains are sup- posed to—you know, the corpse.
VANĚK	I know—

ACTRESS	Yes. And now—imagine that!—this evening in July when the news comes from Prague.
JOURNALIST	If you're still talking about the same misunderstanding, that was in August.
ACTRESS	Well, what's the difference? Anyway, it was summer. That I remember exactly. My son, the older one, was staying with me at the time. I was preparing him for the entrance exam, he's a long-established actor now, my son, you know. I'm older than I look.
VANĚK	I know—
ACTRESS	Oh, you know—??? How did you—?
VANĚK	That is—no—
ACTRESS	Oh, I see—he found it colossally difficult to assert himself against four parents, you see what I mean?
VANĚK	Yes—that is—no.
ACTRESS	All right—Tex, his father, you see, well, he married another colleague, and I married another colleague, Mex, you see. It was really colossally difficult for Matthias, but now even Mr. Grumpo writes well of him—even though really he hates all actors.
	(All laugh, including the Critic; the Poet just grins.)
PLAYWRIGHT	Not all. Some of them he even loves, right?
	(The laughter stops. A few seconds later the Poet laughs out loud. All look at him, the Critic offended.)
MODERATOR	*(Reproachfully to the Poet.)* Dickie—I think—Mr. Forniker—I think—perhaps we shouldn't burden Mr. Vanick with things which have no bearing on today's—
	(She doesn't need to continue, since the Poet is occupied with a slip of paper the Assistant has just brought him. When he is finished with it, he winks at the camera, while the Moderator looks on jealously. The Actress takes a cigarette from her cigarette case. The Journalist wants to light it for her, but she ostentatiously beckons the Waiter over. Then she smokes, looking relaxed. Everyone else is looking at her.)
MODERATOR	It was your turn, Lydia—
ACTRESS	Mine? What was I—? Oh yes, of course! About Matthias.
PLAYWRIGHT	You were playing Ophelia.
ACTRESS	Oh God, I'm completely— *(To Vaněk.)* See, that's why people have to write for us, without a text we are totally—I mean, without us, texts would also be totally—you probably know that too.
VANĚK	I—yes—
ACTRESS	Well, that evening, I'll never forget it, in the intermission Mex said, "Listen folks, we can't keep mum about this, not even in *Hamlet*."

JOURNALIST	About what?
ACTRESS	About this occupation, of course!
JOURNALIST	It wasn't yet a misunderstanding then?
ACTRESS	Then—well, we didn't know anything.
JOURNALIST	What didn't you know?
PLAYWRIGHT	That a counterrevolution was prevented there. Sorry, Mr. Vejnek probably sees it differently, but from this perspective, today's, tomorrow's—
JOURNALIST	From that same perspective, doesn't one have to agree with the occupation of Western Europe?
PLAYWRIGHT	They're here to prevent a revolution!
MODERATOR	*(To the Journalist.)* Mr. Blumann—I think—*(To the Playwright.)* Mr. Rednek—I think perhaps we shouldn't confront Mr. Vanick with problems which are entirely unconnected to today's—Go ahead, Lydia.
ACTRESS	Oh yes—where was I?
MODERATOR	You were playing Ophelia.
ACTRESS	Yes, well, and in the intermission Mex had this wild idea—he sent his assistant to the radio station, but they didn't have the record. We were already playing again—and nothing. And, well, then Mex had an even wilder—between two monologues he—now just imagine that!
CRITIC	It's impossible even to imagine that!—
ACTRESS	Pardon?
MODERATOR	He what between two monologues?
ACTRESS	Sent the fellow to the sport-stadium, to the caretaker. And there they had it! No, that's something I'll never forget! *(She smokes, lost in memory.)*
JOURNALIST	What is?
ACTRESS	Pardon?
JOURNALIST	You still haven't told us what this was all about.
ACTRESS	This occupation, naturally—this misunderstanding.
JOURNALIST	What kind of record was that?
ACTRESS	Oh God, didn't I—? The anthem! The Bohemian national anthem. Mex was buried as Hamlet to the strains of the Bohemian anthem. *(To Vaněk.)* The audience was flabbergasted!
CRITIC	How did the audience know the Czech anthem?
ACTRESS	Perhaps they didn't know it at first, but then they just recognized it.
CRITIC	How was that?
ACTRESS	How—how?? Because the audience isn't stupid, certainly not as stupid as you always think it is. *(To Vaněk.)* Are the critics in your country as utterly convinced that all of us, the audience, the writers, even the actors—who, in the last analysis, only

say what someone else tells them to—that we're all totally demented? Is what they write about you over there just as slanderous?

JOURNALIST   Madam, you seem to forget that in Czechoslovakia they haven't written about Mr. Vanyek at all since that evening.

ACTRESS   *(To Vaněk.)* Well, for that I envy you from the bottom of my heart.

JOURNALIST   About the author Vanyek, that is. About the citizen Vanyek they certainly do. A lackey of imperialism is probably the nicest term they use.

ACTRESS   I hope you didn't put up with that. Here, if anyone has the gall to say something like that about me, I sue and that's that. Only with our freedom it's the same as with yours. Even when, for example, some critic corroborates your total lack of talent, you still can't sue him, no matter what.

MODERATOR   Lydia, I think perhaps we should—

ACTRESS   By all means, Lola, we should be united in our resistance. That's why I was so thrilled *(To Vaněk.)* when you fled, that you protested against our system at the same time.

VANĚK   But—

PLAYWRIGHT   I was pleasantly surprised as well. You know, we were really getting concerned that the so-called dissidents are gravitating more and more to topics which deflect attention from the real problems of this century, whether it's the nuclear threat or the misery in the Third World. Compared to that our problems are peanuts.

ACTRESS   My opinion exactly. I mean, we understand your problems too, that thing with the anthem—I mean—it just goes to show. That's why I'm so happy that with your fleeing to the occupied marshes on the Danube, you condemned our establishment so un—so clearly and expressed your support for the alternative ideals.

VANĚK   But—

JOURNALIST   That's a bunch of baloney! Forgive me, Ms. Greiner, I admire you as an actress, but as a citizen you scare me!

CRITIC   With me it's almost the other way round.

ACTRESS   *(To the Journalist.)* Which—coming from you—I can only be proud of.

JOURNALIST   Oh spare us this tough-talk you've been spouting in public ever since you climbed on the progressive bandwagon; deep down inside you must be happy that, as a rule, our entertainment editor speaks more highly of you than your confederate Mr. Grumpo does.

ACTRESS   Surely you've noticed that I won't let you even light a cigarette for me.

JOURNALIST	Provided there's a waiter on hand.
ACTRESS	If you were the only person in the world, I'd rather stop smoking.
JOURNALIST	Still better than if Mr. Grumpo were the only one; then, I suppose, you'd have to stop acting.
ACTRESS	I'd rather be slammed by Mr. Grumpo than praised by your stink-reactionary paper!
MODERATOR	Lydia—I think—Mr. Blumann—I think—
JOURNALIST	All right, everybody has to decide for himself whether he wants to be a necrophiliac or a flagellant. My business, Ms. Greiner, is to enlighten you to the fact that a man with Mr. Vanyek's personal history and experience can hardly fail to find you and the likes of you ridiculous.*(To Vaněk.)* Isn't that so?
VANĚK	Well—
JOURNALIST	More than ridiculous—dangerous, yes, dangerous! Because he has experienced socialism not the way girls from bourgeois, well-to-do families dream about it but as it really is—brutal, inhuman, bloody, simply murderous. *(To Vaněk.)* Isn't that so?
VANĚK	But—
JOURNALIST	But, above all, that's what I was just going to say, Mr. Vanyek has had a taste of red power and knows what it does to people when all of a sudden there's no camera, no waiter, but only naked force.
PLAYWRIGHT	Naked force can also be nice, right? *(He laughs out loud.)*
JOURNALIST	That a Vanyek flees into the marshes—now if that isn't a pointed message, a dramatic warning, a last appeal to all those as naive as you! The flight of a man this strong ought to make you wonder—assuming you ever do manage to create similar conditions here—whether you wouldn't be the first to flee your country.
ACTRESS	You mean—I?? Very funny! *(She laughs.)* Then I'd find the right words to rouse the masses from up there on the stage— whether someone writes them for me or not!
JOURNALIST	The ones who tried that in Mr. Vanyek's country were all very quickly fired from the stage.
ACTRESS	Then I'll perform in the basement theatres. I'm sure my audience would come with me.
JOURNALIST	There, there's nothing but state theatres—down into the basements. Once you're fired, it's curtains everywhere—the end—adieu.
ACTRESS	Then I'll just act at home, in front of the video camera.
JOURNALIST	Some actress in Prague has already tried that. The police simply evicted everyone from the apartment.

PLAYWRIGHT	More of these old wives' tales!
JOURNALIST	More of these old wives! Is this Snow White sitting in front of you or Ferdinand Vanyek, one of the most important playwrights of our time who—in contrast to the fabricators of artificial problems—writes what he lives and lives what he writes? And after fifteen years of resistance still had to flee? *(To Vaněk.)* Isn't that so?
VANĚK	I didn't—
JOURNALIST	Flee, of course not. My apologies. No one understands better than I that you have to throw a smokescreen over your flight so you don't endanger those who helped with the getaway. If I have to have any dealings over there, it's certainly not to be corrupted by their state cultural organizations but in the name of truth be expelled as quickly as possible—so I can sleep quietly.
PLAYWRIGHT	Are you referring to me?
JOURNALIST	Why are you inferring that I'm referring to you?
PLAYWRIGHT	Because, as everybody knows, I associate with the state organizations you disapprove of.
JOURNALIST	Then why do you ask?
PLAYWRIGHT	Because you were talking about corruption. And that I won't stand for!
JOURNALIST	Why should you? I didn't mention your name.
PLAYWRIGHT	But you meant me! You think I'm a village idiot?! And I know you only too well! *(To Vaněk.)* What this gentleman calls the truth he reports so courageously, that's the proclaimed opinion of the paper's owner you've got to sign together with the paycheque there. Yes, I openly declare that I cultivate and intend to maintain official contacts, and I'm sure if anyone understands and approves of it, it's Mr. Vejnek here. *(To Vaněk.)* I only hope that the years of persecution—the discrepancies between you and the actually existing socialism, that is, haven't embittered you to the point where you too have become a slave of prefabricated opinions, or am I wrong?
VANĚK	I—
PLAYWRIGHT	Me neither. I'm especially certain a man like you understands best that his personal fate, however harsh, must not serve to decelerate, let alone impede the attempts to reconcile the divided world. Or would you deny your colleagues from the state cultural organizations any legitimate right to discuss art and peace with us?
VANĚK	No, but—
PLAYWRIGHT	But that's precisely what prompted many of us to seek contact with the others time after time, notwithstanding the loss

223

	of time, the insults from reactionaries like Mr. Blumann here, but also, unfortunately, the difficulties with people *(To Vaněk.)* like you. And we can look back on genuine accomplishments.
JOURNALIST	For example?
PLAYWRIGHT	For example—something you won't believe—that wherever we go, whether it's Sofia or Moscow, we get such red-carpet treatment it makes one feel like an MP or a minister or goodness knows what—
JOURNALIST	Like Alice in Wonderland.
PLAYWRIGHT	Being, in your own words, intent only on increasing your market value by provoking an expulsion, you may of course find it next to impossible to understand that we are accepted as the true representatives of our people there, because they realize that although we've no questionable political power, we still exert an enormous moral influence.
JOURNALIST	What have you used it for until now?
PLAYWRIGHT	For changing our image from that of a nation of cold-warmongers—despite the likes of you.
JOURNALIST	And beyond that?
PLAYWRIGHT	We think that's the most important thing, because it also unwinds the spiral of eastern armament.
JOURNALIST	And apart from these phenomenal accomplishments in halting the armament race? Has either Mr. Vanyek or Mr. Havel been released from prison one single day earlier as a result of your influence? That time in Sofia you were sitting at one table with the Czech delegation.
PLAYWRIGHT	Only that was about literature, not politics. The other side also refrained from making political accusations so as not to poison the atmosphere. And that's exactly why in the end we were able to push through a resolution that was quite political.
JOURNALIST	And contained the usual blah, as we know.
PLAYWRIGHT	To you peace is all blah, since it doesn't sell as well as war.
JOURNALIST	You and Ms. Greiner are proof that it is indeed possible to live off peace.
ACTRESS	Impertinence!
JOURNALIST	That's what I think. And as far as dispensing with political accusations goes—the suggestion so magnanimously accepted by the other side—who in the West could they have accused of gagging and even incarcerating writers?
ACTRESS	And Nicaragua? What about Nicaragua??
JOURNALIST	That's right.
ACTRESS	You see!
JOURNALIST	There they are thrown into jail by a leftist government.
ACTRESS	What did I say—

PLAYWRIGHT	You said Nicaragua!
ACTRESS	I mean I meant Chile.
PLAYWRIGHT	Or South Africa.
JOURNALIST	There Breytenbach[3] wrote a fat book in solitary confinement. Were you allowed to write in prison, Mr. Vanyek?
VANĚK	No—
JOURNALIST	Exactly. And your flight proves that you have lost all hope of being able to write at all over there, or am I mistaken?
VANĚK	I didn't—
JOURNALIST	Flee, obviously not. Sorry. No one understands better than I that you have to call the flight an abduction to throw the bloodhounds off the scent. But, regardless of the manner in which Mr. Vanyek arrived here, his flight is akin to a siren that must not go unheard.
PLAYWRIGHT	Selling this kind of statement is what you're so highly paid for, that the so-called dissidents are of special importance—I trust Mr. Vejnek won't take it personally—But in the Soviet Union they welcomed us like old friends at the Writers' Association—the amount of caviar alone I saw on the table there! I've never seen anything like it even in our gourmet delicatessens—this simply goes to document how important we seemed to them—all the same, we often sat together until dawn and talked openly, without protocol and napkins, man-to-man.
JOURNALIST	You speak Russian?
PLAYWRIGHT	Me? Of course not. Are you trying to expose me as an agent?
JOURNALIST	I'm just thinking that there must have been interpreters then.
PLAYWRIGHT	Yes, of course, everything was taken care of, intelligent people all of them, spoke as well as you and I.
JOURNALIST	So: a man-to-man talk via a middleman.
PLAYWRIGHT	I see, you're trying to say they were intelligence people!
JOURNALIST	Didn't you say so yourself?
PLAYWRIGHT	I said—intelligent people.
JOURNALIST	Can we agree on intelligent intelligence people?
PLAYWRIGHT	This vile trick of luring people into a trap with your puns won't work with me. You think I'm a village idiot?
JOURNALIST	No, you're not.
PLAYWRIGHT	Good, I'm glad you know it.
JOURNALIST	You've already told me once today.
MODERATOR	Mr. Rednek—I think—Mr. Blumann, I think we shouldn't throw Mr. Vanick—
JOURNALIST	All right, we're just having a conversation, and Mr. Vanyek can learn a few things from it. Well, Mr. Rednek, you were talking man-to-man, what exactly about?
PLAYWRIGHT	I asked them quite frankly what the situation was with these

	so-called dissidents.
JOURNALIST	And they answered quite frankly?
PLAYWRIGHT	Of course—and this will surprise you: they admitted that they exist.
JOURNALIST	But?
PLAYWRIGHT	But what?
JOURNALIST	I thought there was going to be a "but."
PLAYWRIGHT	There's no "but."
JOURNALIST	You don't say.
PLAYWRIGHT	I do say. So it was all the more convincing when they explained that as writers they are of no significance whatsoever—
JOURNALIST	Oh, yes?
PLAYWRIGHT	Oh, no!
JOURNALIST	And how did they substantiate that?
PLAYWRIGHT	Obvious: nobody reads them.
JOURNALIST	Not because nobody publishes them, by any chance?
PLAYWRIGHT	Nobody publishes them because they are completely isolated.
JOURNALIST	Not by the K.G.B. by any chance?
PLAYWRIGHT	That's already a consequence of their extra-literary activities.
JOURNALIST	Their protests against not being allowed to engage in literary activities, by any chance?
PLAYWRIGHT	They are allowed and they do, but apparently find no echo in society.
JOURNALIST	Why is that?
PLAYWRIGHT	Because they've lost touch.
JOURNALIST	How is that?
PLAYWRIGHT	In contrast to the normal writers, who despite many difficulties continue trying to write about the everyday problems they share with their readers, these so-called dissidents deal with unrealistic dreams and elitist concerns. In a word—they are alienated.
JOURNALIST	Do you also consider Sakharov[4] alienated—because isolated?
PLAYWRIGHT	Come on! If you didn't have him, you'd have to invent him! However, shouldn't we be dealing mainly with Mr. Vejnek?
MODERATOR	I was just going to suggest that and ask those who haven't yet taken their turn. Afterwards you, dear viewers, will have the opportunity to give us your opinions; our telephones *(She points to a pile of white slips of paper the Assistant has been bringing in.)* are ringing off the hook. Mr. Grumpo, how do you—I'm afraid now I have to disturb and at the same time excuse you: Mr. Grumpo is under time pressure and has to proofread the next issue of his magazine which is as feared as it is respected. How then do you, Mr. Grumpo, see the question of this—if I may say so—forbidden literature?
CRITIC	*(He does not look at Vaněk even once while speaking.)* I've

	always been against categorizing it. A literature produced under such aspects and consumed minimally is phenomeno-logically of little relevance.
MODERATOR	Precisely which aspects do you mean?
CRITIC	Well, a) since, resultant from atypical coercion, it is relativ-ized from the beginning.
MODERATOR	Which is to say—?
CRITIC	That, to put it simplistically, it forfeits its archetypal substance. And b) generates from this a fatal divergence between itself and the dialectics of the concrete, i.e., between the author and his respective reality, which he then reflects only agnostically.
ACTRESS	My opinion exactly.
MODERATOR	Lydia—I'm afraid—Mr. Grumpo—I'm afraid—you should be more considerate of your viewers, not all of whom are as clever with foreign words.
ACTRESS	Forgive me. I'm supposed to play Nora[5] shortly, and so I'm naturally also studying Freud; that's why I'm so tuned in to this equestrian language.
JOURNALIST	You mean sequestrian.
ACTRESS	And what did I—
MODERATOR	Equestrian.
JOURNALIST	That has to do with horses.
ACTRESS	Dear me, what a slip of the tongue!
JOURNALIST	A downright Freudian one!
	(All laugh politely; the Poet just grins.)
POET	Equestrian language cause great diturbance.
	(The laughter stops. A few seconds later the Poet laughs out loud.)
MODERATOR	*(Reproachfully to the Poet.)* Dickie—I don't—Mr. Forniker—I don't think you need to demonstrate to Mr. Vanick— *(She doesn't need to continue, since the Poet is occupied with a new slip of paper the Assistant has just brought him. When he is finished with it, he winks at the camera, while the Moderator looks on jealously.)*
MODERATOR	Well, then—it's your turn, Lydia.
ACTRESS	Mine—? Where did I stop? Oh yes, *(To Vaněk.)* I was playing Ophelia, that's the—you know—! And Rex was Hamlet. You can believe me, we'd rather not have played at all that evening.
PLAYWRIGHT	Excuse me, Lydia, but you've already told that story.
ACTRESS	This one I haven't told!
PLAYWRIGHT	Yes you have. With the Czech anthem.
ACTRESS	But no! That was *Hamlet* with Mex, I'm talking about the *Hamlet* with Rex— *(To Vaněk.)* that's my current husband, you know, and naturally he made them play the Polish anthem,

	since that was on the day of the Poland-crisis.
MODERATOR	Lydia—I think—Mr. Grumpo—I think it was actually your turn.
CRITIC	It was, actually.
ACTRESS	*(Hand to mouth.)* I'm so sorry! Of course! You were talking about the—the—
POET	Horses.
ACTRESS	Oh God, a poet might be expected to have a sense for assertations.
PLAYWRIGHT	Personally, I prefer associating.
ACTRESS	What did I—
CRITIC	The dissenting writers, I believe, can't deny that their triggering impulses emanate from the intromission of their daily conflict with power. So far, so good. Only that consequentially it leads to a sort of negocentrism, if you see what I mean.
MODERATOR	I do, but please think of our viewers and—
CRITIC	Pleasure. Negocentrism is what I call an egocentrism which is so negative that it no longer allows the artist affected to analyse reality as a self-consistent textuality. The result—texts of reactionary functionality.
JOURNALIST	Are you trying to portray Mr. Vanyek as a political reactionary—
CRITIC	Certainly not. I'm not talking about individuals but about phenomena, aesthetic phenomena. However, as there is no definable aesthetic *per se*, certain repercussions ensue and, *eo ipso*, the text's performance can also be from politically conservative to reactionary.
JOURNALIST	I knew it!
CRITIC	Which might mean the same in tabloid journalism. But to me it is a plausible reason for granting this subsidiary art a certain licence and the dissidents, seeing as they insist on being taken for literati, at least a partial reprieve—and not necessarily brand them as either politically reactionary, which would aggravate their existence in the East, or as aesthetically entirely insignificant, which might devalue them on the Western art market as well. Only then, one has to apply the law of reciprocity and grant the same licence to the other side.
JOURNALIST	Which one?
CRITIC	The official artists of those regions, obviously. Yes, of course. What did they do, that in the world today dissident art can lay a quasi-exclusive claim to morality and truth? *Audiatur et altera pars. Per interim* this other side has neither, although, seen historically, it is *sub conditione* the carrier of progres-

	sion *pro futuro.*
PLAYWRIGHT	With that I have to agree. Isn't that the greatest absurdity in this whole situation that—Mr. Vejnek won't be offended—because of him and a few of his colleagues, one no longer sees the majority of those who came to some agreement with the system, ultimately a socialist system, so the readers over there wouldn't be left entirely without literature? Since my colleague will hardly maintain that only he and his peers make up Czech literature. Or?
VANĚK	No, certainly—
PLAYWRIGHT	Quite. For that you'd have to be better known over there. I'm far from being an ardent Grumpo-supporter—seeing what grumpy articles he writes about me— *(All laugh.)* but his thesis is something I have to subscribe to. Wherever we talked with the so-called official writers, in Bucharest or in East Berlin, we were always immensely impressed by their fierce support of détente. And even in the frankest and most private conversations—
JOURNALIST	Conducted via the interpreter—
PLAYWRIGHT	In Berlin they happen to speak German, which I'm more or less able to understand without an interpreter.
JOURNALIST	But only more or less. If they serve it with caviar.
PLAYWRIGHT	I won't put up with that!
JOURNALIST	But you told us yourself.
PLAYWRIGHT	It's a question of truth, not caviar.
JOURNALIST	The truth is on the other side, that's what Mr. Grumpo said. Only you can't dig that.
PLAYWRIGHT	Digging into caviar was already a result, not a cause. With people who work for détente I'm prepared to eat even caviar. In America I haven't eaten a single gram of caviar, because I would've had to vomit it right back up again, if only on account of Chile and Nicaragua.
JOURNALIST	No writers' association in America could have offered you caviar—Rockefeller, at best.
PLAYWRIGHT	So there. There's one you'd like to be invited by, only for him you're not a big enough fish.
JOURNALIST	About like you for Mr. Grumpo. Wasn't he the one who wrote, "Too bad they don't put on his aphorisms instead of his plays, since they're immeasurably better and, above all, shorter"?
PLAYWRIGHT	Nevertheless, I prefer Mr. Grumpo to you a thousand times over!
JOURNALIST	Take note, Mr. Vanyek, that's what it's like here. Whereas I see Mr. Rednek and Ms. Greiner as rather talented artists, Mr Grumpo considers them zeros. Even so, Ms. Greiner

likes Mr. Grumpo a hundred times and Mr. Rednek even a thousand times better than me. Isn't it touching how much they enjoy being torn to shreds by him? Or are your protestations of loyalty meant to secure better treatment in his trendsetting magazine for the future?

PLAYWRIGHT This I really don't need!

JOURNALIST You're satisfied with caviar.

PLAYWRIGHT And you just can't stomach that!

JOURNALIST No; you already have. And one really has to admire it for not turning, with all the lies fed into this true representative of our free nation by the true writers of the totalitarian regime. When I wanted to meet with the Jewish dissident Buruschwilli recently, he went underground a full two weeks before, staying with fellow Jews so he'd lose his shadows. And still, two minutes into the interview, they nabbed him right in front of my eyes.

PLAYWRIGHT Not because you put the bloodhounds on the right trail, by any chance?

JOURNALIST Maybe.

PLAYWRIGHT And you say that so calmly?

JOURNALIST Why not. My eye-witness-account of the arrest brought his case to the attention of a hundred times as many people as the interview could ever have. There I have to say *(To Vaněk)* that your secretiveness has always bothered me. You repeatedly refused to give me an interview even over the phone. Some of your colleagues took advantage of such an opportunity to the point of self-destruction—I admired that—in order to convey their message to the world through me.

PLAYWRIGHT Even when that made it their last one for a long time? If I talk to someone over there, it's not to put them behind bars but in the name of peace build bridges of understanding—so I can sleep quietly.

JOURNALIST Do you mean me?

PLAYWRIGHT I mean you know who I mean.

MODERATOR Mr. Blumann, Mr. Rednek, if I may pick up on that note to ask our guest what he has to say on this very controversial subject.

VANĚK I—

MODERATOR *(Has just been handed a slip of paper by the Assistant.)* Sorry to have to interrupt you for a moment, our producer is reminding us that we have not as yet responded to any of the numerous phone calls. Before returning to the topic, I would therefore like to read at least a few of the many questions our viewers have called in for you, Mr. Vanick. Now—Mrs. Sieglinde von Stallenberg-Ehrenberger asks if Prague still has its famous

230

tailors. Before the war she used to go there once a year to order a made-to-measure suit for her husband. The firm was next to the Brown House,[6] and Mrs. von Stallenberg-Ehrenberger would like to know whether your suit is perhaps from the same firm and how much it costs today.

VANĚK No, I—

MODERATOR Let me just read all the questions to you, and you can then give a comprehensive reply. Mr. Gosk from Carinthia would be interested to know if the Scharenhort barracks are still standing. He had the pleasure of sojourning there as an N.C.O. during the war. In the vicinity he recalls a park where throngs of beautiful maidens would gather. He himself frequented the pub "U Fleku"[7] and wonders if it is now being patronized by the Soviet occupation forces. Well, Mr. Vanick?

VANĚK You wanted to—

MODERATOR Oh yes, I wanted a comprehensive—! Well. Jiri Pri-bi-li-cek—a fellow countryman, I presume—who wants to welcome you!—Now Mr. Pri-bi-li-cek thinks—ah yes—right—he thinks you should have left twenty years ago when you were still a writer of agitprop loyal to the regime and not only now that you are not raking it in any more.

VANĚK I never was—

MODERATOR I think you better explain that to your countryman in person; it's too delicate and too specific as well. What, however, seems to interest a wide audience—the question comes up one, two, three, four, five, six, seven, eight, nine, ten times— why has your colleague Mr. Forniker not yet said anything, one of our best-known poets whose collection *The Bisexual Trifon* is currently making headlines? I think before Mr. Vanick begins to answer you should perhaps also ask him a question, Mr. Forniker.

POET *(To Vaněk.)* What's there to ask, right? Everything's crystal-clear, right? You already know with whom you have the dubious honour, right? You think you know what it's like to be unfree? Then you'll now get to experience a free variation on that. A model freedom, right? Freedom par excellence. Freedom from here to doomsday. Freedom as such. A freedom for itself that won't tolerate any other freedom because that would mean un-freedom. A fuck-freedom—to use equestrian language—right? Which I don't mean politically. I'm not a supporter of either Mr. Blumann or Mr. Rednek, who might as well be called Blunek and Redmann, right?

PLAYWRIGHT
JOURNALIST *(Simultaneously.)* I won't stand for—

POET Which, however, I also don't mean aesthetically. I'm not a

CRITIC   Your whole aesthetic is an affront to others.

POET   Right. But I do it openly. *(To Vaněk.)* Take a good look at us. Six supra-frustrated would-be world improvers. Flat on their backs most of the time, saying—yes, please. And when it starts smelling of rape, covering up with no-thank-you slogans— afterwards, while their legs are still shaking. We're know-it-alls and hate-them-alls, rebellious accomodators and excessive bedwetters, right? And as we—so our world: mucked up, fucked up, boozed up, doped up, sucked up, used up, lost. Believe me, if I want to feel that I still exist, I have to wing it down to Nepal or Nairobi and spend my last buck—every one of the publishers here is a white shark, right?—on the best room in the best hotel. Then I pull down the blinds so I'm not distracted by any mountains, oceans, deserts, and other kitsch and crap of the sort and take turns reading Homer and writing verses of my own. And when I feel like a piece of ass, it's just as bad. I'm not talking about an amateur fuck here; that died out together with the economic miracle. After all, who wants to dump scarce commodities during a free market boom? I'm talking about the good old whores that supplied real fuck for real money. Just check out the red light district these days. At an extortionate rate all you can buy are remote-control mini-fuck-computers. It's like calling Australia from a phone booth: You throw in a sackful of chips and after thirty seconds of feeble thigh-quivering a sign lights up, "Insert money!" and if 'you're stupid enough to fork out more cash the sign switches to, "Do it yourself!" Right? No, my dear fellow, then I grab the first jet—and I want you to know this—to Warsaw, Budapest, or Prague, yes, mostly Prague—funny that we've never run into each each other there!—and to the first dame that crosses my path I say, "Miláčku!" right? and screw her all night until the plaster falls off the walls—for two pairs of pantyhose, often even for free because she likes my ball-game. Yes, my dear fellow, you've not only retained the holy naiveté of the reformers in your soul while we've turned into dubious third-class deformers, but so far you've also had the good fortune to live in a world where real suffering and consequently also real fucking is still possible—out of a fundamental *joie de vivre* all of us here can only read about, right?

MODERATOR   I think Dickie—Mr. Forniker—is very unjust as far as women in the West are concerned, who, in my opinion, have proven themselves not only in the fight against rearmament and pollution but also—if I may say so—in private intercourse. But that is easily explained, if for the reasons just given he doesn't find enough time to get to know them better, more than three times, that is. On the other hand, I have to confirm that the men from the East still radiate a unique charm. Certainly if a woman wants to experience a primal scream, that's where she has to go. But perhaps that will soon have become unnecessary if more men of your sort, Mr. Vanick, intellectual but at the same time of a gentle manliness— pardon? *(The Assistant has just brought her a message writ-ten on a big piece of paper.)* Ah yes, our producer suggests that I ask the last question so Mr. Vanick can start answering. Well—your admirer, Mrs. Spittelgrubler from Munich—oh yes!—there too you are flickering across the TV screens— has dictated an entire love-letter over the phone, from which I can only read the most important things: "As someone driven from our common homeland I nevertheless don't want to complain about the injustice. Time heals all wounds and as a Christian I have long since forgiven your people for the crimes through which they sinned against the Germans after the war. Instead of questions about blame I have a peaceful question: How does one make the famous Bohemian fruit dumplings?

(In the meantime the Assistant has brought the Poet a telephone, and he is talking quietly and winking at the cam-era once in a while. The Critic is again making corrections. The Actress, Playwright, and Journalist seem all the more interested.)

ALL THREE Yes, how then?

MODERATOR *(Continues reading.)* "I still remember quite well," continues Mrs. Spittelgrubler, "that, corresponding to the order of God's bounty, there were strawberry, apricot, and, finally, plum dumplings. I often dream about their wonderful, sweet smell. As reparation, could you reveal how exactly to pre-pare them?"

ALL THREE *(Taking napkins, manuscript pages, or plain pieces of paper and searching themselves and others for pencils and pens.)* Yes, how?

VANĚK Well, I— *(Expects to be interrupted; when nothing happens he continues, evidently frustrated.)* I'm not really—really, I'm not a—

PLAYWRIGHT Just don't underestimate yourself, Mr. Vejnek, it's been proven that good playwrights are usually also excellent cooks. I cooked for Dürrenmatt[8] once—

ACTRESS Why only playwrights? When Rex cooks—my present husband,

	that is—
MODERATOR	*(Has also availed herself of writing materials.)* I by no means want to cut the discussion off, but I think we are all eagerly waiting for what Mr. Vanick has to—if I may say so—divulge. Please, Mr. Vanick.
VANĚK	*(Unsure whether he will not be interrupted again.)* It—it's quite simple—you pat—if it's strawberries—pat the fruit dry—apricots and plums, on the other hand, must be cut in half—*(They all nod and write.)* and then—you make—
ALL	The dough.
VANĚK	Yes—
ALL	But how?
VANĚK	Quite simply—with—
ACTRESS	Flour. Now I remember; after all, I was in Prague, when was it? Two—no, three years ago, I was shooting there—marvelous city, Prague, a bit run down, but that's what I like, the nostalgic odour of decay, the Fishermen's Bastion and—
PLAYWRIGHT	That's in Budapest; you probably mean the Wawel.
JOURNALIST	That's in Cracow; you probably mean Hradčany Castle.
ACTRESS	Oh yes, Hradčany Castle—but what was it I—
ALL THREE	The flour.
ACTRESS	Oh yes, the flour, well, the Czech colleagues let us in on the secret: It takes a very special kind of flour to make fruit dumplings, namely very finely ground.
CRITIC	*(Looks up from his proofreading.)* You mean—very coarsely ground.
ACTRESS	Not at all, that's the joke, that it has to be very finely ground.
CRITIC	On the contrary: the joke, if you want, is that it has to be very coarsely ground.
ACTRESS	Stuff and nonsense!
CRITIC	This stuff and nonsense I have from my grandmother, née Svobodová.
ACTRESS	Then you're having a lapse of memory, as you often do when you're listing the best actors of today. Want to bet?
CRITIC	With pleasure.
ACTRESS	A bottle of Rothschild?
CRITIC	Two bottles of Rothschild!
ACTRESS	It's a bet!
CRITIC	And who's to referee?
MODERATOR	Your hour has come, Mr. Vanick!
ALL	Yes! Which kind of flour do you use??
VANĚK	I don't— I don't use flour—
ALL	No flour??
VANĚK	I always make them with semolina—
ALL	With semolina??

VANĚK	Or with potatoes—
ALL	*(Shake their heads in distrust and exchange glances of contempt.)*
CRITIC	*(For the first time addressing Vaněk directly.)* But they are sprinkled with toasted breadcrumbs.
PLAYWRIGHT	*(Still talking on the phone.)* With ground poppy seeds.
MODERATOR	Dickie, what do you— Mr. Forniker, what do you know about—
PLAYWRIGHT	Me? Nothing. But Mimi does!
MODERATOR	Which Mimi?
PLAYWRIGHT	*(Pointing to the receiver.)* The last whore who sells a decent fuck in this country—active in Bohemia before she fled from the Russians.
MODERATOR	Mr. Vanick, now you have to arbitrate again. What are real fruit dumplings sprinkled with: toasted breadcrumbs or ground poppy seeds?
ALL	Yes! What are they sprinkled with?
VANĚK	I—with grated curd cheese—
ALL	*(Outraged.)* Curd cheese!!
ACTRESS	*(To Vaněk.)* Are we both talking about Bohemian fruit dumplings?
VANĚK	Yes—
ACTRESS	Oh God, well now. When did you flee?
VANĚK	I didn't—
ACTRESS	I know. See how quickly one loses the habit? And how quickly everything changes? I assure you that now they use flour for the dumplings, very finely ground flour.
CRITIC	They use coarsely ground flour—guaranteed.
PLAYWRIGHT	*(Still holding the receiver.)* What's definite is that you sprinkle them with ground poppy seeds.
CRITIC	The truth is, you sprinkle them with toasted breadcrumbs.
ACTRESS	If we phone up Tex we'll know in a minute.
PLAYWRIGHT	I thought you said Rex was the great cook?
ACTRESS	Yes, with meat, Mex with fish, but Tex is the pastry chef.
CRITIC	Only none of them an actor.
PLAYWRIGHT	What do you know about good theatre?!
JOURNALIST	What do you know about true dissidents?!
ACTRESS	What do you know about real caviar?!
MODERATOR	What does a prostitute know about honest cooking?!
PLAYWRIGHT	What do you know about a good fuck?!
	(The violent dispute grows more and more violent. The reproaches are being repeated more and more loudly until there is almost a scuffle. The lights change to blue. Having noticed that Vaněk is gone, everyone freezes in mid-movement.)

NEWSCASTER   *(Voice-over.)* According to eye-witness accounts made by people occupying the marshes and later confirmed by local police, a naked, unidentified man tried to cross the relatively cold Danube in the early hours of the morning. He was heading for Czechoslovakia. Of interest in this connection is a report from the Czechoslovak News Agency that has just reached us. According to this, the well-known playwright Ferdinand Funyek, who under mysterious circumstances left his home country a few days ago, is supposed to have just as mysteriously returned. In accordance with the three-year prison-term imposed on him for his defection, he was immediately committed to a medium-security prison as a recidivist. *(Darkness. The familiar sign-off signature of the Austrian Broadcasting Corporation concludes the comedy.)*

THE END

NOTES

1. *Safari* is the first play Pavel Kohout has written in German.
2. The occupation of the marshlands along the Danube near the Czechoslovak border took place during December 1984 and part of January 1985, when thousands of Austrian protesters gathered there in an attempt to prevent the construction of a hydro-electric power plant. The result was that the Austrian government postponed construction plans, and this unique ecological area has been, for the time being at least, preserved.
3. Breyten Breytenbach (born in 1939 in the Republic of South Africa and now living in Paris) is widely recognized as one of South Africa's leading writers. He has published many volumes of fiction, essays, and poetry in English and Afrikaans. From 1975 to 1982 he was imprisoned in South Africa on charges of terrorism.
4. See note 6 to *Permit.*
5. Nora Helmer is the central character of Henryk Ibsen's play *The Doll's House.*
6. The Brown House—a house on one of Prague's main streets, called so because during the German occupation (1939-45), it was used as the headquarters of the Nazi Party authorities.
7. "U Fleku" is the most famous and oldest of Prague's beer halls.
8. Friedrich Dürrenmatt (born 1922), well-known Swiss dramatist.

VÁCLAV HAVEL

Light on a Landscape*

In the 1970's it was customary (and a good custom it was) for several of my writer-friends to spend one summer weekend with me in my country cottage every year. After 1969 they all had found themselves in a situation similar to mine; that is to say, they were banned in their native country and publicly disgraced for their beliefs concerning society. At these gatherings we used to, among other things, read our new works to each other. In the course of about two days before our meeting in 1975, and mainly to have something to read on that occasion, I wrote the one-act play *Audience*. The inspiration came from personal experience—my employment in a brewery the year before—and the play was intended, as may be evident, primarily for the entertainment of my friends. Indeed, it is little more than a dialogue between the so-called "dissident" writer Vaněk (who works in a brewery) and his superior, the brewmaster. Though the latter is invented, obviously many of my own experiences—and not only those from the brewery—went into his making.

It never occurred to me that the play might be saying something (more or less significant) to other people, people who do not know me or my situation and who are ignorant of my having worked in a brewery. As it turned out, I was—as I had, after all, been a number of times before in regard to my literary work—mistaken: the play was successful not only with my friends but, also, having by various ways soon penetrated the relatively broad consciousness of the Czech public, also won its esteem. At times, it has even happened that total strangers, people in restaurants or casual hitchhikers I picked up, not only knew it but also had extracted from it pieces of dialogue, which they then used—in addition to short quotations or paraphrases—in

* In the Czech original Havel's essay is untitled. This is the translators' title.

various situations (in some cases as a sort of password among people spiritually akin). This wide domestic acclaim naturally pleased me, the more so as it occurred under conditions which made it impossible for the play to be published or performed publicly in my country. But what pleased me most is that something apparently happened which, I think, does or should occur with all art, namely that the work of art somehow exceeds its author, or is, so to speak, "cleverer than he is," and that through the mediation of the writer—no matter what purpose he was consciously pursuing—some deeper truth about his time reveals itself and works its way to the surface.

Stimulated by this experience, I later wrote two more Vaněk plays, *Unveiling* and *Protest.* All three have since been staged by many theatres in divers countries, and, in spite of the rather special and unusual circumstances from which they originated, they have turned out to be generally intelligible. The third one, *Protest,* however, was actually written after a discussion with my friend Pavel Kohout as a counterpoint to his *Permit* (likewise a Vaněk play). These two were originally written with the intention of having them staged together, something that eventually did happen. Later, when I was already in prison, Kohout wrote another Vaněk piece, *Morass,* and at approximately the same time my friend Pavel Landovský composed *Arrest.* Later still, after his release from the prison in which we had served time together, Jiří Dienstbier, another of my friends, wrote a Vaněk play as well.

If I am to make some marginal comments on the whole Vaněk series, it might, above all, be appropriate to emphasize that Vaněk is not Havel. Of course, I have transferred into this character certain of my own experiences, and I have done so more distinctly than is usual among writers. Undoubtedly, I have also implanted in him a number of my personal traits or, more precisely, presented a number of perspectives from which I see myself in various situations. But all of this does not mean that Vaněk is intended as a self-portrait. A real person and a dramatic character are entirely different things. The dramatic character is more or less always a fiction, an invention, a trick, an abbreviation consisting only of a limited number of utterances, and subordinated to the concrete "world of the play" and its meaning. In comparison with any living person, even the most enigmatic and psychologically most rounded character is hopelessly inadequate and simplistic. On the other hand, however, he should also exude something a real person cannot possibly possess: the ability always to say something perspicuous and essential about "the world as it is"—all within the context of the few lines of dialogue and the few situations that make up his entire being.

This holds true for Vaněk as well, perhaps more so than for many another dramatic character. Vaněk is really not so much a concrete person as something of a "dramatic principle": he does not usually do or say much, but his mere existence, his presence on stage, and his being what he is make his environment expose itself one way or another. He does not admonish anyone in particular; indeed, he demands hardly anything of anyone. And in spite of this, his environment perceives him as an invocation somehow to declare and justify itself. He is, then, a kind of "key," opening certain — always different — vistas onto the world in which he lives; a kind of catalyst, a gleam, if you will, in whose light we view a landscape. And although without it we should scarcely be able to see anything at all, it is not the gleam that matters but the landscape. The Vaněk plays, therefore, are essentially not plays about Vaněk, but plays about the world as it reveals itself when confronted with Vaněk. (This, I must add, is an *ex post facto* explanation. While writing *Audience,* I was not aware of this, and I did not plan things that way beforehand. It is only now that, removed in time and faced with Vaněk's literary and theatrical existence of several years, I have come to realize it.)

From what I have just said about Vaněk, it of course follows that the Vaněk of different plays and, even more so, the Vaněk of different authors is not always quite the same character. While it is true that as a "principle" or "dramatic trick" he moves from play to play, the principle is used differently every time, and as a character he is therefore always someone slightly different. The writers impress on him their own varied experiences, they perceive him in the framework of their individual poetics, perhaps they even project into him their varying interpretations of the man who was the original model. In short, every writer is different and writes differently; consequently, he has his own Vaněk, different from the Vaněks of the others.

For me, personally, all that remains is to be pleased that, having discovered — more unconsciously than on purpose — the "Vaněk principle," I have inspired other Czech writers who, as it happens, are also my friends, and have provided something of a key for them to use in their own way and at their own responsibility. And if the present collection of Vaněk-plays says — as a whole — something about the world in which it was given us to live our lives, then the credit should be given collectively and in equal measure, to all the authors involved.

Hrádeček, July 25, 1985

Translated by Milan Pomichalek and Anna Mozga

PAVEL KOHOUT

The Chaste Centaur
(Havel's Vaněk and Vaněk's Havel)

To Václav Havel on the occasion of his fiftieth birthday.

Investigating world drama, a theatre criminologist would be bound to discover a great many instances of theft of character, some of which have even had to be settled in court as plagiarism. To list all the appropriations from authors who, long dead, left their characters to be dealt with at will by their heirs would prove a nigh-impossible task. Except for Ferdinand Vaněk, however, I do not know of any figure playwrights have borrowed with the kind approval of the hero's original father.

I was sitting in Václav Havel's hillside cottage that summer day when, for the "entertainment of friends," as he remarked with characteristic modesty, he read his one-act play *Audience.* In it he used the character of Vaněk as a means of describing to us the lot of a brewery worker—his own. With characteristic immodesty, I note that it was I who, after the reading, drew his attention to the fact that he had discovered a vehicle for translating concrete information about concrete people and problems in a concrete period into a dramatic form capable of sustaining life on stage.

The world-wide acclaim received by the play soon proved right both author and listener, the latter—by the same twist of fate that expelled both men from the Czech theatre—also a playwright. And when Vaněk performed equally successfully in a second play, *Unveiling,* I tentatively asked his creator for permission to use him in recording my own experiences. He not only agreed willingly but also actively endorsed the proposal. Out of this conversation grew the idea for a jointly composed evening of theatrical entertainment. In the autumn of 1979 the world première of his *Protest* and my *Permit,* collectively named *Tests,* took place in the Akademietheater in Vienna.

By that time Václav Havel was already in jail. As a homage to him, I wrote another Vanĕk play, *Morass,* and persuaded our common friend Pavel Landovský to contribute *Arrest,* yet another play structured around the hero whom we three have come to pass back and forth among us like a challenge-cup. This pair we provisionally named *Rests.* Five years later still when, for the first time, I felt the need to reflect in dramatic form the experience of my involuntary stay in the West—a consequence of a trip to Vienna—I added to the hitherto formed sequence my third work, *Safari.*

How can one explain the fact that a writer who has never been in want of his own ideas employs the dramatic principle of a colleague—and does so three times? If we disregard my natural affiliation with a group of authors ruled by the great William and, in our century, presided over by Brecht—both of whom considered the scenic adaptation of the works of others as no less of a creative adventure than the treatment of an original theme—I personally see two causes.

Distance in time has confirmed my belief that the initial impulse was generated jointly by the state of society and that of my own life. I was—and feel I still am today, in this other world—a member of a small but amazingly vital community, one forged by far more than the voluntarily chosen and collectively borne lot of exiles in their own country. In this extreme situation, people with entirely different personal histories and ideas discovered themselves as well as each other. Without surrendering their own convictions, they learned to understand others; without losing the traits of their individuality, they found what they have in common.

Although, taken superficially, Václav Havel and I seem to be almost polar opposites in terms of personality and political inclinations, our friendship has become one of the dominant factors in my life. The nature of our understanding is a topic for another and more important essay, one reflecting on the possibility of a consensus among all of Czech society. The two of us have clearly answered this question in the affirmative, and it appears to me that taking over the character of Ferdinand Vanĕk was an expression of my need to meet Václav Havel also in the writer's most intimate sphere—in creation. A Freudian philosopher would probably delight in calling this a manifestation of abnormal sexuality. In fact, through the psychology of his/my hero and with my typewriter as the only tool, I established a much closer and more permanent relationship with my friend than anyone could possibly achieve in bed.

That is why I am certain of the second cause of my attraction to and as yet undiminished relations with the dramatic principle of *Audience,* which has held firm under the threefold pressure added by me. After all, what is the essence of its aesthetics? Vanĕk. And what is the essence of Vanĕk? Havel. And the essence of Havel?

During the eight long years I have not seen him, half of which he has spent behind bars, the original has surely changed; but the essence is bound to have endured. To describe it as accurately as possible, I must once again resort to intimate vocabulary: chastity. At first, this may sound ridiculous—considering that I belong to those most familiar with the friend's renaissance personality, his eager penchant for every joy life has to offer. But for a long time I have also known that there is a chastity of a higher order. Both Havel and his fictional twin brother Vaněk have everything that makes a man a man, but they have retained the soul of a child.

Even a child knows how to do wrong, how to hurt, pretend, and lie, but to the child these actions are dictated by instant need or emotion, not moral corruptness, which is only acquired later. When a child tries to deceive or, more still, to harm, he usually does so with guileless awkwardness, eliciting compassion. A man with the soul of a child does not always elicit compassion in human conflicts, but neither does he forfeit the sympathy of others. Furthermore, in key confrontations such as the one presently taking place in Czechoslovakia, he unconsciously irritates both the bureaucratic (equal: police) apparatus as well as the mass of his fellow citizens.

Omnipotent authority is faced with a shy, polite, even obliging intellectual of a visibly non-athletic cast, the like of which it has come to deal with expeditiously, if he be furnished with the soul of an ordinary man— commonly a mixture of cowardice and cynicism—and therefore amenable to a bargain. But when authority enters, this man does not rant and rave; he neither quarrels nor exchanges blows; he does not even lie. At the most, he is silent, if the truth might hurt someone other than himself. When authority displays its candies of all flavours and whips of all sizes, it at first misses his quiet "No," and when it finally hears it, it does not believe. It shows him its instruments; it uses them.

Before his trial ever began, Václav Havel was offered *laissez passer* to New York. The fury he unleashed by his persistence in saying "No" brought down on him a (for such a delicate man astronomical) term of four-and-a-half years in prison. Only slightly before the term expired was he released, a seriously ill man they feared might die in prison. Ferdinand Vaněk has inherited his disposition.

To once critical intellectuals, the overwhelming majority of whom have by now come to an arrangement with authority, he poses no less of a problem. To them he is an inconvenience greater than authority itself since he proves them guilty of a life-sized lie: guilty in front of the world, their families, and even themselves. Whereas authority knows his momentary powerlessness, to this group of despondents Václav Havel is a very real danger—because the future threatens to prove him right, and that will necessarily mean a condemnation of them. They hate him, but at the same time, just to be sure, they obsequiously curry favour with him, only to slander and denounce him the next moment.

Like Havel at times in real life, Vaněk is a "reagent" on stage. His mere appearance whips others on to fervent activity and elicits cascades of words that are supposed to habilitate or rehabilitate them, to convince or convict him. The less they tolerate him, the more they invite him; the fewer questions he asks, the more answers they provide; the less he blames them, the more stubbornly they defend themselves; the more he calms them, the more agitated they get; the more magnanimous he is, the more aggressive they become, and yet—the more they try to hold him back when at last he wants to remove his irritant self from their presence. It is precisely his departure they obviously fear most—the Brewmaster in *Audience,* the couple in *Unveiling,* and the writer Staněk in *Protest* as well. As if departing together with him were their secret hope—that through him the world might once again become a more decent place, and they more decent people.

No matter how different the life and style of the authors who have appropriated Vaněk so far, each of their Ferdinands preserves symptomatic traits of his spiritual father. Invariably, each and every one of them is in essence Havel portrayed by different painters, including himself.

A good portrait or self-portrait is never as descriptive as a photograph, but it can present a more truthful depiction and, by eliminating secondary ornaments and focusing only on essentials, reveal the immutable centre of the subject's personality. It is in this sense that Ferdinand Vaněk is an artistic artefact, a skillfully crafted *dramatis persona* escaping the fluidity of life and functioning in accordance with the laws of the theatre. The transposition of Havel's chastity from life to drama via this prototype in all three original plays is proof of an artistic blessing of the highest degree. This is precisely where Havel-Vaněk is the most truthful embodiment of Vaněk-Havel, something of a popular reincarnation of the centaur Cheiron.

My last piece, *Safari,* summons him on a first investigation of Western society. At the end of the play I, honest debtor that I am, return him to the country of his original owner. He cannot cross over to me a second time; I can only rejoin him. This I hope for; but I also believe that he will not wait, that he will, shyly yet without hesitation, enter into further plays which, in turn, will chart the features of our time on the blank map of contemporary Czech theatre.

Vienna, April 1986.

Translated by Milan Pomichalek and Anna Mozga.

PAVEL LANDOVSKÝ

Ferdinand Havel and Václav Vaněk

In my mind the dramatis persona—and today already the archetype—of "Vaněk" is associated exclusively with the persona—and today already the archetype—of "Havel." When in 1976 I introduced the Vaněk-character into my play *Sanitární noc**—his first appearance outside Havel's one-act plays—I did it rather to get even with my friend Václav because he had put me (name and all) into his play *Audience,* something which inflicted on me a remarkable popularity in almost all of the theatrical world. As recently as 1983, when the French "superstar" actor Daniel Gelen was on tour in Vienna, playing the part of Vaněk (in the play *Protest*), he did not search out the man who at that time was the Austrian minister of culture, but immediately wanted to meet that guy Landovský, who on late-night binges had roamed through Prague with Václav Havel and prevented him from writing yet another work of genius. This is popularity on the border between alcoholism and moral licentiousness. But I am content, for in the theatrical profession it is accepted that "a bad reputation is a good reputation."

I am on such intimate terms with Václav Havel that dealing with the character Ferdinand Vaněk as a symbol of something other than the real Václav Havel would be an insoluble problem for me. Havel's thinking, a computer of at least the twelfth generation, has been programmed to reflect in an almost mirror-like harmony the ordinary life of this century; thus I don't want to get involved with it—not even as a meliorator or discoverer of new possibilities. For that I respect my friend too highly.

It is worthwhile, after all, to note that Vaněk has been dislodged from Havel's last two plays first by Professor Kopřiva and then by Doctor Foustka.**

When Václav Havel was in jail, Ferdinand Vaněk visited me a few times in Vienna, but it has been a long time since he last appeared. In my opinion, he has probably moved from Prague to Havel's Hrádeček near Vlčice, and there he and Václav chat about what was, what no longer is, and what may some day be again. But who knows?

Written on Friday, 20 June 1986, in the Akademietheater
in Vienna, dressing room number 4, during the performance
of Václav Havel's play *Temptation.*

Translated by Milan Pomichalek and Anna Mozga

* Translators' note: During "sanitation night" a public place would be closed for cleaning purposes.
** Professor Kopřiva (Professor "Nettle" in English) is the protagonist of Havel's *Largo desolato*; première at the Akademietheater in Vienna, April 1985. Doctor Foustka is the protagonist of Havel's *Pokoušení* (Temptation); première at the Akademietheater in Vienna, May 1986.

JIŘÍ DIENSTBIER

On *Reception*

Until late that night we hung out in the shower room, trying to convince them that it simply wouldn't do for us to denounce ourselves and that, as far as they were concerned, the prospect of getting parole wasn't worth it. Once they started informing, they might continue doing so for the rest of their lives. If it leaked out that we dictated the reports to them, they wouldn't get paroled anyway. And God knows what else might happen to them.

Every so often an overseer dashed through, grunting something to the effect that we should beat it. They seemed to be exceptionally considerate; apparently they were in the know. Otherwise, at least some of them would not have let such an opportunity go by; catching us at prohibited activities was a treat for them. And spending the night in the washroom was forbidden.

Without our co-operation, they insisted, they wouldn't accept the assignment. But maybe the choice wasn't theirs anymore. It's what they wanted. For them it was an even more fundamental question than for us. Either they'd go home on parole or not. The terms they'd been sentenced to were long. They'd write the reports, regardless, and they wouldn't stop pressing us. Or, at least, they'd keep telling us what it was they put into the reports. And why kid ourselves? We wouldn't say no; we'd be too curious. So there was a practical motive as well.

On the outside we couldn't have cared less what stories were passed on about us or by whom. We acted publicly and without concealing anything. The only secrets left to be told were private ones. Sometimes the result was marital troubles, but in most cases the police couldn't even count on that. When during interrogation they pointedly asked a friend of mine, "Mr. X, do you cheat on your wife?," X, without batting an eyelid, replied, "And don't you, major, sir?"—which put an end to the issue.

But in prison danger is always imminent. I myself experienced it often. One time, for instance, a stoolie, not knowing what to write, decided to get even with one of the pedagogues—that is what the wardens are called. In his report he fabricated something about my considering the pedagogue a fancy clodhopper. He greatly enjoyed himself. The pedagogue's colleagues, the addressees of the report, also had fun at the man's expense. And then I did, too. True, the pedagogue couldn't punish me (or he would have revealed the identity of the informer), but he missed no opportunity of making my life miserable.

"I'll write you a new *Audience,*" I jokingly said, after Václav, the play's author, had dictated his first report. And when we said good-bye to each other on the Bory prison-yard, I repeated my joke. If I ever took it seriously, then it was only to the extent that I planned a parodic sketch to welcome him back to civilian life.

Months passed, and I realized that there would be no fun and no "welcome-parody." More and more it became clear to me that, in fact, this whole thing wasn't about prison—and even less about a concrete one—and that neither is this anecdote.

Actually, the world of the prison hardly differs from the world surrounding it. Only, in it behaviour patterns, relationships between people, and social stratifications become glaringly apparent. Goodness, therefore, is of more consequence and evil is more evil, brutality more brutal, hypocrisy repulsive at first sight. When hair and civilian clothes are shed, the masks fall along with them. Of course, nearly everybody immediately tries to put on another one, but the new mask is dreadfully transparent. The least awkward thing is confronting the discomfort with one's own face.

And so I started to write. At first I wanted to leave out Vaněk and the Brewmaster and all references to Havel's play. But then I changed my mind. Moved into different situations, familiar characters are, naturally, changed; but the point I wanted to make by presenting them is that a man's ethics and sense of responsibility do not rest only on abstract principles, that they always relate to concrete people, even if these be scoundrels, or maybe mostly unfortunates.

As someone once said: our lives are like a canvas on which we spread, now more, now less skillfully, our paints.

And the same applies to this play. What in it succeeds and to what extent— that I cannot judge.

Prague, May 1986

Translated by Milan Pomichalek and Anna Mozga

International Performances of Vaněk Plays

(excluding productions as television and radio plays)

Václav Havel, *AUDIENCE* performed, in the respective languages, in Australia, Austria, Belgium, Canada, Denmark, England, Finland, France, Germany, Greece, Holland, Iceland, Israel, Italy, Jugoslavia, Japan, Norway, Poland, Sweden, Switzerland, Turkey, and the United States.

Václav Havel, *UNVEILING* (original Czech: *Vernisáž*) same as *Audience*.

Václav Havel, *PROTEST* performed, in the respective languages, in Austria, Belgium, Canada, Denmark, England, France, Germany, Holland, Iceland, Jugoslavia, Norway, Poland, Sweden, Switzerland, and the United States.

Pavel Kohout, *PERMIT* (original Czech: *Atest*) performed, in the respective languages, in Austria, Canada, Germany, Norway and Sweden.

Pavel Landovský, *ARREST,* performed in German, in Austria and Germany.

Pavel Kohout, *MORASS* (original Czech: *Marast*) performed in German, in Austria and Germany.

Première Performances of Vaněk Plays

(all these performances in German translations)

Václav Havel, *AUDIENCE*: October 9, 1976, Akademietheater des Burg-theaters, Vienna (performed with *Unveiling*).

Václav Havel, *UNVEILING* [*Vernissage*]: October 9, 1976, Akademietheater des Burgtheaters, Vienna (performed with *Audience*).

Václav Havel, *PROTEST*: November 17, 1979, Akademietheater des Burgtheaters, Vienna (performed with Pavel Kohout's *Permit*).

Pavel Kohout, *PERMIT* [*Attest*]: November 17, 1979, Akademietheater des Burgtheaters, Vienna (performed with Václav Havel's *Protest*).

Pavel Landovský, *ARREST*: October 11, 1981, Akademietheater des Burgtheaters, Vienna (performed with Tom Stoppard's *Every Good Boy Deserves Favour*).

Pavel Kohout, *MORASS* [*Morast*]: March 27, 1982, Deutsches Theater in Göttingen (performed with Pavel Landovský's *Arrest*).

The Editor

MARKETA GOETZ-STANKIEWICZ is Professor of Germanic Studies and Comparative Literature at the University of British Columbia. She is the author of *The Silenced Theatre: Czech Playwrights without a Stage,* (Toronto, 1979); she edited *The Filtre of Translation,* special issue of the *Canadian Review of Comparative Literature* (1980), and *Dramacontemporary: Czechoslovakia* (New York, 1985). She has also written essays on modern German and Czech literature.

The Translators

VERA BLACKWELL is a well-known translator of several of Havel's full length plays. Her translations of all three Vaněk plays by Havel were staged and broadcast in Britain, North America and Australia. She lives in New York.

JAN DRABEK is a Canadian writer among whose novels are *Whatever Happened to Wenceslas* (1975), *Report on the Death of Rosenkavalier* (1977) and *The Statement* (1982). His translations from Czech include Ivan Klíma's play *Games* for *Dramacontemporary: Czechoslovakia* (1985) and Zdena Salivarová's *Ashes Ashes All Fall Down* (1987). He lives in Vancouver, B.C.

ANNA MOZGA is a doctoral student of German and Theatre at the University of British Columbia. In addition to her translation work from Czech and German, she has written poetry. She lives in Vancouver, B.C.

JAN NOVAK is a Czech/American writer whose *Striptease Chicago* appeared in the original Czech in 1983 with Sixty-eight Publishers, Toronto; his *The Willys Dream Kit*, written in English, was suggested for the Pulitzer Prize in 1985. His translations of *Audience* and *Unveiling* (included in this volume) were staged in Chicago in 1986. He lives in Chicago.

VERA PECH translated the Czech writer Milan Uhde's monodrama *A Blue Angel* for *Dramacontemporary: Czechoslovakia*. She lives in Vancouver, B.C.

PETER PETRO, Associate Professor of Slavonic Studies at the University of British Columbia, is the author of *Modern Satire: Four Studies* (1982). He has translated several literary texts from Czech and Slovak, and has written numerous essays on aspects of modern Czech, Slovak, Russian and Comparative literature. At present he is writing a *History of Slovak Literature*. He lives in Vancouver, B.C.

MILAN POMICHALEK is a student of psychology at the University of British Columbia. He is currently collaborating with Anna Mozga on translations of philosophical and literary Czech prose. He lives in Vancouver, B.C.

JOSEF SKÁLA, who is a Professor in the Faculty of Medicine of the University of British Columbia, has adapted, directed, and acted in various Czech plays. Among his roles on the stage and in radio plays is the part of Ferdinand Vanĕk, which he performed in the Kitsilano Theatre production of Havel's *Protest* and Kohout's *Permit* in 1984. He lives in Vancouver, B.C.

Bibliographical Notes

These notes include only the four authors' dramatic works, world premières in the plays' respective languages, productions of particular importance in English, and first publications in Czech, English or German. When no language is indicated, the performance or publication is in the original Czech. Theatre companies are mentioned only for important productions in English. Translators as well as publishers are listed only if the performance or publication was in English. Nearly all the texts mentioned, unless they were published officially in Czechoslovakia prior to 1968 (the year of the Soviet invasion), have been published in one of the *samizdat* editions in Czechoslovakia. These typescript publications have not been included.

JIŘÍ DIENSTBIER

Než upečeme selata [*Before We Roast the Piglets*], (1967).
Vánoční dárek [*The Christmas Present*], (1977).
Kontest [*The Contest*], (1978).
Hosté [*The Guests*], (1978).
Příjem [*Reception*], publication (in English): in this volume.

Except for *Reception* [*Příjem*], Dienstbier's plays have not been translated into English. All, however, circulate in *samizdat* editions in Czechoslovakia.

VÁCLAV HAVEL

Autostop [*The Hitch-hike*], with Ivan Vyskočil; première: Prague, 1961; publication: Prague, Dilia, 1961.
Nejlepší rocky paní Hermanové [*The Best "Rock" Years of Mrs. Herman*], with Miloš Macourek; première: Prague, 1962.

Zahradní slavnost, première: Prague, 1965; publication: Prague, Orbis, 1962; in English as *The Garden Party* (trans. Vera Blackwell), London, Cape, 1969.

Vyrozumění, première: Prague, 1965; in English: London, Orange Tree Theatre, 1977; publication: Prague, Dilia, 1965; in English as *The Memorandum* (trans. Vera Blackwell), London, Cape, 1969; New York, Grove Press, 1980.

Ztížená možnost soustředění, première: Prague 1968; in English: London, Orange Tree Theatre, 1980; publication: Prague, Orbis, 1968; in English as *The Increased Difficulty of Concentration* (trans. Vera Blackwell), London, Cape, 1972.

Spiklenci [*The Conspirators*], première in German: Baden Baden, 1974; publication: in *Hry 1970-77,* Toronto, Sixty-Eight Publishers, 1977.

Audience, première in German: Vienna, 1976; in English: London, Orange Tree Theatre, 1977; publication: in *Svědectví* XII:51, 1976, also in *Hry 1970-77;* in English as *Conversation* (trans. Vera Blackwell), in *Index on Censorship,* Autumn, 1976; also in *Sorry...,* London, Eyre Methuen, 1978.

Vernisáž, première in German: Vienna, 1976; in English: London, Orange Tree Theatre, 1977; publication: in *Hry 1970-77;* in English as *Private View* (trans. Vera Blackwell), in *Sorry...*

Žebrácká opera [*The Beggar's Opera*], première: Horní Počernice, Czechoslovakia, 1975 (amateur actors; one performance only); in Italian: Trieste, 1976; publication: *Hry 1970-77.*

Horský hotel [*The Mountain Chalet*], première in German: Vienna, 1981.

Protest, première in German: Hamburg, 1978; in English: London, Orange Tree Theatre, 1980; publication: in *Dramacontemporary: Czechoslovakia* (trans. Vera Blackwell), New York, Performing Arts Journal Publications, 1985.

Chyba [*The Mistake*], première in Swedish: Stockholm, 1983; publication: in *Svědectví,* XVIII:69, 1983.

Largo desolato, première in German: Vienna, 1986; in English: (trans. Marie Winn), New York, Public Theatre, 1986; (adapted by Tom Stoppard), Bristol, Old Vic Theatre, 1986; publication: Munich, Obrys/Kontur Pmd, 1985; in German: Reinbek bei Hamburg; 1985.

Pokoušení, première in German: Vienna, 1986; in English: Stratford on Avon, The Other Place, Royal Shakespeare Company, 1987; publication: Munich, Obrys/Kontur Pmd, 1986; in English: *Temptation* (trans. George Theiner), in *Index on Censorship,* Vol. 15, no. 10, 1986.

PAVEL KOHOUT

Taková láska [*Such A Love*], première: Prague, 1957; publication: Prague, 1958.

Dobrá píseň [*The Good Song*], première: Prague: 1952; publication: Prague, 1952.

Cesta kolem světa za 80 dní [*Around the World in Eighty Days*] (based on Jules Verne's novel of the same title), première: Prague, 1962; publication in German: in *Theaterstücke,* Lucerne, 1980.

Josef Švejk (based on Jaroslav Hašek's novel *The Good Soldier Švejk),* première: Prague, 1963; publication: Prague, 1966.

Válka s mloky [*War with the Newts*] (based on Karel Čapek's novel of the same title), première: Prague, 1963; publication: in *Divadlo,* Prague 1963.

August August, august, première: Prague, 1967; in English: Minneapolis, "Théâtre de la jeune lune," Southern Theatre, 1986; publication: Prague, 1968; in German: in *Theaterstücke.*

Evol, première in German: Graz, 1970; publication in German: in *Krieg im dritten Stock, Evol,* Lucerne and Frankfurt, 1970.

Válka ve třetím poschodí [*War on the Third Floor*], première in German: Vienna, 1971; publication in German: in *Krieg im dritten Stock, Evol;* in *Listy,* XIV:3, 1984.

Ubohý vrah, première in German: Düsseldorf, 1973; in English: *Poor Murderer* (trans. H. Berghof and L. Luckinbill), New York, Ethel Barrymore Theatre, 1976; publication in German: Lucerne and Frankfurt, 1972; in English: *Poor Murderer,* New York, Penguin, 1977.

Pech pod střechou [*Bad Luck under the Roof*], première in German: Ingolstadt, 1974; publication in German: Ingolstadt, 1974; in *Listy,* XIII:3, 1983.

Požár v suterénu, première in German: Ingolstadt, 1974; in English: Vancouver, Canada, Kitsilano Theatre Company, 1983; publication, in *Listy,* XII: 3-4, 1982; in English: (trans. Peter Stenberg and Marketa Goetz-Stankiewicz), in *Dramacontemporary: Czechoslovakia,* 1985.

Ruleta [*Roulette*], (based on the story *Darkness* by L.N. Andrejev), première in German: Lucerne, 1975; publication in German: Kassel, 1975.

Amerika (with Ivan Klíma), (based on Franz Kafka's novel with the same title), première in German: Krefeld, 1978.

Play Macbeth — A Tragedy Without Intermission After William Shakespeare, première: Living-room-theatre, Prague, 1978; performed in English in various theatres in Britain, the United States, and Canada.

Colas Breugnon (based on Romain Rolland's novel with the same title), première in German: Linz, 1978.

Atest, première in German: Vienna, 1979; in English as *The License* (trans. Peter Tegel): London, Orange Tree Theatre, 1980; publication: in *Listy,* XVI:3, 1986; in English: first published in this volume.

Maria zápasí s anděly [*Maria Struggles with the Angels*], première in

German: Vienna 1981; publication in German: Kassel, 1981.

Marast [*Morass*], première in German: Göttingen, 1982; publication in *Listy*, XV:3, 1985; in English: first published in this volume.

Malý August [*Little August*] (a version of *August August, August* for children), première in German: Wilhelmshaven, 1982.

Chudák Cyrano [*Poor Cyrano*] based on Edmond Rostand's play *Cyrano de Bergerac*), première in Dutch: Antwerp, 1982.

Hráč a jeho štěstí [*The Gambler and His Luck*] (based on Dostoyevsky's novel *The Gambler*), première in German: Hamburg, 1983.

Velká hra na javora [*The Big Maple Tree Game*] (based on Mircea Eliade's novel *Pe strada mantuleasa*, translated into English as *The Old Man and the Bureaucrats*), première in German: Basel, 1984.

1984 — Noční mura [*1984 — A Nightmare*], (based on George Orwell's novel *Nineteen Eighty Four*), première in English: Edmonton, Canada, 1984.

Vzpomínka na Biskaj [*Memories of the Bay of Biskay*], première in German: Vienna, 1985.

Kellermann, written in German in 1985. Not performed or published to date.

Safari, written in German in 1986; not yet performed, first published in this volume.

PAVEL LANDOVSKÝ

Hodinový hotelier [*Rooms by the Hour* (free translation)], première in Polish: Warsaw, 1970; publication: in *Jiné komedie a Sanitární noc*, Toronto, Sixty-Eight Publishers, 1982.

Chudobinec aneb případ pro vesnického policajta [*The Poorhouse or a Case for a Village Policeman*]; publication: in *Jiné komedie a Sanitární noc*.

Supermanka [*Superwoman*]; première in German: 1979; publication: in *Jiné komedie a Sanitární noc*.

Sanitární noc [*Closed for Disinfection*], première in German: Bonn 1978; publication: in *Jiné komedie a Sanitární noc*.

Objížd'ka, publication in English as *Detour* (trans. Ewald Osers), in *Drama-contemporary: Czechoslovakia*, 1985.